THE SCIENCE
AND PRACTICE
OF WELLNESS

"In *The Science and Practice of Wellness*, the Jains make a strong case that mental wellness is far more than mental health and is indeed important for all of us, irrespective of the presence or absence of psychiatric disorders. The beauty of their book is that it is based on their own practice and research from which they both provide the evidence to prove their beliefs but also give the reader a step-by-step approach on how to incorporate wellness interventions in clinical practice. Bravo on writing a gem of a book on wellness that is both evidenced-based as well as practical."

—**Leonard Calabrese**, D.O., Head of Clinical Immunology, Cleveland Clinic

"Diminished wellness is ubiquitous among persons with medical/mental disorders, as well as in the general population. Drs. Saundra and Rakesh Jain have written an erudite, encyclopedic, thoughtful, and accessible book about wellness. Their empathy and humanity emanates and surrounds each chapter. The global epidemiologic transition has invited the need for this kind of authoritative text about resiliency, wellness, and positive mental health."

—**Roger S. McIntyre**, M.D., FRCPC, Professor of Psychiatry and Pharmacology, University of Toronto

A NORTON PROFESSIONAL BOOK

THE SCIENCE AND PRACTICE OF WELLNESS

*Interventions for Happiness, Enthusiasm,
Resilience, and Optimism (HERO)*

RAKESH JAIN AND SAUNDRA JAIN

W. W. NORTON & COMPANY
Independent Publishers Since 1923

All royalties paid to the authors are donated to mental health charities.

Copyright © 2020 by Rakesh Jain and Saundra Jain

All rights reserved
Printed in the United States of America
First Edition

For information about permission to reproduce selections from this book, write to Permissions, W. W. Norton & Company, Inc., 500 Fifth Avenue, New York, NY 10110

For information about special discounts for bulk purchases, please contact W. W. Norton Special Sales at specialsales@wwnorton.com or 800-233-4830

Manufacturing by Sheridan Books
Production manager: Katelyn MacKenzie

ISBN: 978-0-393-71365-7

W. W. Norton & Company, Inc., 500 Fifth Avenue, New York, N.Y. 10110
www.wwnorton.com

W. W. Norton & Company Ltd., 15 Carlisle Street, London W1D 3BS

1 2 3 4 5 6 7 8 9 0

This book is dedicated to our loving parents:
Prabha and Gulab Jain, and Martha and Harvey Whitehead.

Contents

PART 1
The Science of Mental Wellness

PART 2
Principles of the Wellness-centric Clinician

Acknowledgments

Wellness is a major force for good. It impacts us in multiple ways: our family, our friends, and of course, our patients. During our personal journey in developing a mental wellness program, our patients have been our best teachers, and we gratefully acknowledge their many contributions to our growth as clinicians. Their fortitude in the face of the often unspeakable suffering inflicted by their mental health disorders is both awe-inspiring and a source of motivation. Their courage and resilience inspired us to step outside of our own complacency and embrace mental wellness, and their gentle pleas asking what more they can do to get better launched our voyage into the world of wellness. Dear patients, we are forever grateful.

Our close friends Charles Raison, Vladimir Maletic, Andrew Penn, Noel Gardner, and Clay Jackson—collaborators, frequent dinner companions, and all-around good human beings—in their own ways have profoundly shaped our vision and thinking. Besides their friendship, which we greatly value, we have benefited from their scientific rigor and deeply humanistic thinking. Betsy Burns, also a treasured friend and collaborator, is a consistent and enthusiastic cheerleader in our efforts to write on the topic of wellness. We are grateful to you all, dear friends.

An unsung hero in our journey in this field of mental wellness is Randy Robbin, a quiet man who prefers not to receive credit for what he does for others. He is one of the most important reasons for our success in researching and teaching others about the importance of wellness. For nearly a decade he has generously provided us with a platform to present our research and clinical findings and has afforded us the opportunity to interact with thousands of mental healthcare professionals. Because of his genuine modesty, he may never willingly acknowledge the large role he played in our professional development, but truthfully, he is one of the most important reasons for our success. Thank you, Randy.

Dr. Dilip Jeste, a past president of the American Psychiatric Association, who has graciously penned the foreword to this book, has been a significant influence in our lives. A thoughtful man, he has taught us over the years that mental wellness is of paramount importance to us as clinicians and to our patients. He was the first to show us that even "fuzzy" topics such as optimism, purpose in life, and resilience can be scientifically studied. His groundbreaking research in wellness and successful aging has been a great influence in our professional and personal development, and we are continually inspired by his humanity and first-rate scholarship in all things pertaining to mental wellness. We are lucky to have a mentor like him in our lives. We are forever grateful, Dilip.

Expressing gratitude is reportedly one of the best mental wellness exercises. So, following our own advice, we want to express gratitude towards a number of wonderful people in our lives. For us it's extremely easy to be grateful to our parents and our families for all the mental wellness they bring to our lives. We are exceedingly blessed to have parents like Prabha and Gulab Jain, and Martha and Harvey Whitehead. Our siblings, Shilpa, Bobby, Willie, Vicki, Pam, and "Sis," are forever part of our wellness-filled lives. Thank you all. Of course, our son, Nick, his lovely wife, Brett, and their bundle of endless happiness and joy, our grandson Max, are all part of our web of mental wellness and connection. Our nieces, nephews, and cousins, including Lori, Natasha, Lynsie, Chris, Kim, Blake, Allison, Elizabeth, Kristen, Kori, and many others, each contribute mightily to our personal wellness. They are all amazing people, and we are very fortunate to call them family.

Deborah Malmud is our editor at W. W. Norton & Company, and if not for her gentle prodding to submit a book proposal, this body of work would never have become a reality. Thank you, Deborah, for believing in the topic of mental wellness and in this book. Deborah understood our fear and hesitation in taking on a project of such magnitude. She used positive and persuasive affirmations to convince us to move forward, and as you can see, her persuasive powers worked!

Finally, as coauthors, as partners, and as a married couple, we acknowledge each other's influence on our personal development in the field of mental wellness. We are true partners in this project, with each of us bringing our life and professional experiences to the table, influencing and shaping each other for the better. Our personal and professional lives have been hugely transformed by our scientific exploration of the field of mental wellness.

And we thank you, dear reader, for your interest in wellness. We sincerely hope your patients will benefit from the thoughts and suggestions offered in this book.

Foreword

Shifting the Focus of Healthcare to Wellness by Promoting Positive Psychosocial Factors[1]
Dilip V. Jeste, M.D.

Some medical specialties are defined by the diseases their practitioners study and treat—e.g., oncology or rheumatology. Others are defined by the unique skill sets of their practitioners—e.g., orthopedic surgery or interventional radiology. The usual dictionary definition of psychiatry falls in the former category: psychiatry is defined as the medical specialty that focuses on study and treatment of mental illnesses. I believe this is unfortunate because it stigmatizes the patients who see a psychiatrist by labeling them as mentally ill people. Equally importantly, it diminishes the value of psychiatrists (as well as clinicians from related mental health fields such as psychologists, social workers, psychiatric nurses, and others) as experts in mental illnesses only. These are all experts in mental health, which does encompass mental illnesses, but goes far beyond. Only a minority of the population suffers from mental illnesses but every single person has mental health, a critical component of which is wellness.

So, how should psychiatry be defined? It should be defined by the unique skill set that psychiatrists and other mental health specialists possess—i.e., behavior modification. We use pharmacological and psychosocial treatments to rectify the most severe behavior problems like delusions, hallucinations, suicidality, and disabling anxiety, to name a few. But just as we seek to mitigate such pathological behaviors, our interventions can also help promote healthful behaviors that lead to improved mental health, including wellness.

Over the years, I have become increasingly convinced that medicine in general (and psychiatry in particular) need to move away from their disease-oriented model and shift to a prototype that emphasizes well-being and happiness through promotion of positive psychosocial factors like resilience, optimism, social engagement, and wisdom. I call this Positive Psychiatry, which derives its inspiration from Positive Psychology, but is more focused on health, biology, and interventions (Jeste & Palmer, 2015; Summers & Jeste, 2018). Current clinical psychiatric practice and training are mainly restricted to diagnosis and treatment of mental illnesses, while today's psychiatric research focuses primarily on elucidating the underlying pathology and therapeutic interventions to treat psychiatric disorders. Positive Psychiatry is the science and practice of psychiatry that seeks to understand and promote well-being through assessment and interventions to promote positive psychosocial factors (Jeste et al., 2015).

The United Nations has formally recognized pursuit of happiness as a fundamental human goal; yet, little attention has been paid to assessing and enhancing happiness among people with serious mental illnesses like schizophrenia, bipolar disorder, and major depression. A positive change in attitude toward serious mental illnesses is necessary among clinicians and scientists in order to facilitate a similar change in attitude among our patients and their families. It is important for the field to appreciate that psychiatric therapeutics need not be restricted to addressing psychopathology, and that compensatory, lifestyle-focused, and resiliency pathways provide important therapeutic targets that can positively impact neurobiology and enhance personal fulfillment (Cohen et al., 2017). In other words,

Positive Psychiatry for serious mental illnesses is not an oxymoron, but a sorely needed approach to fully addressing the toll of these disorders in terms of suffering and reduced well-being.

There is considerable evidence that positive psychosocial factors have as strong, if not stronger, impact on *enhancing* patients' well-being as common health risk factors such as obesity, hypertension, sedentary lifestyle, and smoking have on *reducing* their well-being (Diener et al., 2011; Schutte et al., 2016; Wiley et al., 2017). Provision of effective interventions to strengthen the positive factors in psychiatric patients could substantially increase the frequency of recovery in individuals with serious mental illnesses.

A number of recent studies (Edmonds et al., 2018; Palmer et al., 2014; Van Patten et al., 2019) have reported that, while the average self-reported levels of happiness, resilience, and wisdom among people with schizophrenia were lower than those in healthy comparison subjects, there was considerable within-group heterogeneity, with about a third of the individuals with schizophrenia having levels of these factors similar to those in their healthy counterparts. Notably, happiness, resilience, and wisdom scores in the schizophrenia group were associated with better mental and physical health.

I am honored that Drs. Rakesh and Saundra Jain asked me to write the foreword for this new and exciting book on *The Science and Practice of Wellness*—an area close to my heart. Dr. Rakesh Jain is an internationally-renowned clinician, researcher, and educator, while Dr. Saundra Jain is an outstanding psychotherapist and teacher. Together this couple have given birth to a brilliant monograph that is comprehensive, scholarly, and yet easily understandable to any student of mental health. What is rare about this book is the marriage of scientific research with an intimately personal, warm, and lucid writing style. Drs. Jain combine the findings of their own research with that conducted and published by other researchers in the field.

As they have described eloquently, Drs. Rakesh and Saundra Jain both come from "traditional" professional backgrounds in terms of their training. But about 20 years ago they came to the realization that something was amiss in their patients' lives. Many of their patients, benefitting from the treatments the authors provided, achieved remission from a majority of their mental illness symptoms, but still reported that something was missing in their life, even though symptomatically and functionally they were better. These patients lacked a feeling of happiness, joy, and contentment. The authors shared their patients' angst and it became the driver for their efforts over the to better understand wellness in mental health, ultimately leading to the creation of interventions to improve wellness in these patients. Drs. Jain appropriately stress that they have not abandoned the "traditional" psychopharmacological and other treatments for psychiatric disorders, but rather, they have added wellness-centric interventions as another tool to enhance wellness.

The authors conducted a considerable amount of original research in mental wellness and presented their findings at national and international conferences. Their careful work resulted in a formal, manual-based wellness program that is being practiced in multiple centers and private practices around the country. As the authors mention, this book is a result of their lifetime's work on wellness—and it is simply remarkable, energizing, and uplifting.

The orderly and well thought out progression of the theme of wellness through the 12 chapters in the book is truly impressive. The authors start out by defining what they aptly call the "Wellness Deficit Disorder." Next, they describe the scientific principles of wellness in mental health, and examine neurobiological underpinnings of wellness as well as its relationship with inflammation, a biological mechanism that may be at the core of many physical, mental, and cognitive disorders. The hypothesis that wellness has a positive impact on inflammation, thereby reducing the risk of major disorders, illustrates the authors' noteworthy ability to tie psychosocial constructs with hard-core biology. Science requires use of validated measures and it is heartening that Drs. Jain stress the value of measurement-based wellness-centric care. For a new approach to succeed, educating the primary stakeholders is critical. Accordingly, the authors discuss in detail the ways in which wellness concepts should be introduced to the patients, so as to facilitate their practical implementation. Using a memorable acronym (HERO), they describe the four key attributes of wellness: happiness, enthusiasm, resilience, and optimism. Next, they consider specific wellness-centric interventions related to exercise, mindfulness, sleep, social connectedness, and nutrition. Finally, they describe the innovative wellness-centric program that the authors have developed over a period of many years, called The WILD 5 Wellness Program. Several scientific studies support its validity. Importantly, from a clinical perspective, the authors go on to discuss the various lessons learned from the WILD 5 Wellness Initiative, and how the wellness interventions can be used in clinical practice. One of the chapters is a highly thoughtful summary of the ways in which we can create symbiotic relationship between psychopharmacology and wellness in routine practice.

There are a number of keen insights that a reader can obtain from this volume. Wellness is a global, human need desired by everyone. Yet, recent studies show that, during the past several decades, stress levels have been increasing and wellness levels have been dropping, especially in the U.S., impacting both mental and physical health. The modern epidemics of opioid crisis, loneliness, and suicide clearly reflect the social anomie and growing stress across all age groups. Indeed, for the first time in decades, the average lifespan in the U.S. has decreased. People with schizophrenia have been known since Kraepelin's time to have significantly shorter lifespan than the general population. Sadly and embarrassingly, this mortality gap between persons with schizophrenia and the community at large has *increased* by about 30% since the 1970s (Lee, Liu et al., 2018).

The good news, however, is that wellness-centric positive psychiatry interventions can produce lasting results. In the shorter run, these can be added to the commonly used treatments including psychopharmacology. My personal hope is that in the near future, evidence-based wellness-enhancing interventions, which could be behavioral, psychosocial, biological, and technological, will come to replace the current therapies that are either ineffective or have major limitations.

A recent study (Lee, Martin, et al., 2018) found that high levels of resilience in adulthood seemed to negate the adverse impact of childhood adversity on mental and physical health and even blood-based metabolic biomarkers in adults with chronic schizophrenia. This suggests a possibility that interventions to promote resilience in later life may have the potential to mitigate long-lasting negative consequences of stressful events in earlier life. Of course, this is a speculation at this time, and carefully designed intervention studies are warranted to test such hypotheses.

To conclude, there is an urgent need for psychiatry to expand its focus on positive outcomes like wellness and positive psychiatric factors like resilience, optimism, and wisdom. This book is an excellent step in that direction. I want to compliment Drs. Rakesh and Saundra Jain for putting together a timely, insightful, and thought provoking monograph that should be of great value to anyone interested in the topic of mental health.

References

Cohen, A. N., Hamilton, A. B., Saks, E. R., et al. (2017). How occupationally high-achieving individuals with a diagnosis of schizophrenia manage their symptoms. *Psychiatric Services, 68*(4), 324–329.

Diener, E., Chan, M. Y. (2011). Happy people live longer: Subjective well-being contributes to health and longevity. *Applied Psychology: Health and Well-Being, 3*(1).

Edmonds, E.C., Martin, A.S., Palmer, B.W., et al. (2018). Positive mental health in schizophrenia and healthy comparison groups: relationships with overall health and biomarkers. *Aging & Mental Health, 22*, 354–362.

Jeste, D.V., Palmer, B.W. (Eds). (2015). *Positive psychiatry: A clinical handbook.* American Psychiatric Publishing, Inc: Arlington, VA.

Jeste, D.V., Palmer, B.W., Rettew, D.C., et al. (2015). Positive psychiatry: Its time has come. *Journal of Clinical Psychiatry, 76*, 675–683.

Lee, E.E., Liu, J., Tu, X., et al. (2018). A widening longevity gap between people with schizophrenia and general population: A literature review and call for action. Special Issue. *Schizophrenia Research, 196*, 9–13.

Lee, E.E., Martin, A.S., Tu, X., et al. (2018). Childhood adversity and schizophrenia: The protective role of resilience in mental and physical health and metabolic markers. *Journal of Clinical Psychiatry. 79*(3).

Palmer, B.W., Martin, A.S., Depp, C., et al. (2014). Wellness within illness: Happiness in schizophrenia. *Schizophrenia Research, 159*, 151–156.

Schutte, N. S., Palanisamy, S. K., and McFarlane, J. R. (2016). The relationship between positive psychological characteristics and longer telomeres. *Psychology and Health, 31*, 1466–1480.

Summers, R. and Jeste, D.V. (Eds). (2018). Positive psychiatry: A casebook. American Psychiatric Publishing: Washington, D.C.

Van Patten, R., Lee, E.E., Daly, R., et al. (in press). Assessment of 3-dimensional wisdom in schizophrenia: Associations with neuropsychological functions and physical and mental health. *Schizophrenia Research.*

Wiley, J. F., Bei, B., Bower, J. E., & Stanton, A. L. (2017). Relationship of psychosocial resources with allostatic load: A systematic review. *Psychosomatic Medicine, 79*, 283–292.

[1]   This work was supported, in part, by the Sam and Rose Stein Institute for Research on Aging at the University of California San Diego.

Introduction:
Mental Wellness in Clinical Practice

As definitions go, the World Health Organization's definition of *health* (WHO, 1948) is truly eye-opening: "A state of complete physical, mental and social well-being, and not merely the absence of disease or infirmity." In just a few elegant words, the WHO affirms the importance of wellness, mental and otherwise, as the truest form of health and establishes that the mere absence of disease or infirmity is not considered a state of health. In other words, to live a happy, healthy, and fulfilling life, wellness is an imperative.

Wellness as an imperative has weighty implications. The WHO's definition of health certainly cannot be written off as a millennial "feel-good fluff" statement, as achieving optimum wellness is the goal of every human being's existence—in fact, it is one of our most prized possessions. It is the pursuit of wellness, in all its forms, that motivates nearly every action we take.

It is also sadly true that mental wellness, in all its forms—happiness, enthusiasm, resilience, optimism, and so on—is on a slow and steady decline in our society. Recent Gallup pole data reveal a worrisome downward slide in happiness, despite our demonstrable rise in wealth and prosperity (Gallup, 2018). Why is this happening? What are its implications? How do we fix this? These are all important questions.

Mental wellness levels are even lower in patients in our psychiatric and psychotherapy practices, where the issue of mental wellness has risen to a crisis level. We have identified at least five reasons that many of our patients are afflicted by a "Wellness Deficit Disorder":

The Diagnostic and Statistical Manual'*s model focuses on mental illness, not mental wellness.* While the *DSM* has many strengths, it focuses *only* on mental illness and not on mental wellness to any substantive degree. This is a serious shortcoming, as mental health professionals consider the *DSM* the final arbiter of what constitutes mental health. Mental wellness is the flip side of mental illness, yet it gets scant mention in the *DSM*.

Clinical training programs narrowly focus on symptom resolution. Clinical training programs in psychiatry, psychology, social work, nursing, and counseling almost exclusively focus on training clinicians to treat mental illness symptoms and offer no training in techniques to enhance mental wellness.

Clinicians aim only for symptom resolution. Not focusing on mental wellness leads to less than ideal clinical outcomes and a missed opportunity when it comes to offering the best possible care. Pause for just a second and ask yourself these two questions:

· Is your only personal goal in life to have the mere absence of depression, anxiety, and stress, or do you want more?

· Besides the absence of depression, anxiety, and stress, do you also crave things such as happiness, enthusiasm, resilience, and optimism?

We suspect that you too want *both* the absence of mental illness *and* the presence of mental wellness. And our patients ultimately have the same goals. Wellness-centric interventions, enhancing happiness, enthusiasm, resilience, and optimism, work synergistically with psychiatric medications and psychotherapies such as cognitive-behavioral therapy aimed at reducing symptoms of depression, anxiety, and so on. Including these interventions in our treatment plan can enhance outcomes for our patients.

Patients expect only symptom reduction from their clinicians. Patients under-standably turn to their clinicians for direction and goal setting in the treatment-planning process. With the prevailing clinical culture focusing exclusively on mental illness symptoms, patients expect, at best, symptom resolution and not the full attainment of mental wellness. This is truly a lost opportunity, because heightened mental wellness confers huge protection from relapse of virtually all mental health disorders.

Clinicians' lack of resources and guides on how to incorporate mental well-ness into clinical practice. Clinicians who sincerely desire to augment their traditional treatments with wellness-centric interventions have few resources to support their efforts. Those wishing to give their patients tangible materials as a "wellness prescription" often find an inadequate supply of such resources. This book aims to help address this problem, a legitimate shortcoming in the field.

About Ourselves

Stepping outside of one's comfort zone is never easy. By the time we were approaching our late thirties, we both were engaged in successful, busy practices in psychiatry and psychotherapy. We were well-liked and well-respected in our local and national communities, and we were well on our way to developing national reputations as educators and presenters on cutting-edge medication and nonmedication therapies in mental health. We were settling into a comfortable groove, and life was humming along just fine.

But there was a fly in the ointment. A decade or so into practice, we started noticing a trend in our patients. Even though their symptoms were improving, and they were grateful for our efforts to help, we started noticing that a distressingly high percentage of patients were relapsing and becoming symptomatic again. *What were we doing wrong? Why were our patients slipping out of remission?*

Once we became aware of this, we began seeing another trend in our patients: many had become the "walking wounded." These patients were lucky enough to lose most, if not all of their psychiatric symptoms, but they simply had no zest for life—they were not happy, content, enthusiastic, or joyful. They did not look forward to things. Mind you, they no longer had any meaningful symptoms of mental health problems, but they were not living a life they considered fulfilling.

This was the beginning of our humbling journey into mental wellness. First, we tentatively explored the topic, ever on the defensive that anyone might suggest "traditional" psychiatry was doing something wrong. We discovered several research papers on mental wellness that helped explain our patients' dilemma but were simply getting no play in mainstream psychiatry. After cautious months of reading and meeting several thought leaders in their fields of expertise, we hesitantly started exploring the issue of mental wellness with patients in our own clinical practice. We tread carefully, concerned that our patients might regard us as "flaky" or "new age" or see us as abandoning the traditional bounds of psychiatric thinking and practice. But this was not the case—far from it.

We discussed with our patients the concepts of mental wellness, including happiness, enthusiasm, resilience, and optimism—which we named the "HERO" traits—and how this positively impacts outcomes and functioning. Our patients enthusiastically embraced wellness-centric conversations, often saying things like, "Now you really get me!" and "Why didn't we talk about this stuff before?" We can think of no time when patients rolled their eyes as we began a conversation about wellness and how it might lead to positive outcomes. Patients appreciated that wellness interventions might make their medications work better. And we were gratified that our patients' responses to adding wellness-centric interventions to the other treatment modalities were hugely positive.

This inspired us to gain true expertise in this area and develop a wellness program that we started incorporating into our traditional practice of psychiatry and psychotherapy. We named the wellness program "WILD

5 Wellness," which stands for Wellness Interventions for Life's Demands, incorporating the five wellness interventions that are the most studied, with the best wellness outcome data in individuals suffering from psychiatric disorders: exercise, optimized nutrition, optimized sleep, mindfulness, and social connectedness. We also included daily positive psychology exercises to build certain core competencies in the HERO positive psychology traits: happiness, enthusiasm, resilience, and optimism. We discuss the elements of the WILD 5 Wellness program in detail in Part 2 of this book, and the science behind the interventions in Part 1.

Early in the development of the WILD 5 Wellness program, we found there was a lack of quality mindfulness exercises designed to reduce psychiatric symptoms and improve mental wellness. To solve this challenge, we recorded our own guided mindfulness meditation audio tracks, which we made available to our patients so they could hone their skills in mindfulness practice. We also shared these audio tracks with other clinicians at no cost as a resource to their patients. A link to these mindfulness tracks can be found in the resource section of this book.

We were not content just to develop this wellness program; we also wanted to test it in various settings. Over the last few years, we and others have researched the WILD 5 Wellness program in diverse groups of patients. A large number of individuals who did not have a psychiatric illness but wanted to further improve their mental wellness also participated in the various WILD 5 Wellness studies, and they too saw significant improvement in their levels of HERO traits and mental wellness. The positive results of each of these studies are discussed in detail in Part 2 of this book.

We have presented our research findings at multiple national and international meetings, with enthusiastic reception by our professional colleagues. Our initial concern, that our colleagues in traditional psychiatry would ostracize our "radical" thinking, did not materialize. In fact, many mental health clinicians have adopted the WILD 5 Wellness program into their clinical practices. The WILD 5 Wellness program is now being used in a variety of settings, from psychiatric practices to chronic pain centers.

About This Book

As you might have guessed, it was our colleagues who first gently encouraged us, and then insisted that we put our experiences into a book about mental wellness. The result is the book you currently hold in your hands. In this book our goal is to share all that we have learned, to arm you with resources to augment your own practice with wellness-centric interventions, to enhance essential mental wellness traits, such as happiness, enthusiasm, resilience, and optimism, in your patients.

In the upcoming chapters we share information about the positive impact that mental wellness can have on our patients, as well as the negative impact that lack of wellness can inflict. Part 1 explores the science and neurobiology of wellness and how it affects us both mentally and physically—the interconnected mind-body. Part 2 focuses on the core elements of using a wellness-centric approach with patients receiving mental healthcare, including reviews of contemporary scientific studies of mental wellness interventions. And in Part 3, we describe some of the positive effects of incorporating a wellness-centric approach into your practice, including tips and suggestions for successfully applying these interventions, how to incorporate them with psychiatric medications, and success stories from both clinicians and patients. The resource section in this book provides you with access to patient-friendly mental wellness resources. Because this is a book written for clinicians by clinicians, we offer you the means and the tools to successfully integrate wellness-centric interventions into your practice.

Please note that throughout the book we illustrate our approaches and ideas with case studies from our own experiences. The case studies we describe, although derived from actual patients in our practice, are composites—they do not represent transcripts of actual sessions, and we use fictitious names. They nonetheless exemplify approaches and dialogue we have found effective in our practice.

THE SCIENCE
AND PRACTICE
OF WELLNESS

CHAPTER 1

Making the Case for a Wellness-centric Approach to Mental Health

As mentioned in the introduction to this book, the World Health Organization (WHO, 1948) defines *health* as "a state of complete physical, mental and social well-being, and not merely the absence of disease or infirmity." Thus, optimum health, or *wellness*, involves not just the absence of illness—the absence of disease, the absence of infirmity, the absence of pain—but also the presence of well-being: physical wellness, including strength, endurance, and vitality, and mental wellness, including happiness, enthusiasm, resilience, and optimism: all the elements we need to thrive and to experience a joyful, exuberant existence.

This distinction between the presence of wellness and the absence of illness is critical, to both our patients and ourselves, as we hope to demonstrate in this chapter. Here we make the case for the need, the ease, and the benefits of including mental wellness interventions in psychiatric and psychotherapeutic practice, to improve well-being not only for our patients but also for ourselves and our practices.

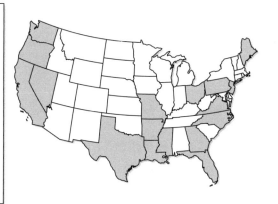

States Where Mental Wellness Has Declined:

Alaska, Hawaii, Nevada, Oregon, Arizona, Washington, California
South: Louisiana, Mississippi, Arkansas, South Carolina, Georgia, Texas, North Carolina, Florida
East: Maine, New Jersey, Pennsylvania, Virginia
Midwest: Missouri, Ohio

No States Had an Improvement in Mental Wellness

FIGURE 1.1: American wellness: 2017 rankings. Mental wellness declined in many places in 2017, and no states showed an increase.　Sources: Gallup Share Care (2018), https://wellbeingindex.sharecare .com/wp-content/uploads/2018/02/Gallup-Sharecare-State-of-American-Well-Being_2017-State-Rankings_ FINAL.pdf. Accessed June 30, 2019

The Societal Decline in Mental Wellness

Gallup regularly conducts surveys of mental wellness in America. In 2018 it published a report revealing some worrisome trends: "Other mental health metrics such as clinical diagnosis of depression, suffering from little interest or pleasure in doing things and significant daily worry all had noteworthy increases in 2017" (Gallup Share Care, 2018, p. 8). When Gallup examined mental well-being in each of the fifty U.S. states, it found that, in this land of plenty, with an abundance of wealth and prosperity, *no* state had improved in well-being, and a significant number had actually worsened (Figure 1.1). This is a damning indictment of our overall American mental health. With mental illness symptoms increasing and mental wellness declining, perhaps it is not hyperbole to diagnose America at large as suffering from a "Wellness Deficit Disorder."

From a global perspective, in a 2017 survey, the United States ranked number 14 (Helliwell, Layard, & Sachs, 2017). American happiness scores have clearly declined from 2006 to 2016 (Figure 1.2). The survey offered

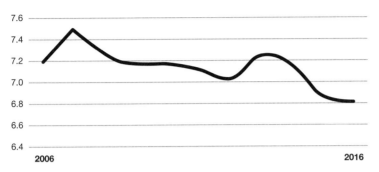

FIGURE 1.2: U.S. Happiness Score: 2006–2016.

this insight specifically aimed at American levels of happiness: "The central paradox of the modern American economy, as identified by this: income per person has increased roughly three-fold since 1960, but measured happiness has not risen. The situation has worsened in recent years: per capita GDP is still rising, but happiness is now actually falling" (Helliwell, Layard, Sachs, 2017, p. 179).

Mental health patients also clearly suffer from a mental wellness deficit. Giovanni Fava (2016), a preeminent thinker in the field of psychiatry and mental wellness, defines *euthymia* as a state characterized by a lack of mood disturbances and feeling cheerful, calm, active, and interested. Thus, euthymia is not just the elimination of psychiatric symptoms but also an abundance of mental wellness, such as cheerfulness, interest in life, and resilience. Simply diminishing mood disorder symptoms to zero is not euthymia. If achieving a true state of euthymia is the goal, then more is needed, and that "more" is enhanced levels of mental wellness (Fava[a], 2016).

The mental wellness deficit our patients experience is actually worse when they have a comorbid condition. Spinhoven and his research colleagues (2015) looked at both happiness and emotional well-being in patients with major depression, an anxiety disorder, or both conditions. Happiness and emotional well-being were decreased in those with either disorder, compared to controls, but was decreased even more in individuals who had both major depression and an anxiety disorder—and many if not most patients in psychiatric practices are afflicted with comorbid disorders. Another noteworthy finding from this study is that even patients in remission of symptoms of psychiatric illness still had low levels of mental wellness compared to controls—simply eliminating symptoms of mental illness is not sufficient. Mental wellness must also be a focus of our clinical interventions.

Mental Wellness and the *DSM*

One of the American Psychiatric Association's best-known contributions to the psychiatric and the mental health community is the *Diagnostic and Statistical Manual of Mental Disorders* (*DSM*), currently in its fifth edition. It would be hard to overestimate the importance of the *DSM* to psychiatry and to the world at large, as psychiatrists from around the globe understand and view mental disorders through the lens of the *DSM*. It is the language of psychiatric thinking, and it guides clinicians on how to conceptualize and treat psychiatric disorders.

Psychiatry is a specialty where, as yet, there are no laboratory or radiological markers for any of its disorders—*none*. The best we have are the lists of psychiatric symptoms from the *DSM* to guide our clinical decision making. And the contemporary practice of psychiatry and psychotherapy are disease-centric: they have bravely taken on the mantle of fighting all the disorders listed in the venerable *DSM*—well over 300 diagnoses are listed in the nearly 1,000 pages of the fifth edition of the book. In our mission to fight and stamp out these disorders, these specialities have done much to reduce the suffering of millions of patients around the world. Psychiatry valiantly continues to look for new options, pharmacological or otherwise, to treat serious and disabling psychiatric disorders, and psychologists and psychotherapists similarly continue to develop new forms of non-medication treatments to address a variety of mental health psychopathologies.

Despite its immeasurable value, one of the *DSM*'s great shortcomings is that it considers only the presence of certain symptoms of illness as the definition of a disorder. *It completely ignores mental wellness.* This significant limitation of the *DSM*'s approach to defining mental health contributes to clinicians focusing on illness and overlooking wellness. Mental wellness is significantly and negatively impacted by psychiatric disorders, but wellness deficits, as opposed to illness symptoms, are not listed in the *DSM* criteria for the various mental disorders. As a consequence, our conceptualization of what constitutes a mental disorder is severely constricted. This results in the following contemporary thought process: psychiatric disorders are a collection of symptoms; evidence of successful treatment of these disorders is the absence of these symptoms; therefore, remission of these symptoms is our highest goal of treatment. Wellness is completely missing from this conceptualization and thus from clinical interventions.

And studies have revealed a mismatch between what clinicians offer patients and what patients truly desire. Demyttenaere and colleagues (2015) examined this issue in depth. They first asked clinicians who had been trained in the *DSM* model to list their top five priorities when treating patients. Ranking their responses resulted in the following overall list of clinician priorities for their patients:

1. Eliminate negative feelings (blue mood, despair, anxiety)
2. Not feeling down, depressed, or hopeless
3. Regain interest/pleasure in doing things
4. Not having symptoms disrupt social life/leisure activities
5. Not feeling tired/having little energy

They focus on the very items from the *DSM* that constitute a disorder like major depression. Then the researchers asked patients to describe their top five needs from treatment:

1. Feeling that life is meaningful
2. Able to enjoy life
3. Feeling satisfied with yourself

4. Able to concentrate
5. Eliminate negative feelings (blue mood, despair, anxiety)

Note the discrepancy between the clinicians' list and the patients' list of priorities: the clinicians' list of priorities is not wellness-focused, while the patients' list clearly is. Patients ranked improvement in various aspects of mental wellness as the top three items that they desire most from treatment. Even patients suffering from a debilitating disorder like major depression reported a desire for improvement in mental wellness, not just an absence of illness symptoms.

Other studies reveal this same mismatch between clinician and patient priorities from the treatment of psychiatric disorders. Zimmerman and his team (2006) conducted a survey asking patients, outside of earshot of their clinicians, what they desire as the top areas of improvement in their psychiatric disorder:

1. Presence of positive mental health, such as optimism, vigor, self-confidence
2. Feeling like their usual, normal self
3. Return to usual level of functioning at work, home, or school
4. Feeling in emotional control
5. Participating in and enjoying relationships with family and friends

Just like in the Demyttenaere and colleagues study (2015), patients seem acutely aware they have a "Wellness Deficit Disorder" and desire improvement. In fact, they seem to rank it even higher than psychiatric symptom resolution. The top five most important factors ranked by patients do not even mention the absence of symptoms of depression (which came it at number six on this patient list of priorities). It's not that patients suffering from psychiatric disorders want one or the other—an increase in positive mental health or a decrease in mental illness symptoms. They want and desire *both*.

Wellness in Psychiatry, Psychology, and Society

Despite the focus in symptom remission in most clinical approaches to mental health, some in the world of psychology and psychiatry have recognized the importance of mental wellness and are asking clinicians to consider mental wellness as an important issue.

Hoyman's Model of Integrated Well-being

One of the early thought leaders, Howard Hoyman, authored an influential article titled "Rethinking an Ecological System Model of Man's Health, Disease, Aging, Death" (Hoyman, 1975), published in the *Journal of School Health*. He laid out a model that integrates mental well-being with social, physiological, and spiritual elements. Figure 1.3 demonstrates the 4-component model of well-being proposed by Hoyman.

Hoyman's work has been highly influential in the world of wellness, laying the foundation by establishing that wellness is multifactorial and based on a number of interdependent factors: social, personal, mental, and physiological. Others have used his specific model to implement and refine various wellness programs (Demiris, 2013), and we were strongly influenced by it in creating our own WILD 5 Wellness program (described in Part 2).

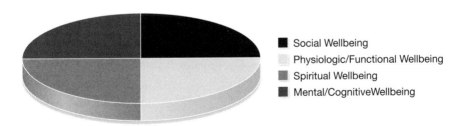

Social Wellbeing
Physiologic/Functional Wellbeing
Spiritual Wellbeing
Mental/CognitiveWellbeing

FIGURE 1.3: Hoyman's Model of Wellness

SAMHSA and Wellness

The Substance Abuse and Mental Health Services Administration (SAM-HSA) is an important part of the US federal government's response to the needs of individuals with mental illnesses. SAMHSA (2016) has identified the following areas as components of wellness:

- **Emotional:** coping effectively with life and creating satisfying relationships
- **Environmental:** good health by occupying pleasant, stimulating environments that support well-being
- **Financial:** satisfaction with current and future financial situations
- **Intellectual:** recognizing creative abilities and finding ways to expand knowledge and skills
- **Occupational:** personal satisfaction and enrichment from one's work
- **Physical:** recognizing the need for physical activity, healthy food, and sleep
- **Social:** developing a sense of connection, belonging, and a well-developed support system
- **Spiritual:** Expanding a sense of purpose and meaning in life

Focus on Mental Wellness in Other Nations

Recognizing that the mental wellness trait of happiness was important to its citizens, the United Arab Emirates (UAE) took an innovative step: in 2016 its prime minister, Sheikh Mohammed bin Rashid Al Maktoum, announced the appointment of Ohood bint Khalifa Al Roumi as the country's first minister of state for happiness—the same governmental level as the minister of defense and the minister of finance (UAE, 2019). The minister of happiness is charged with finding ways to improve life satisfaction and mental wellness among the UAE citizens.

Like many countries, Bhutan (a tiny country in Southeast Asia) uses gross domestic product as a measure of its wealth. But unlike other countries, Bhutan instituted a new measure in 1972 called the Gross National Happiness index (Bhutan GNH, 2019). The country conducts regular national surveys of its citizens' happiness and mental wellness and designs its national policies to achieve sustained gains in these measures. Venezuela, too is addressing mental wellness at a governmental level by creating a cabinet-level position called the Ministry of Supreme Social Happiness in 2013 (Business Insider, 2013).

In early 2018, the United Kingdom became the first developed Western country to address this issue by establishing a cabinet-level position titled the Minister of Loneliness (UK Government Press Release, 2018). Like most Western countries, the United Kingdom is becoming alarmed at the dropping rates of mental wellness and the increasing social fragmentation and loneliness in its population. The Minister of Loneliness and her staff are charged with creating societal-level interventions to reduce social isolation and improve mental wellness.

Workplace Wellness Programs

Most, if not all, Fortune 500 companies have robust employee assistance programs (EAPs), as do many midsize companies. EAPs provide a range of assistance to employees, from dealing with work-life stressors to even legal matters, and all are commendable pursuits. In most EAPs, there is no significant attention paid to mental wellness, and we are aware of no EAPs that directly help their clientele target mental wellness traits such a happiness, optimism, enthusiasm, purpose in life, etc. At the government level, federal and state employees also typically have access to EAPs and the wellness programs offered by them. Thus, a large portion of American workers have access to some type of wellness program. Ultimately the organization stands to benefit from the employees' enhanced wellness.

The Negative Impact of Low Mental Wellness

Given how many clinicians already have too much on their plates, isn't the goal of driving patients' symptoms into remission enough, without also taking on the task of improving mental wellness? Yet research shows that mental wellness directly affects symptoms of mental illness.

For example, Menezes and colleagues (2013) assessed a cohort of 5249 participants from Pelotas, Brazil. They examined happiness, a component of mental wellness, on a scale of 1 (lowest) to 7 (highest). Individuals who scored less than 2 on this scale had a 55% risk of depression, those with a score between 2 and 3 had a 34.8% risk of depression, and the risk kept declining—in those with a happiness score of 7 it was only 1.6%. Thus, the risk of developing depression is 34 times greater in those who reported significant unhappiness than in those reporting high levels of happiness. This suggests that considering mental wellness as a modifiable risk factor may reduce the risk of recurrence of a psychiatric disorder, no matter the treatment philosophy.

Another study shows us the importance of well-being not just to an individual but for those connected to that person. A group of researchers (Tough, Siever, Benzies, Leew, & Johnston, 2010) examined maternal mental well-being and developmental difficulties in children and found that 37% of children born to mothers with low mental health (such as sadness, apathy) had developmental difficulties, compared to 17% of children born to mothers with better mental health (such as happiness, contentment).

Psychiatry and psychotherapy, in addition to targeting mental disorders, is also concerned with health behaviors, such as smoking. Steptoe and colleagues (2009) examined the interaction of mental wellness and health behaviors in individuals from the United States, Eastern Europe, and Asia. In each of the three groups, the percentage of non-smokers was higher among individuals who were "very satisfied" with life compared to those who were dissatisfied or who felt neutral. Thus, mental wellness appears to positively impact not just mental health but also health behaviors.

How Mental Illness and Mental Wellness Intersect

Mike Slade, a prominent researcher in the interaction of mental illness and mental wellness, has a helpful model to expand our understanding of mental wellness (Slade, 2010). He distinguishes high mental illness symptoms, and low mental illness symptoms. The traditional approach in psychiatry and psychotherapy is to move patients from high mental illness through treatment to low mental illness. Once this is done, treatment has been successful.

But according to Slade, this approach doesn't account for the overall well-being of the patient. His model also shows low subjective well-being at the bottom and high subjective well-being at the top. Thus, in Slade's model, individuals with essentially no mental illness symptoms, but without high subjective well-being symptoms, are at best in the "incomplete mental health" category, which he describes as "languishing." In other words, well-being and mental illness interact. Having high subjective well-being symptoms and high mental illness symptoms is also an inadequate state of mental health, which Slade labels as "struggling." Only those patients who have both *low* mental illness symptoms and *high* subjective well-being, are considered optimum, and are labeled as "flourishing."

This is an elegant way for us to conceptualize both mental illness and mental wellness. It is not that one is more important than the other. Rather, they are equal partners in achieving the best possible mental health for our patients.

HERO Wellness Traits: Results of a National Wellness Survey

To measure mental wellness in the United States, we undertook a large nationwide survey of American mental health (Jain et al., 2016[a]). We wanted to see how people in the fifty U.S. states self-assessed the important mental wellness traits of happiness, optimism, resilience, and optimism—what we now call the HERO wellness traits (more on this in Part 2).

A total of 757 people from across the United States, men and women from the ages of 18 to 86, completed the anonymous survey about the state of their mental health in the previous week. Among these 757 partici-pants, 490 individuals (170 males, 320 females) reported neither a mental health disorder nor a chronic physical pain condition, and 169 individuals (32 males, 137 females) reported having a mental health condition in the last six months; 146 individuals (42 males, 104 females) reported chronic pain, and 48 individuals (9 males, 39 females) reported both a mental health disorder and chronic pain. Each of these individuals filled out an online survey of their mental well-being by answering a number of ques-tions, with their responses ranging from 0, not at all, to 10, the highest possible score.

The initial results are summarized in Table 1.1. Respondents who reported having a mental health condition in the last six months showed deficits in wellness traits, and in overall assessment of wellness, compared with respondents who had no mental health condition.

TABLE 1.1 RESULTS OF OUR ONLINE SURVEY ON MENTAL WELLNESS: SELF-ASSESSMENT OF MENTAL WELLNESS TRAITS

	Mean score[a]		Mean deficit for respondents with a mental health condition
Mental Wellness Trait	Without a mental health condition (*n* = 490)	With a mental health condition (*n* = 169)	
Happiness	6.5	4.9	25%
Enthusiasm	5.9	4.6	22%
Resilience	7.2	5.9	18%
Optimism	6.5	5.0	23%
Overall	7.4	5.5	26%

[a] The HERO wellness traits (happiness, enthusiasm, resilience, and optimism) were measured by the HERO Wellness Scale: a Likert scale from 0 to 10, with 0 being the lowest and 10 being the highest/best score.

We also examined respondents' desired levels for each of the HERO wellness traits (Table 1.2). We divided the study results into four groups: those with no mental health problems, those with mental health challenges, those with chronic pain conditions, and those with both mental health challenges and chronic pain conditions. For each of the HERO traits, the desired levels were near identical, no matter the group. There is a powerful lesson here for all clinicians: *Human beings, irrespective of whether or not they have a physical or mental disorder, desire about the same levels of happiness, enthusiasm, resilience, and optimism.*

TABLE 1.2 RESULTS OF OUR ONLINE SURVEY ON MENTAL WELLNESS (N = 757): AVERAGE DESIRED LEVELS FOR THE HERO WELLNESS TRAITS

Group	Desired HERO Wellness Trait[a]			
	Happiness	Enthusiasm	Resilience	Optimism
No Condition Group (*n* = 490)	7.8	7.5	8.3	8.0
Mental Health Condition Group (*n* = 169)	7.8	7.5	8.2	7.8
Chronic Pain Group (*n* = 146)	7.6	7.3	8.3	7.8
Both Mental Health + Chronic Pain Group (*n* = 48)	7.4	7.0	8.2	7.6

[a] *The HERO wellness traits (happiness, enthusiasm, resilience, and optimism) were measured by the HERO Wellness Scale: a Likert scale from 0 to 10, with 0 being the lowest and 10 being the highest/best score.*

We also asked our respondents how important they considered these mental wellness traits. You will notice we asked how *important* they considered a wellness trait, and not how much they *desired* it. This is a crucial point as desired levels can be higher than its perceived importance, and as we wanted a clear, accurate picture of how important wellness traits were to our participants, we made a decision to ask the questions accordingly. We were struck by two findings:

- The level of importance participants ascribed to mental wellness traits such as happiness, enthusiasm, resilience and optimism were all in the range of 7 to 9 (on a scale of 0–10)
- The level of importance was similar for all individuals, whether or not they had a mental health condition

Double-Hit Disorders

The vast majority of individuals in clinic populations suffer from both the presence of mental illness and the absence of mental wellness—a "double-hit" condition. Although some individuals in clinical settings possess significant mental illness symptoms and thankfully have no deficits in mental wellness, research data and clinical experience indicate these are a small minority.

Our position is that *all* psychiatric disorders are in reality dual-pathology conditions: they involve both an increase in psychiatric illness symptoms and a decrease in mental wellness traits. Yet as we described above, the *DSM*-based model focuses on the former and entirely ignores the latter. Consider, for example, the *DSM* criteria for one of the most common of all psychiatric disorders, major depression. The *DSM* lists nine criteria, and all nine appropriately talk about the illness aspects of this devastating disorder. However, not a single item lists the absence or reduction of mental wellness traits, such as happiness, enthusiasm, optimism, or resilience.

In the traditional clinical view of the relationship between mental illness and mental wellness (Figure 1.4A), clinicians treat these as completely separate entities. Psychiatrists and psychotherapists are charged with tackling the symptoms of mental illness because patients were thought to be afflicted *only* with mental illness. We propose to treat mental illness and mental wellness as overlapping, interactive facets of overall mental healh (Figure 1.4B), an approach supported by multiple scientific studies, as we describe throughout this book.

If psychiatry and psychotherapy start seeing psychiatric disorders as "double-hit" conditions, then we would devote resources to addressing *both* conditions. Viewed from this perspective, recovery would mean that mental illness symptoms (negative traits) diminish *and* mental wellness (positive traits) increase, in separate but parallel trajectories (Figure 1.5). This has strong potential to significantly improve outcomes: results from research by ourselves and others show that, when both mental illness and mental wellness issues are addressed, patients demonstrate global benefit and do so quickly, often in as little as 30 days (described in Part 2).

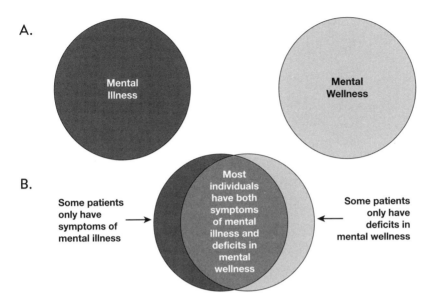

FIGURE 1.4: **A**, The traditional clinical view of mental health sees mental illness and mental wellness as separate, mutually exclusive entities. **B**, A model that views our patients' mental illness and mental wellness as overlapping, interactive facets of overall well-being.

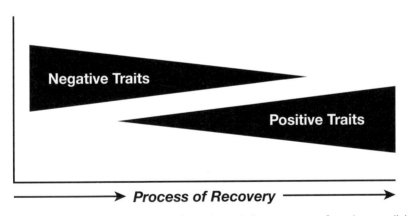

FIGURE 1.5: Mental illness symptoms (negative traits) are separate from but parallel to mental wellness (positive traits). The y-axis represents magnitude of the traits, and the x-axis represents time for the recovery process: negative traits diminish and positive traits increase as recovery proceeds.

Incorporating Wellness in Mental Health Practice

In the classic American tradition, all new movements in time give birth to a countermovement, and the same is true for the wellness movement in the scientific and lay community. Recently, some have expressed skepticism about the current focus on mental wellness, and some of their arguments are worthy of consideration. Take, for example, an article by Gruber and colleagues titled "A Dark Side of Happiness? How, When, and Why Happiness Is Not Always Good" (2011). Popular books such as *The Happiness Trap: How to Stop Struggling and Start Living* (2007) by Russ Harris and Steven Hayes raise similar concerns. Solid arguments are laid out in these articles and books warning us that the mindless pursuit of mental wellness and happiness can worsen mental health, not improve it.

We agree that a blind fidelity to mental wellness, at all costs and with no rhyme or reason, is neither appropriate nor in anyone's best interests. However, we offer the following reasons for why focusing on and enhancing mental wellness is beneficial for most individuals, which we elaborate on throughout this book:

1. Individuals with a higher degree of mental wellness have better physical and mental health. They tend to live longer, have less risk of depression, anxiety, and other mental health challenges. They are more resilient in the face of stressors, and they are better able to parent and contribute to society at large.
2. Individuals with higher levels of mental wellness have better relationships and are more productive at work. We do not find any convincing or persuasive evidence that reveals people with high degrees of mental wellness are less productive, less driven or are less happy in life. We are simply not persuaded that mental wellness comes with a negative impact on work or school performance.
3. Survey after survey in the United States and from overseas show that people from all walks of life highly rank wellness, happiness, and

contentment (all traits of positive mental health) as top life goals. If the masses believe that mental wellness is important, and they strongly desire it, is it really fair to say they are uniformly wrong?

4. Data indicate that even those suffering from a devastating condition like depression desire wellness. In fact, studies reveal depressed patients crave well-being and often rank the need for mental wellness over mere symptom resolution.

5. Even our patients who are in remission still report that "something was missing" from their treatment experience. Furthermore, results from our national survey indicate the importance of mental wellness and the need to adopt wellness-centric interventions. Improvement in mental wellness leads to global improvement in functionality, work productivity, sleep, eating behaviors, and less depression and anxiety.

As we discussed above, patients afflicted with psychiatric disorders rank mental wellness improvement quite highly—often even higher than the resolution of the symptoms of depression. Multiple patient surveys reveal the need to broaden our vision and our interventions. While psychopharmacology is quite often the most judicious way to treat a patient's psychiatric suffering, there is limited evidence that psychopharmacology alone addresses the mental wellness needs of our patients.

In psychiatry and psychotherapy, clinicians often use augmentation strategies to enhance treatment effects. This is by necessity, as suboptimum responses often occur with our interventions. Most augmentation interventions are usually additional medications or, less commonly, psychotherapy. Yet if wellness deficits are so common and have such a negative impact on our patients, why not consider wellness-centric interventions as an augmentation therapy?

For wellness interventions to gain wide acceptance in psychiatry and psychotherapy, they need to demonstrate scientific validity to all the stakeholders in mental health, including psychiatrists, family practitioners, rheumatologists, pain specialists, psychiatric nurse practitioners, physician assistants, psycho-therapists, psychologists, social workers, nurses, administrators, policy mak-ers, and of course, patients and their family members. As has often been said before, good ideas are a dime a dozen, but good ideas that are based in science and demonstrate strong outcomes data are the ones that end up changing things for the better in our practices. Thankfully, wellness-centric applications in mental health treatment have a solid scientific basis. This book examines the evidence derived from epidemiological studies, including patient surveys; clinical outcomes studies; neurobiological and imaging studies; and wellness-centric interventions as anti-inflammatory agents.

Before the professional community accepts an intervention for clinical utilization, it demands evidence for its effectiveness and safety. Therefore we subjected wellness-centric interventions to a high level of scrutiny, exam-ining two emerging concepts: positive psychiatry and positive psychology. We also examined clinical studies conducted around the world which eval-uate the impact of wellness-centric interventions in patients with psychiatric disorders. It is our hope that, with such a deep, unbiased assessment of the evidence, you will embrace wellness as one of the central tenants of treat-ment of your patients.

We offer seven reasons that we think will persuade you to incorporate wellness-centric interventions into your clinical armamentarium, elaborated in Part 1 of this book on the science of mental wellness:

- Patients who have higher levels of mental wellness, have lower rates of psychiatric symptoms, such as depression, anxiety, etc.
- Patients with higher levels of mental wellness are more likely to engage in healthy behaviors, such as lower rates of smoking, exercis-ing more often, etc.
- Patients with higher levels of mental wellness show greater resil-ience to stress
- Patients with higher levels of mental wellness are less likely to have an excessive cortisol response when exposed to stress

- Inflammation both at rest, as well as stress-induced inflammation, is lower in patients with higher levels of mental wellness
- Individuals with higher levels of mental wellness live longer and have healthier telomeres on their chromosomes, as compared to individuals with lower levels of mental wellness
- Patients rank mental wellness as one of their highest treatment priorities

Part 2 then discusses the core principles incorporating elements of mental wellness and the HERO wellness traits into your wellness-centric practice, offering practical tools for implementation. Part 3 rounds out the book by offering tips gleaned from our clinical experience and examples from both clinicians and patients who have benefited from adding a wellness focus to their clinical experience.

As you read through this book, we ask that you consider what might happen if you did the following when meeting with your patients:

- Initiate conversations about both psychiatric illnesses and mental wellness deficits at nearly every visit
- Measure both mental illness and mental wellness symptoms at baseline and periodically thereafter
- Provide patients with reading materials and clear directions on how to incorporate these practices on a regular basis
- Adopt an active coaching model of interaction and motivation enhancement, and encourage patients to continuously "aim higher" for full recovery

Imagine what this type of approach might offer your patients as you read through the science and practice of wellness we describe. It is our hope that, once you have read this book, you will not just imagine but plan and succeed in incorporating these concepts of mental wellness in your practice, to the benefit of your patients and yourself.

PART 1

The Science of Mental Wellness

Our understanding of the science of mental and physical wellness has grown by leaps and bounds and is poised to have profound effects on how all aspects of healthcare are studied, measured, and delivered—to the benefit of our patients. In Part 1 of this book, we review the science behind the relationship between mental wellness and physical well-being, and provide a background for our review of principles of mental wellness interventions in Part 2. Chapter 2 examines how the brain and the body are interconnected and interact to both produce and respond to varying levels of mental wellness. Chapter 3 takes a closer look at how mental wellness impacts inflammation in particular, which has been found to have a profound relationship with our mental states. Chapter 4 rounds out Part 1 by describing how these interconnected systems unite to help us maintain our health and wellness.

CHAPTER 2

Mental Wellness and Brain-Body Connections

In contrast to the narrowly focused, brain-centric thinking prevalent in psychiatry and psychotherapy, a wider, more inclusive, and ultimately more accurate view of both mental illness and mental wellness views the brain-body as a unified organ. The intimate and synergistic relationship between the brain and the body is not just an issue of scientific curiosity—it also helps us expand our therapeutic options.

For example, the vagal nerve, or cranial nerve X, is a major part of the parasympathetic system (which in turn is part of the autonomic nervous system). It originates in the midbrain, has connections to the limbic system, and then, like a mighty river, leisurely meanders through our body, with major connections with the heart, gastrointestinal organs, spinal column, urinary system, and reproductive organs. The vagal nerve, which uses acetylcholine as its major neurotransmitter to signal and control various functions, impacts both brain function and body function. This is how emotions and thoughts impact the body, and how in turn the body can impact the brain and the mind.

This bi-directional relationship extends to disease states as well. During states of stress and depression, the parasympathetic system is in an imbalanced state, which contributes to heightened depression and anxiety, insomnia and disturbed sleep, increased heart rate, gastrointestinal disturbances

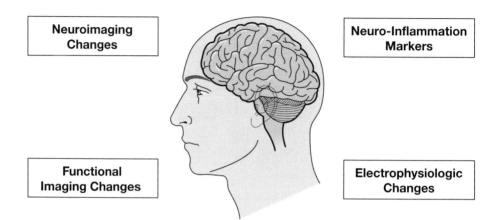

FIGURE 2.1: Tools to examine the neurobiology of mental wellness

like excessive gastric acid production, diarrhea, irritable bowel symptoms, sexual disturbances, and increased bodily pains, among others. Wellness-centric interventions, as described throughout this book, can reverse this abnormal mind-body communication, thereby ameliorating symptoms of a psychiatric disorder, as well as enhancing mental wellness markers.

As noted in Chapter 1, mental wellness deficits are prevalent in all fifty states in the United States and are even more evident in our clinical populations. However, *wellness deficits are reversible*, as demonstrated by multiple neurobiological studies in the field of wellness, involving neuroimaging, functional imaging, neuroinflammatory markers, and electrophysiologic changes, measured via brain and body metabolites, autonomic nervous system tone, and many other methods (Figure 2.1).

Psychiatric Disorders and the Brain

As we look at studies from the fields of major depression, bipolar disorder, and schizophrenia, a common theme emerges: the human brain is negatively impacted by these disorders in enumerable ways. Generally speaking, the brain structures primarily targeted by psychiatric disorders

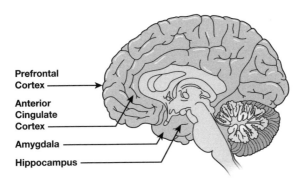

Prefrontal
Cortex

Anterior
Cingulate
Cortex

Amygdala

Hippocampus

FIGURE 2.2: The brain structures primarily targeted by psychiatric disorders.

include the prefrontal cortex, the anterior cingulate cortex, the hippocampus, and the amygdala (Figure 2.2):

> *The prefrontal cortex* (PFC) gives us the very core of who we are as humans. The PFC is the largest lobe of the brain, sitting behind the forehead and just above the eyeballs, and its importance in mental wellness is unmatched. It is unusually large in human beings, and it is responsible for many of the higher functions that make us human: intelligence, motivation, drive, and our ability to work in groups like no other species in history. The PFC is divided into a few distinct anatomic and functional regions, including the dorsolateral PFC, the ventromedial PFC, and the orbitofrontal PFC. These areas play prominent roles in much of the research in wellness.
>
> *The cingulate cortex*, a narrow band of gray matter that straddles the C-shaped corpus callosum, is important for processing emotions. It is a small structure but of great importance in psychiatry and mental wellness. The cingulate cortex, and particularly the anterior cingulate cortex, is involved with regulation of both negative and positive emotions. The subgenual region of the cingulate cortex is an important organ in mood processing—in deep brain stimulation treatment

of depression, electrodes are often placed in this region. The anterior cingulate cortex is also involved in the processing of pleasurable stimuli.

The hippocampus is a brain structure shaped like a seahorse, hence its name: *hippocamp* is Greek for seahorse. The hippocampus plays a central role in creation of memory, emotional processing, and stress management, and it is often damaged by chronic and unremitting psychiatric disorders. There is convincing evidence that depression reduces hippocampal volume and that wellness interventions increase it. The hippocampus plays an impressive role in controlling the functioning of the major mind-body pathways: the autonomic nervous system (ANS), the hypothalamic–pituitary–adrenal (HPA) axis, and the neuro-immune system.

The amygdala, which lives deep in the recesses of the brain and is the size and shape of an almond, is an extremely important member of the mood and anxiety circuit. It deals with automatic fear responses and is often implicated in anxiety disorders, rage reactions, and emotional dyscontrol. When functioning in a healthy state, the amygdala helps with threat assessment by managing threat-opportunity situations. However, when the amygdala misperceives threat, it becomes overactive, which leads to heightened fear and a strong startle response. The ultimate result of this hyperactivity is increased mental illness and decreased mental wellness.

The "Triple Highways" of Bi-directional Communication

The HPA Axis

The hypothalamic–pituitary–adrenal (HPA) axis, one of the great systems in the human body, could be considered one of the prime members of the neuroendocrine system. Figure 2.3 illustrates the three members of the HPA axis and the various hormones that help these structures communicate

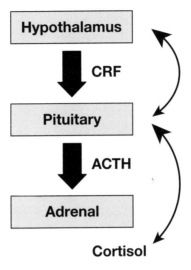

FIGURE 2.3: The hypothalamic-pituitary-adrenal (HPA) axis feedback loop. The three elements of the HPA axis communicate via the hormones corticotropin-releasing factor (CRF), adrenocorticotropic hormone (ACTH), and cortisol.

with one another. Despite being located in different parts of the body, the hypothalamus and pituitary in the brain and the adrenal glands, one above each kidney, function as a single system.

> *The hypothalamus*, situated just below the large thalamus (hence the name *hypo*thalamus), has several tasks in mood and mental wellness regulation and is the fountainhead of the HPA axis. The hypothalamus secretes the hormone corticotropin-releasing factor (CRF), to direct the pituitary to produce its own signaling hormone in the HPA axis cascade. The hypothalamus in turn is directed to increase or decrease CRF production by several other organs in the brain, most notably the hippocampus. In fact, the hippocampus's control over the hypothalamus is so strong that this system has been called the HHPA (hippocampal–hypothalamic–pituitary–adrenal) axis. This HPA axis's connection with the hippocampus is especially important to behavioral health and mental wellness because

the hippocampus is where we store memory and is the organ most likely to be adversely affected in acute and chronic stress situations. The HHPA axis is not merely a physiological axis but also a neurobehavioral pathway responsive to our state of mental health and wellness, negative or positive.

The pituitary gland is connected to the brain via the pituitary stalk, dangling below the brain in its own bony cradle at the base of the skull. Among its very long list of duties and tasks, the hypothalamus signals to the pituitary to increase its production of adrenocorticotropic hormone (ACTH). ACTH diffuses into the bloodstream, making its way to the adrenal cortex, which it directs to produce cortisol. Thus, the pituitary is a go-between for the hypothalamus and the adrenal gland.

The adrenal glands are structures that sit right above the kidneys. The inner part of the adrenal glands, called the medulla, produces norepinephrine and mineralocorticoid hormones. The outer layers of the adrenal gland, called the adrenal cortex—the final member of the HPA axis—respond to the direct commands of the ACTH released from the pituitary by producing cortisol, essential for maintaining optimum physical and mental health. Both very high and very low cortisol levels are harmful to mental health and well-being. Excess circulating cortisol is found in states of high mental illness and in states of low mental wellness. The consequences of chronically elevated cortisol levels include disturbed sleep, fatigue, weight gain, greater susceptibility to infections, increased vulnerability to stress, and impaired glucose tolerance, among many others.

The HPA axis is not just a unidirectional system. As you can see in Figure 2.3, cortisol has inhibitory effects on the pituitary, which in turn has inhibitory effects on the hypothalamus. This decreases the production of CRF and ACTH, which in turn leads to lower production of cortisol by the adrenal glands. This system of checks and balances is designed to keep cortisol in a healthy range. However, in both high mental illness and in low mental wellness states, this feedback loop's functioning is faulty, with both the pituitary and the hypothalamus exhibiting resistance to the inhibitory effects of the high circulating cortisol levels. Without this inhibition, the production of CRF and ACTH continues unabated, leading to further production of cortisol in a vicious cycle.

To best understand how important the HPA axis is to mental health, we need look no further than examples of unusually weak or unusually strong activity of the HPA axis: Addison's disease, caused by underperforming adrenal glands, and Cushing's disease, a classic example of excessive functioning of the adrenal cortex, with resultant excess cortisol. These disorders present with physical symptoms, but depression, anxiety, and insomnia also are common in both. In fact, with Cushing's disease frank psychosis is a possibility.

Mental health has a similar relationship with the HPA axis. In states of both high mental distress and lower mental wellness, the HPA axis is generally overactive, which triggers a cascade of events leading to less optimal physical and mental health. It is important to note that mental health biologically impacts the hippocampus, an important member of the limbic system. The hippocampus modulates HPA axis functioning (the HHPA axis) and thus is a direct line of communication for emotions, adversity, and wellness to the very core of the HPA axis's functioning.

Autonomic Nervous System

The autonomic nervous system (ANS) is the unsung hero of mind-body health, illness, and wellness. The term "autonomic" denotes its relative independence from the other parts of the neurological system, such as the motor and the sensory systems. It controls and modulates many factors crucial for our mental and physical well-being, such as heart rate, respiration, gastrointestinal motility, digestion, pupil size, urination, defecation, blood pressure, sweating, anxiety, and emotional reactiveness. Fortunately, measurable positive changes in the functioning of the ANS can be created by specific wellness interventions, such as mindfulness practice, improved sleep hygiene, physical exercise, and other interventions discussed throughout this book.

The ANS arises from the midbrain and spinal column, below the level of the cerebral cortex. The ANS "listens" to and is modified by the cortex, the part of the neurological system we use to think and create memories and generate emotions and feelings, but we are usually unaware of it as it functions "automatically" in the background. Mental wellness interventions leverage this intimate back-and-forth relationship between the ANS and the cerebral cortex.

The ANS has two major components: the sympathetic nervous system (SNS) and the parasympathetic nervous system (PNS):

The Sympathetic Nervous System.   The SNS is the cornerstone in the human fight-or-flight system critical to survival and functioning. When activated by a sudden and unexpected physical or mental stressor, the SNS releases two neurotransmitters: norepinephrine and epinephrine. Massive surges of these transmitters cause a coordinated response, with increased heart rate, pupil dilation, increased blood flow to the muscles, and other changes needed for a successful fight-or-flight response.

The SNS fires at a low steady rate, even when not engaged in a fight-or-flight response, to continuously manage alertness, blood pressure, and other critical elements of functioning. The SNS response during acute mental stress is healthy and positive, but only if the stressor is acute and dissipates rapidly. If the stress is chronic or extreme, then the SNS can get "stuck" in high gear, as happens with posttraumatic stress disorder (PTSD). Many symptoms of PTSD, such as feeling jumpy, irritability, poor sleep, and hypervigilance, are all courtesy of an overactivated SNS.

Another kind of stress devastating to the normal functioning of the SNS is chronic, low-grade, randomly occurring psychological stress. An example might be a woman whose spouse randomly yells and berates her, but then calms down and feels remorseful. After repeated such events, the SNS can stay overactivated for prolonged periods. And this phenomenon has both physiological and psychological consequences, including greater risk of hypertension and cardiac events. An overactive SNS also negatively impacts mental health and mental wellness as a component of panic disorder, major depression, and generalized anxiety disorder, as well as lower rates of the HERO wellness traits: happiness, enthusiasm, resilience, and optimism.

The SNS also has the ability to impact literally every member of the immune system, including bone marrow, spleen, and thymus gland. Even macrophages, the foot soldiers of the inflammatory system, have norepinephrine receptors studded on their cell walls and produce pro-inflammatory cytokines in response to SNS signals.

The Para-Sympathetic Nervous System.   The PNS is the great balancer to the SNS within the ANS (Figure 2.4). The exquisite balance between these two systems is crucial for optimum physical and mental health, and many mental wellness interventions positively improve the tone of this crucial system. The PNS is widely distributed throughout the human body and is responsible for modulating a huge number of functions, literally from head to toe.

Several cranial nerves have parasympathetic functions and control such critical functions as pupil size, salivation, and even the production of tears. But without question, the real star of the PNS is the tenth cranial nerve: the vagal nerve. This impressive cranial nerve descends from the midbrain to innervate multiple structures, such as the larynx, heart, gastrointestinal system, liver, spleen, urinary system organs, and both male and female sexual organs.

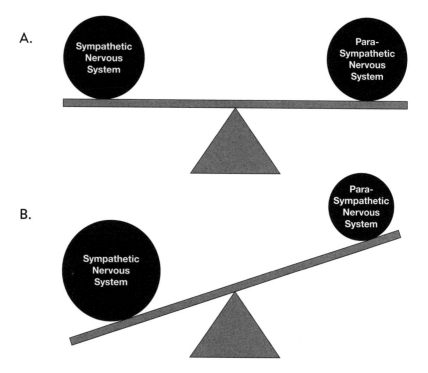

FIGURE 2.4: **A**, The ANS in balance: the PNS balances the SNS's response to stress. **B**, The ANS in stress, mental distress, and low mental wellness: the dysregulated SNS overwhelms the balancing force of the PNS.

The neurotransmitter acetylcholine is the main chemical messenger of the PNS, and many organs possess acetylcholine receptors, taking their direct cues from the PNS. Acetylcholine receptors are widely distributed in the brain and are densely located in the prefrontal cortex, where they impact cognition; in the limbic system, where they impact mood, anxiety, and stress management; and in the various structures of the pons and medulla, which control wakefulness, alertness, concentration, attention, and food satiety. And, like the SNS, the PNS is deeply intertwined with the inflammatory system, starting with the bone marrow, spleen, and the thymus gland, which have acetylcholine receptors that respond to activation of the PNS, leading to an anti-inflammatory response.

ANS dysregulation has negative consequences for both mental and physical health—so much of the brain and body, so richly innervated by both the PNS and the SNS and studded throughout with their receptors, can be negatively impacted. Both the SNS and PNS are crucial in mental health and mental well-being; they balance each other, often exerting equal and opposing forces. Both acute and chronic low-grade stressors can adversely impact the ANS: mental illness and lowered mental wellness both are associated with an excessively strong sympathetic (SNS) drive and a weakened parasympathetic (PNS) drive. Successfully restoring ANS balance involves interventions that lower SNS tone and/or heighten PNS tone.

The fountainhead of both the SNS and PNS neurons anatomically resides in the midbrain, where neurons that produce serotonin, norepinephrine, and dopamine reside and interact with one another and with systems throughout the brain. This shared neurobiology is designed so that none of these neurotransmitter systems operate as truly autonomous entities; rather, they respond to one another to maintain homeostasis. The ANS has reciprocal ties with these neurotransmitter systems, and via this pathway the ANS impacts both mental illness and mental wellness.

The hippocampus has a strong ability to control the ANS, just as it does with the HPA axis. The hippocampus is rich in norepinephrine and acetylcholine receptors—the primary neurotransmitter messengers of the SNS and PNS, respectively. The hippocampus is deeply involved in memory, stress, and mood management; hence, there is a bi-directional relationship between the ANS and the hippocampus. In individuals with significant mental health challenges, the pathology in the hippocampus spills over to the ANS system, which then affects other parts of the brain and the body. Conversely, individuals with a higher degree of mental wellness have optimum hippocampal function, which has a positive effect on the ANS.

Inflammation: The Evolutionarily Ancient Messenger System

Many people are surprised to learn that inflammation plays an important role in the bi-directional communication between the brain and the body. Human beings possess an inflammatory system that is highly adaptive, similar to the ANS and the HPA axis. Our success as a species is in many ways due to our ability to create a balance between the pro-inflammatory and the anti-inflammatory response systems. Many of us think inflammation primarily protects us from bacteria and viruses, which of course it does. But studies have now revealed that the inflammatory system has also evolved to help us manage our emotional, mental, and physical wellness.

The Traditional View of Inflammation.   Inflammation was once thought only to be part of our bacterial and viral infection fighting system, having nothing to do with the brain or the mind. The blood-brain barrier was thought to keep the immune system out of the cerebral cortex. And since the brain has no lymphatic system and no macrophages or lymphocytes, traditional approaches to mental health that focus only on the brain had no need to account for inflammation.

This traditional view is understandable, given the history of how we understand our physiology. Inflammation as a phenomenon is not new to the medical sciences, with thinkers as far back as the ancient Egyptians and Greeks reporting on the four classic signs of inflammation: *rubor* (redness), *calor* (temperature), *tumor* (swelling), and *dolor* (pain). Early physicians noticed that the body had a very characteristic system of defense that started and ended in the body. This inflammatory response to an infection was usually caused by an invading bacteria, and the organ most accessible to visual inspection at that time was the skin. Later, with the invention of the microscope and the advent of animal models to study disease processes, it became apparent the body was very good at detecting invading foreign, harmful, and noxious elements such as bacteria and mounting both a quick and a slow cascade of defense activities.

This defense mechanism over time came to be called the immune system. The quick response system was called the innate immune system, and the slow system came to be called the adaptive immune system. Over decades, many more members of this immune system were identified and cataloged. The lymphatic system and its tributaries were identified. Various cells in the circulating blood system were identified, and white blood cells (WBC) in particular were accurately seen as important players in the immune system's functioning.

The Modern View of Inflammation. Advances in microscopy, cell and receptor labeling, and functional magnetic resonance imaging (MRI) have led to a clearer understanding of how the brain and body interact via the immune system. These advances have changed the way we view inflammation, which is now considered a key part of mental health and well-being and is reversing some long-held assumptions:

> *The immune system does more than just protect against foreign invaders.* Clinicians noticed that patients with AIDS, who were extremely susceptible to infections due their HIV-ravaged immune system, also had a surprisingly large incidence of depression, anxiety, sometimes psychosis, and occasionally even frank dementia. By the early 1990s it became clear that much of this psychopathology resulted from heightened inflammation in the body. There is a bi-directional line of communication between the brain and the body. The body, when inflamed, can provoke the brain into producing more inflammation, and the brain, when stressed, either acutely or chronically, can make the body mount a clear and measurable pro-inflammatory response.
>
> *The immune system does not end at the blood-brain barrier.* Recent advances show that the brain is continuously "sampling" the body's environment for inflammation status, by allowing WBCs to enter the

lymphatic system circulating around the brain and by receiving cytokine signals from the body. Far from being immune isolated, the brain and body maintain an active bilateral relationship to ensure both the brain and the body are continuously aware of each other's inflammatory status.

White blood cells have access to the cerebral cortex. Early microscopic studies of the brain showed no overt presence of WBCs. The blood-brain barrier was deemed to be impermeable and impenetrable for WBCs. Later research showed several ways WBCs and their messengers have continuous access to the central nervous system, particularly during enhanced inflammation or psychological stress.

Inflammatory molecules can cross the blood-brain barrier. Initially, the inflammation response was thought to involve only WBCs, but now we know that cytokines are chemical signals produced by the WBCs and many other immune cells, are as important as the WBCs in producing inflammation. These chemicals are small molecules and have access to the brain.

The brain has lymphatic drainage. Lymphatic channels course through the cerebral cortex, collecting debris and sending it off to the body's lymphatic system, where the spleen and other organs sample what comes out of the brain and use this information to maintain a harmonious inflammatory status. The human brain's lymphatic system may be particularly active at night, like a night shift cleaning crew.

Major Players in the Inflammatory System.   Bone marrow, thymus, and the spleen are vital members of the inflammatory system: each houses the progenitor cells for the various members of the inflammatory system. The bone marrow is where white blood cells (leukocytes) and macrophages mature and are released into the circulation. The thymus gland, nestled in our chest just behind the sternum, is a nursery for lymphocytes. The spleen is where we store the vast majority of macrophages, which can maintain specific memories of emotions for several decades.

None of these cells enter the central nervous system themselves but send their messages to the brain via chemical messengers known as cytokines. These signaling molecules can be broadly classified into two groups: pro-inflammatory and anti-inflammatory. Cytokines can easily and quickly cross into the central nervous system and have access to all the important cells in the human brain—especially the brain's immune cells, called microglia—thus affecting mental health. Elevated levels of cytokines can increase depression, anxiety, and sleep disruption as well as damaging joints and various tissues.

> *T lymphocytes, B lymphocytes, and natural killer (NK) cells* are each negatively impacted by stress, especially chronic emotional stress. NK cells are a type of specialized lymphocytes from the innate immune system that possess no immunologic memory, but are tasked with attacking tumor cells and viruses in the body. NK cell functioning is altered by both acute and chronic stress. Lymphocytes produce both antibodies and cytokines, which can be disrupted in states of high mental illness and low mental wellness. Research has revealed that states of heightened emotional distress, such as high levels of anxiety and depression, impair lymphocytes' main tasks of phagocytosis and chemotaxis. The dysregulated production of these cell lines creates the negative impact of mental illness on inflammation, and "taming" these cells is an important therapeutic goal of mental wellness interventions.
>
> *Macrophages* are larger (*macro*) than many of the other cells of the immune system, although there are fewer of them in the blood than the other immune cells. Once macrophages leave the bone marrow, most burrow into the spleen, but a few patrol the bloodstream, alert

for threat and danger signals. Once these peripheral circulating macrophages detect any such signal, they signal other macrophages, which grow larger and secrete lots of cytokines to recruit other parts of the immune system. Once the danger signal passes, macrophages shrink and cytokine levels return to normal. However, in situations of psychological stress, macrophage activity is chronically elevated, leading to considerable distress and damage.

Microglia are brain-based immune cells. From an evolutionary perspective, microglia and macrophages are closely linked and have similar characteristics and behaviors, possessing primary responsibility for immune functioning in their respective organs. Macrophages are part of the family of WBCs (which also includes leukocytes and lymphocytes), and microglia cells are part of the family of glia cells (which also includes astrocytes and oligodendrocytes). Macrophages and microglia both produce and have receptors for several inflammatory cytokines and thus communicate with each other across the blood-brain barrier. Peripheral inflammation impacts brain inflammation, and brain-based conditions such as psychiatric disorders, stress, and low mental wellness create heightened inflammation in both the brain and the body.

Cytokines are important members of the inflammatory system. These pro-inflammatory and anti-inflammatory molecules are produced by a large number of diverse immune cells. During states of optimum physical and mental health, pro- and anti-inflammatory cytokines maintain a balance. But the body misperceives states of heightened emotional stress as threats and responds by producing elevated amounts of pro-inflammatory cytokines. If the stress is chronic, this elevation of pro-inflammatory cytokines alters the balance in the autonomic nervous system, making the SNS more dominant in the ANS and causing the HPA axis to induce the adrenal glands to produce more cortisol, weakening the control exerted by the pituitary gland and the hippocampus. Multiple studies have found lower levels of inflammatory cytokines in those with higher levels of mental wellness traits.

Treating the mind/brain helps reduce body inflammation. Several studies, described in Chapter 3, demonstrate that both brain-centric interventions, such as cognitive-behavioral therapy and mindfulness-based cognitive therapy, and body-centric interventions, such as physical exercise and optimized nutrition, reduce inflammation, in both the brain and the body.

CHAPTER 3

Mental Wellness and Its Impact on Inflammation

There is striking evidence that systemic inflammation is present in a number of psychiatrically ill patients. In many patients, systemic inflammation is both the cause and the result of psychiatric disorders. There is also substantial evidence that lack of mental wellness can be pro-inflammatory, and vice versa: higher levels of mental wellness diminish inflammation.

The Mental Health Effects of Inflammation

Vogelzangs and colleagues (2014) studied individuals suffering from major depression, measuring levels of inflammatory markers (C-reactive protein and the cytokines IL-6 and TNF-α) and metabolic markers (waist circumference, triglycerides, HDL cholesterol, blood pressure, fasting glucose). Then they divided these patients into two groups: those with less than four and those with four or more of these pro-inflammatory conditions. Individuals in the higher marker group had more than *six* times greater odds of having chronic depression.

Psychopharmacology and cognitive-behavioral therapy both exert a positive anti-inflammatory response. In a meta-analysis of 32 studies with 1137 patients treated with "classic" antidepressants such as SSRIs or SNRIs, Więdłocha and colleagues (2017) examined inflammatory markers in these patients. Antidepressant therapy did significantly decrease levels of some well-known inflammatory markers, including IL-4, IL-6, and IL-10, but did not have significant effects on other critical inflammatory markers, such as the cytokines IL-2, TNF-α, and IFN-γ or the inflammatory protein CRP. This result was confirmed by another large meta-analysis of the impact of antidepressants on inflammation status in those with major depression (Kopschina Feltes, 2017).

A comprehensive review of 23 studies of CBT's impact on anti-inflammatory markers conducted by Lopresti and colleagues (2017) found that in 14 of these studies, at least one inflammatory biomarker responded positively to CBT. Although three studies revealed an increase in such markers, and no change was found in the remaining six studies, this is an overall positive finding. Three of these 23 studies also found that the level of pretreatment inflammation impacted benefits derived from the CBT: the treatment was less effective in those individuals who had higher baseline levels of inflammation.

Another study implies that it is not the antidepressants themselves that are anti-inflammatory, rather it is the mental health benefit derived from successful anti-depressant therapy that exerts an anti-inflammatory response. Lindqvist and colleagues (2017), in an interventional study in patients with major depression found that unmedicated patients had blood levels of IL-6, a well-known inflammatory cytokine, that were much higher than in normal controls. They then offered 22 of the 55 patients therapy with an SSRI antidepressant. Individuals who responded to the SSRI therapy showed a significant decrease in IL-6 levels during treatment, but SSRI non-responders showed a small increase in IL-6. Thus, pharmacotherapy may possess anti-inflammatory effects, but only if it is clinically effective; if it does not clinically improve symptoms, it does not appear to exert any anti-inflammatory effects.

A pharmacology-based study looked at using baseline levels of the inflammatory marker C-reactive protein (CRP) to help make treatment decisions. In a pharmacological interventional study in patients with

MDD, Jha and colleagues (2017) looked for response and remission rates with different treatments—SSRI monotherapy or SSRI plus bupropion therapy. Some patients were "matched" to the SSRI plus bupropion treatment arm if they had a CRP level greater than 1, or matched to just SSRI non-therapy treatment if not; other patients received these therapies without using CRP guidance. Patients who were not matched had a remission rate of 30.9 percent, but patients who were matched with CRP levels in mind had a remission rate of 53.1%—matching treatment to inflammatory status improved remission by 22.2%.

Wellness Interventions and Their Anti-inflammatory Effects

Several wellness interventions have proven anti-inflammatory effects: mindfulness, physical exercise, sleep optimization, optimized nutrition, enhanced socialization, and positive psychology.

Physical Exercise and Inflammation

If we could give every individual the right amount of nourishment and exercise, not too little and not too much, we would have the safest way to health.

    —HIPPOCRATES

The benefits of physical exercise on the body have been scientifically discussed for decades. Exercise is sometimes thought to be the perfect "polypill": it has a large number of benefits on multiple aspects of bodily functions, including heart health, bone health, obesity, glycemic control, systolic blood pressure, muscle hypertrophy, and even risk of certain cancers such as colon cancer (Schon & Weiskirchen, 2016).

Additionally, the impact of physical exercise on brain health is considerable, with a large body of evidence revealing that the brain also responds positively to this intervention. The hippocampus in particular appears to react in response to physical exercise by becoming hypertrophic, possibly because exercise elevates levels of BDNF (Erikson et al., 2011). The benefits from hippocampal enlargement are obvious: greater stress resilience, and improved memory and mood. Studies actually support all of these conclusions. Exercise is an important intervention for addressing symptoms of mental illness and for improving mental wellness (Carek, Laibstain, & Carek, 2011).

Physical exercise also has positive anti-inflammatory effects. Schon and colleagues conducted an extensive review of physical exercise's positive effects on the body, finding that exercise also impacts the immune system at multiple levels (Schon & Weiskirchen, 2016), decreasing lymphocytosis and numbers of circulating monocytes, sources of inflammatory cytokines, among many other effects:

- Reduces the expression of toll-like receptors (TLR) by macrophages and monocytes, thereby making them less likely to over produce inflammatory cytokines
- Reduces the intrusion of macrophages, which are activated monocytes, into adipose tissue, thereby reducing adipose tissue produced inflammatory substances
- Shifts the macrophage cell lineage in adipose tissue from type M1, which produce pro-inflammatory cytokines like TNF-alpha, to type M2, which produce anti-inflammatory cytokines such as IL-10

Much more is known about the impact of exercise on the immune system. For example, it has both short- and long-term effects (Goh, Goh, & Abbasi, 2016). Short-term exercise can actually elevate inflammation by increasing both the pro-inflammatory and anti-inflammatory cytokines (van de Weert-van Leeuwen, Aret, Ent, & Beekman, 2013). However, with longer-term exercise, pro-inflammatory cytokines, such as IL-6, TNF-alpha, and IL-1beta, are significantly decreased, while levels of anti-inflammatory cytokines, such as IL-10 and TGF-beta, are increased.

Regular exercise is also associated with larger brain volume, improved cognition, reduced risk of mental disorders, and heightened mental wellness.

Nutrition and Inflammation

Let food be thy medicine and medicine be thy food.

HIPPOCRATES

It is certainly true that we are what we eat, especially when it comes to our levels of inflammation. Both macronutrients (carbohydrates, proteins, fats) and micronutrients (vitamins, minerals) play a role in the inflammatory cycle. Over the last few decades, diets in the developed Western world have shifted toward far too many macronutrients (particularly carbohydrates) and far too few micronutrients (lower consumption of vitamins, particularly from the vitamin B family). Concurrently, rates of multiple inflammatory disorders, such as rheumatoid arthritis, atopic dermatitis, and asthma, have risen sharply, which parallels the worsening of American nutrition. Perhaps not a coincidence, the incidence of psychiatric disorders, which are at least partly based on inflammation, has also risen sharply.

Two studies looked at the connection between obesity and depression, from two different angles: whether obesity increases the risk of depression, and whether depression makes one prone to obesity. The answer is, quite conclusively, yes to both (Simon et al., 2008; Pan et al, 2012): as depression severity rose, so did the risk of obesity, and as body mass index (BMI), a good marker for obesity and excessive macronutrient intake, rose, so did the risk of depression. Another study showed that BMI of 30 or greater (which qualifies as obesity) is a risk factor for multiple psychiatric disorders (Simon et al., 2006), increasing the risk of having major depression by 21%, bipolar disorder by 47%, generalized anxiety disorder by 20% and panic disorder by 27%.

An increased BMI is related to not only a greater risk for depression but also a lower response to antidepressants. One study looked at antidepressant treatment response rates in three groups of individuals, with BMI of less than 25 (not overweight), 25–30 (overweight), and greater than 30 (obese). The group with the lowest BMI had the best response to antidepressants; the highest BMI group had the least response, and the middle BMI group was in between (Kloiber et al., 2007).

The thread connecting obesity, depression, and antidepressant response is inflammation. Shelton and Miller (2010) have demonstrated that in obesity a higher degree of inflammation is produced by macrophage invasion of adipose tissues, with a resultant higher production of inflammatory substances such as IL-6, and the resultant increased risk of sickness behavior/major depression.

Micronutrients, defined as vitamins (fat-soluble vitamins such as vitamins A and D, and water-soluble vitamins such as the B vitamins) and minerals (iron, magnesium, zinc, etc.), are also related to inflammation: suboptimum ingestion of micronutrients results in elevated inflammation (Thurnham & Northrop-Clewes, 2016). Emerson and Carbert (2018) conducted a large cross-sectional study on the role of micronutrients in mental health. They looked at daily consumption of fruits and vegetables in 37,071 patients and its association with three mental health outcomes: anxiety and/or mood disorders, being distressed, and having good self-rated overall mental health. They found a positive co-relationship between consumption of the micronutrient rich foods and both risk of mental illness and levels of mental wellness. Inflammation connects the elevated risk of mental health challenges to diminished micronutrient ingestion: Suchdev and colleagues (2017) found that nutrition is indeed linked to levels of inflammation and the resultant negative consequences to the brain and body.

Inflammation and its links to psychiatry and mental wellness are the purview of a new branch of psychiatry, called nutritional psychiatry, which is growing by leaps and bounds (Marx, Moseley, Berk, & Jacka, 2017). The evidence that macronutrients and micronutrients impact human inflammation, mental illness, and mental wellness is compelling, and the birth of nutritional psychiatry as a subspecialty will help us learn more about how to offer better care to our patients by reducing mental illness and increasing mental wellness.

Sleep and Inflammation

Sleep that knits up the raveled sleave of care
The death of each day's life, sore labour's bath
Balm of hurt minds, great nature's second course
Chief nourisher in life's feast

　—SHAKESPEARE, *MACBETH*

Shakespeare, in just four short lines, tells us nearly all we need to know about sleep. Even hundreds of years ago, and without the benefit of the neurobiological advances we have today, he surmised sleep healed the hurt mind and is the chief nourisher in life's feast—and his observations apply as well to the impact of sleep on inflammation.

Insomnia is associated with elevated inflammation. In a meta-analysis on this topic, Dr. Irwin and colleagues conducted a systematic search of 72 primary research articles that characterized sleep disturbance and assessed inflammation by levels of circulating markers (Irwin, Olmstead, & Carroll, 2016). To assess for insomnia and sleep disturbance they utilized self-reported symptoms and questionnaires. In terms of inflammatory markers, they looked at the two best-studied markers, CRP and IL-6. They found a statistically significant relationship between sleep disruption and inflammation, with both CRP and IL-6 showing elevation.

In a landmark paper, Irwin (2015) describes the inter-relationship between the autonomic nervous system (ANS) and the HPA axis, and found both are upregulated in states of sleep disruption. As described in Chapter 2, these two systems have direct links to nearly every member of the immune system, and any state of ANS disruption, such as that caused by insomnia, immediately upregulates the immune system, resulting in increased inflammation.

It has long been known that individuals with chronic insomnia have a higher risk of developing dementia, a disorder with known inflammatory underpinnings, primarily as elevated tau protein levels in the brain. A large meta-analysis of over 5000 patients revealed insomnia does elevate the risk of dementia (de Almondes, Costa, Malloy-Diniz, & Diniz, 2016). Insomnia is definitively associated with abnormalities in amyloid protein and in the creation of tau pathology (Sprecher et al., 2017). The process by which insomnia causes this inflammation-mediated damage in the brain is becoming better understood. There appears to be diminished glymphatic clearance in the brains of individuals who sleep poorly, leading to higher exposure for neurons and astrocytes to inflammatory substances, and ultimately to earlier cell death—the very pathology of dementia (Lucke-Wold et al., 2015).

On the other hand, treatment of insomnia appears to exert a quick, significant, and sustained anti-inflammatory effect. Heinzelmann and colleagues (2014), in an observational study of 66 U.S. military personnel who presented for evaluation of sleep disturbance, examined the relationship between reported sleep changes and serum concentrations of the well-known inflammation markers IL-6 and CRP. Then they offered these individuals any and all appropriate treatments—pharmacological, non-pharmacological, or both—and examined changes in CRP and IL-6 between baseline and follow-up. About half of the participants returned to restorative sleep, and about half did not. Only the group that had improved sleep had improved levels of both CRP and IL-6 concentration; the other group actually showed a tendency for worsening of their inflammatory markers.

While insomnia and disturbed sleep are clearly inflammation provokers, sleeping excessively is also a source of inflammation. In a systematic review, Irwin (2016) found higher inflammation, as measured by levels of CRP and IL-6, was associated with longer than normal sleep duration. For practicing clinicians this is an important finding: our therapeutic goal is to help patients get the ideal amount of sleep, not too much and not too little.

Mindfulness and Inflammation

The ancient Eastern tradition of mindfulness has become popular all over the globe, and both lay and professional publications have spent a lot of time highlighting its many virtues. Studies have also shown it has an impact on inflammation. Carlson and colleagues (2007) published a study of 49 patients with breast cancer and 10 with prostate cancer who were enrolled in an 8-week mindfulness-based stress reduction program that incorporated relaxation, meditation, gentle yoga, and daily home practice. This study also included a large number of inflammation markers. Participating in mindfulness practices not only reduced perceived stress in these participants but also reduced levels of inflammatory markers such as interferon gamma, and this effect was detectable even ten months after the formal end of the mindfulness practice intervention. This study also found mindfulness practice reduced the number of interferon gamma producing T lymphocytes.

A meta-analysis specifically examined the effects of mindfulness on five aspects of inflammation (Black & Slavich, 2016): circulating and stimulated inflammatory proteins, cellular transcription factors and gene expression, immune cell count, immune cell aging, and antibody response. They assessed results from twenty studies with a total of 1602 patients. Four out of these five parameters showed a positive response to mindfulness practice, including reductions in the cellular transcription factor NF-κB and in CRP and increases in CD4+ T cell count (in HIV-diagnosed individuals) and in telomerase activity. Interestingly, this meta-analysis did not find convincing data on the impact of mindfulness on antibodies or interleukins.

Inflammation is deeply tied to the stress response. A meta-analysis on mindfulness altering markers of the stress response examined forty-five studies that met their exacting standards for inclusion in the analysis (Pascoe, Thompson, Jenkins, & Ski, 2017). They found that systolic blood pressure was reduced in mindfulness practitioners and that focused-attention meditators had reduced levels of cortisol, C-reactive protein, heart rate, and TNF-alpha. There is an emerging understanding of how mindfulness practice may decrease inflammation: another study revealed mindfulness may actually increase the connectivity between the posterior cingulate cortex and the dorsolateral prefrontal cortex. In fact, the degree of this connectivity explained 30% of the reduction in interleukin 6 (IL-6) levels (Creswell et al., 2016).

Social Connectedness and Inflammation

I define connection as the energy that exists between people when they feel seen, heard, and valued; when they can give and receive without judgement; and when they derive sustenance and strength from the relationship.

—BRENÉ BROWN, UNIVERSITY OF HOUSTON
GRADUATE COLLEGE OF SOCIAL WORK

Brené Brown's astute observations on the importance of social connectedness and its impact on human functioning are now well accepted in both mental health and medicine in general. Good human health is strongly dependent on an individual's level of social connectedness.

Robbins and colleagues (2003) studied 38 African American women who lived in an inner-city environment and were infected with the HIV virus. They measured their degree of social connectedness, and blood counts for CD4 cells, a type of lymphocyte impacted by the HIV infection. This is what they found: women who have higher satisfaction from their social connectedness had better CD4 counts at baseline, and over time their levels of these critical cells declined less than in women with lower social connectedness. Another important finding from this study was that the quality of social connectedness matters more than the quantity: merely having a lot of Facebook friends may not have a significantly positive impact on mental and physical health.

Boen and colleagues (2018) used the University of North Carolina Health Registry/Cancer Survivorship Cohort to examine both inflammation levels and degree of social connectedness. Mortality after a diagnosis of cancer was reduced among individuals who felt more connected to their social milieu. They also found evidence that inflammatory processes may be the link between social support satisfaction and mortality among individuals with cancer: individuals with higher social support had lower levels of the inflammatory markers CRP, IL-6, and TNFα.

Another well-known marker of inflammation, fibrinogen, is a clotting factor that when elevated poses significant challenges to human health. A study examined fibrinogen levels and the degree of social connectedness of individuals, utilizing a unique research methodology called human social network (Kim, Benjamin, Fowler, & Christakis, 2016). They found that greater social connectedness led to lower fibrinogen levels and that the negative, pro-inflammatory impact of low socialization was worse than the smoking status of an individual.

Social rejection, that is, feeling socially ostracized from one's social milieu and environment, has emerged as devastating to an individual's mental health. In today's modern Western societies, loneliness and social rejection have emerged as one of our greatest threats, and it appears its negative impact on the human body and mind is partly mediated by inflammation. Slavich and Irwin (2014) have written eloquently about this phenomenon, and they persuasively implicate inflammation as the mediator of this negative impact. They found that pro-inflammatory cytokines were the key mediators in this effect, in turn eliciting profound behavioral changes, such as sad mood, anhedonia, fatigue, psychomotor retardation, and social-behavioral withdrawal.

It appears low social connectedness causes higher inflammation, and the reverse also appears to be true. One study (Das, 2016) attempted to explore this issue using the 2005–2006 and 2010–2011 waves of the U.S. National Social Life, Health, and Aging Project data set, and found that heighted inflammation may set up an individual to suffer negative consequences through multiple mechanisms—such as causing them to feel more fatigue, more depression, more apathy—all collectively leading to lower socialization.

Positive Psychology and Inflammation

Positive psychology is a new but already vast field of study and research. Multiple human traits are thought to be part of the ideal makeup of an individual with high levels of positive psychological traits, including elements of happiness, enthusiasm, resilience, and optimism—the HERO wellness traits.

In a study from Japan, researchers assessed 160 volunteers for levels of happiness and levels of interferon alpha (IFN-γ), a pro-inflammatory cytokine (Matsunaga et al., 2011). Compared to individuals with low levels of perceived happiness, happy individuals had lower levels of IFN-γ. Another group of researchers examined if higher levels of happiness exert an anti-inflammatory effect in individuals who were purposefully exposed to experimental stressful situations. Panagi and colleagues (2018) measured levels of happiness in 140 people with type 2 diabetes, as well as blood levels of various inflammatory markers. Although findings were mixed, greater daily levels of happiness significantly predicted lower baseline and lower post-baseline levels of IL-6. Taken together, the evidence supports the notion that happiness directly leads to lower inflammation.

Another study using a completely different methodology found very similar results: in a sample from the Normative Aging Study cohort, Kim and colleagues (2016) examined different sets of inflammatory markers and found higher levels of happiness and satisfaction in life was inversely related to levels of inflammation.

Another crucial component of positive psychological traits is optimism. One study attempted to assess if high levels of optimism were associated with lower levels of inflammation. Roy and colleagues (2010) analyzed data from the Multi-Ethnic Study of Atherosclerosis (MESA), a study of 6814 persons aged 45 to 84 years. They measured levels of dispositional optimism, along with many biomarkers of inflammation, such as levels of IL-6, fibrinogen, and homocysteine. They found that more optimistic individuals had lower concentrations of IL-6, fibrinogen, and homocysteine, and that pessimism was associated with higher systemic inflammation.

Taken together, the evidence connecting inflammation to many elements of mental wellness—mindfulness, physical exercise, sleep optimization, optimized nutrition, enhanced socialization, and positive psychology—is strong and has clear clinical implications. Part 2 of this book discusses how this relationship can be leveraged to both reduce psychiatric symptoms and improve mental wellness.

CHAPTER 4

Unifying Health, Illness, and Wellness

The neurobiology of wellness manifests throughout the body, from DNA to organ function, including the brain. The burgeoning field of wellness neurobiology has been fruitful for those interested in mental wellness and its biological signature. Research has found that it affects longevity, development and recovery from cancers, health of the cardiovascular system, and brain size, organization, and function. The field of psychoneuroimmunology is a great unifier of studies in health, illness, and wellness, encompassing the "triple highways" of bi-directional communication, the hypothalamic–pituitary–adrenal (HPA) axis, autonomic nervous system (ANS), and immune system—as one of us found out through personal experience.

Psychoneuroimmunology as a Unifier in Health and Illness

The psychoneuroimmunological (PNI) system, comprising interactions among the HPA axis, ANS, and immune system, is a complex, integrated system connecting multiple parts of the brain and the body (Figure 4.1).

Let's examine the various components of the PNI system that are unified in both health and disease states. We can start out with any of the three components of the PNI system (the immune system, the autonomic

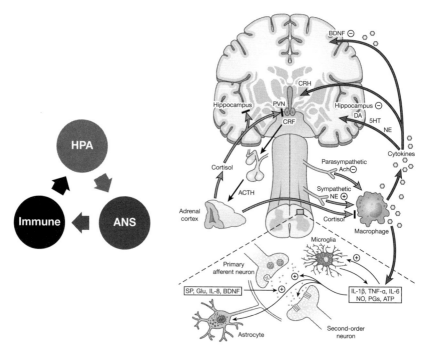

FIGURE 4.1: The psychoneuroimmunological (PNI) system comprises the HPA axis, the ANS, and the immune system, each responding to the others to achieve mental and physical well-being. Abbreviations: 5HT, Ach, ACTH, ATP, BDNF, CRF, DA, Glu, IL-1β, IL-6, IL-8, NE, NO, PGs, PVN, SP, TNF-α.   Source: Jain et al. (2011)

system, and the HPA axis), as these systems are so well interconnected that the relationship between them is non-linear and non-hierarchal in nature. It is instead a circular relationship of three equals who all carry the power to influence each other for better or for worse. As you examine Figure 4.1, it is abundantly clear there is a web of interconnectedness between these systems. We begin our journey with the hippocampus, a brain structure intimately involved in the processing of emotions and memories, and a vital member of the limbic system. The hippocampus, based on its perception of positive or negative emotions and thoughts, then influences the functioning of the hypothalamus, which is the very fountainhead of the HPA axis (hypothalamic–pituitary–adrenal axis). Corticotropin releasing factor

(CRF) hormone released from the hypothalamus directs the pituitary gland to release its own hormone, adrenocorticotrophic hormone (ACTH), which signals the adrenal glands to produce cortisol. Cortisol exerts an inhibitory effect back on the brain at the periventricular nucleus (PVN) and hypothalamus, thereby completing the HPA loop.

The two central members of the autonomic system, the sympathetic system and the para-sympathetic system, arise from the sub-tentorial portion of the brain and from the spinal column, from which they spread out to nearly every part of the human body. The sympathetic system (SNS) uses norepinephrine (NE) as its chemical messenger, and the para-sympathetic system (PNS) uses acetylcholine (Ach) as its own unique chemical messenger. You will note the sympathetic system induces macrophages to produce more inflammatory cytokines, while the para-sympathetic system does the complete opposite by signaling macrophages to produce less inflammatory cytokines. We should take note that cortisol also exerts an inhibitory effect on macrophage mediated release of cytokines.

We now turn to the inflammatory system, where the body-based immune cells—macrophages, and brain-based immune cells—microglia, are the primary producers of inflammatory cytokines. Elevated cytokines impact the brain by negatively impacting three monoamines of prime importance in the control of mood: dopamine (DA), norepinephrine (NE), and serotonin (5-HT). These elevated cytokines also negatively affect the functioning of the hippocampus, and are implicated in lowering the levels of an important brain neurotrophic factor: brain-derived neurotrophic factor (BDNF). In the brain, microglia are the prime producers of cytokines such as IL-6, TNF-alpha, IL-1beta, and IL-8. Activated microglia in turn activate astrocytes, which then produce excessive glutamate. Neuronal functional in the brain is also negatively impacted with intrasynaptic alternations in signaling chemicals such as substance P (SP), glutamate (Glu), nitrous oxide (NO), prostaglandins (PGs), and adenosine triphosphate (ATP).

The optimal functioning of the PNI system is critical to health and mental wellness. When one part of the PNI system is not functioning optimally, the rest of the system kicks in to establish balance and restore health; if it cannot achieve balance, this causes significant havoc in brain-body functioning. In large part, PNI disruptions explain why individuals with various body disorders like rheumatoid arthritis, inflammatory bowel disorder, diabetes, and even certain cancers have high rates of "classic" brain-based disorders such as depression and anxiety.

A Personal Experience with PNI Disruption

Recently, one of us (RJ) had a personal experience with PNI disruption. After experiencing minor blood electrolyte abnormalities, his clinician ordered several tests to better understand the issue. One of the tests ordered was the adrenocorticotropic hormone (ACTH) challenge test, which may be familiar to many readers. As described in Chapter 3, ACTH is the hormone produced by the pituitary to direct the adrenal gland cortex to produce more cortisol. The ACTH challenge test is administered by injecting a small amount (250 micrograms) of ACTH intramuscularly, with serum cortisol measured at baseline, and after 30 minutes and 60 minutes. A normal result is a sufficient cortisol response produced by this challenge.

> On a Monday at 9 a.m., the nurse administered the ACTH injection intramuscularly. As she was pushing the somewhat large needle into a muscle, rather off-handedly she said, "Some people have the jitters and sweats after this shot, but it goes away in a couple of hours." This was the first I had heard of any such reaction. The ACTH injection certainly did provoke my adrenal glands to produce more cortisol: my baseline serum cortisol shot up in 30 minutes and went even higher at 60 minutes—I "passed" my ACTH test with flying colors! It was quite impressive how even a small amount of ACTH could command my adrenal gland to produce so much cortisol in such a short period.
>
> Despite her caution about me feeling jittery or sweaty, nothing happened, at least not initially. I felt fine at the two-hour mark, but this honeymoon phase didn't last long. Around 5 p.m. that evening, unexpectedly,

I started feeling significant and unrelenting levels of tiredness, lethargy, muscle aches like I had just run a marathon, low mood, and overall feeling quite "blah." I had a low-grade fever, my heart raced, and I had real trouble sleeping that night. I felt tired and jumpy at the same time. This injection clearly affected my entire being—both mind and body. *What was happening to me?*

Upon researching my experience the next day, it became clear that the nurse was not completely accurate. In fact, my research revealed that many people experience exactly what I was experiencing. This massive increase in cortisol was disrupting my PNI status and was in fact causing my symptoms. Disruption in one system, in this case the HPA axis, causes the other two systems, the ANS and the immune system, to overreact. All of my symptoms could easily be explained by these triple PNI disruptions. I was personally living through what I had been theoretically teaching others for some years. It was a very uncomfortable experience, but it gave me huge respect for what happens to individuals who have unrelenting PNI disruptions over months and years.

While all these novel experiences were interesting, the resultant impact on my mental wellness was the most remarkable of all. I didn't just feel "blah"—I found myself being far less optimistic and enthusiastic. I was easily overwhelmed, felt my resilience slipping, and I was distinctly less happy. It was as if the PNI disruptions poked a hole in the bottom of my proverbial barrel of mental wellness and drained it. It was a most unusual experience.

It took about a week before this PNI insult receded and equilibrium was restored. This experience has profoundly increased our respect for the PNI system and helped us appreciate that disruptions to any aspect of the PNI system—HPA axis, ANS, and immune system—are not just abstract concepts. Our patients with both high mental illness symptoms and low mental wellness traits are also quite likely facing these PNI challenges, in a lesser but more chronic manner.

The Neurobiology of Wellness

A large number of studies have demonstrated how varying degrees of mental wellness affect our body, in addition to specifically impacting the PNI system. Levels of mental wellness affect DNA, longevity, development and recovery from cancers, heart health, and brain function.

DNA and Mental Wellness

DNA was once thought to remain unchanged from birth to death. But now we know that, while the basic DNA structure—its nucleotide sequence—remains essentially stable for life, frequent changes occur to DNA methylation and acetylation, which regulate how genes are transcribed from the DNA and conducted by RNA. Methylation reduces transcription, and acetylation enhances transaction, thereby controlling and regulating RNA activity that leads to peptide and protein generation.

There is now considerable evidence that states of high psychological stress and low mental wellness disturb the delicate balance between DNA methylation and acetylation, thereby leading to a chain of negative reactions; for example, neurotransmitter production is impaired, production of pro-inflammatory cytokinesis is increased, production of anti-inflammatory cytokines is decreased, and levels of neurotrophic substances (which promote growth of dendrites and synapses) drop. The impact of all of these DNA-driven changes are felt far and wide in the brain and the body. Thankfully, the reverse is equally true: higher levels of wellness traits are associated with improved DNA health, as demonstrated by optimized methylation and acetylation patterns (Barker, 2018).

Telomeres, another vital part of DNA, are structures that cap off the ends of our chromosomes. DNA lives in tight coils housed in the 23 pairs of chromosomes humans possess. As we age, telomere length tends to diminish. A striking finding from the world of neurobiology is that our mental health strongly affects telomere length: low mental health is associated with shorter telomere length, but improved mental health is associated with improved telomere length, which slows the aging process of the DNA (Schutte, Palanisamy, & McFarlane, 2016).

Mental Wellness and Longevity

Many studies from multiple continents around the globe have revealed that individuals with higher levels of mental wellness live longer and are less prone to chronic physical conditions, have less weight gain, are less likely to smoke, and generally are more likely to engage in pro-health behaviors of all types. This positive impact of mental wellness on longevity is dose proportionate: every degree of greater mental wellness appears to generate further increased longevity. This is not surprising, since mental wellness improves ANS tone, modulates cortisol tone in the HPA axis, decreases inflammation, and improves DNA production and telomere length, among other benefits. Enhanced mental wellness is associated with longer and better quality of life.

Mental Wellness and Oncology

Individuals with higher degrees of mental wellness have lower rates of developing cancers, and if cancer were to develop, individuals with higher degrees of wellness have better survival rates. First, individuals with higher degrees of mental wellness are less likely to smoke, have better nutrition, and exercise more—all behaviors that reduce the risk of developing cancers. Second, individuals with a higher degree of mental wellness have better modulation of the PNI system—when it functions optimally, the risk of developing cancers is reduced. Third, mental wellness has a positive impact on DNA methylation—an abnormally functioning DNA is the prime cause of malignancy. Similar factors are thought to be at play once cancer develops, giving individuals with a higher degree of mental wellness a higher survival rate (Massetti, Thomas, King, Ragan, & Lunsford, 2017).

Mental Wellness and the Cardiovascular System

People faced with great emotional stress can literally die of a broken heart. There is great overlap between mental health and the cardiovascular system. The heart's blood supply is influenced by the ANS, and inflammation negatively influences heart function through multiple mechanisms—cytokines such as IL-1, IL-6, TNF-alpha, among others, can contribute to ischemic heart disease by impacting cardiac muscle cells involved with contractility (Bartekova, Radosinska, Jelemensky, & Dhalla, 2018). Both the ANS and the immune system are directly influenced by mental health—individuals with mental health disorders have higher rates of cardiovascular events.

The heart is connected to the ANS in other ways, too. The sinoatrial node (SA node) of the heart is its pacemaker, and it receives profuse input from the ANS: the sympathetic nervous system (SNS) accelerates heart rate and the parasympathetic nervous system (PNS) decreases it. In states of mental distress, the SNS dominates the PNS, and heart rate is accelerated. Conversely, in states of heightened mental wellness, PNS tone optimally balances the SNS, heart rate is lowered, and heart rate variability is increased. Heart rate variability, the variability that occurs from beat to beat as the heart responds to varying bodily conditions, is a sign of good cardiovascular health; its decrease is associated with poor cardiovascular outcomes. Poor mental health decreases heart rate variability, and good mental wellness increases it.

Mental Wellness and Brain Function

Enclosed in the bony skull, the functioning brain is not visible to the naked eye. Other than from postmortem examinations, for centuries we knew nothing about the structural changes or functional alterations as the brain and body respond to the environment, whether during heightened distress or when experiencing positive emotions. Today we have several ways to peer into functioning brains without doing any harm. Techniques such as computed tomography (CT) scans, volumetric magnetic resonance imaging (MRI), and functional MRI are completely changing our understanding of the brain and its intimate relationship with feelings, thoughts, and emotions.

In one of the earliest studies on the neurobiology of mood disorders, a research group led by Yvette Sheline, a psychiatrist at Washington University School of Medicine in St. Louis, conducted a pioneering study. Sheline and colleagues (1999) examined hippocampus volume in women suffering from major depression and how it related to the actual amount of time these women experienced depression during their lifetimes. They found that the longer a person had experienced depression, the smaller the hippocampus—this was the first evidence that depression affected brain structure. They replicated the study and found the same results in a completely different group of patients. Later studies revealed no relationship between the age of the women and the size of the hippocampus or between hippocampus size and the duration of depression treatment (Sheline, Mittler, & Mintum, 2002)—the only effect on the hippocampus was related to states of untreated depression.

This finding of diminished hippocampal volume in depressed individuals has been consistent since that first study and was noted even in one of the world's largest meta-analysis of three-dimensional brain MRI data. Schmaal and colleagues (2016) compared 1728 patients with major depression and 7199 controls from 15 research studies worldwide. Compared to controls, those with depression had significantly lower hippocampal volumes.

One possible explanation for this result was that a smaller hippocampus may predispose people to depression, a possibility that Sheline and colleagues' studies could not rule out. Another group of researchers examined this same issue, following patients longitudinally for up to three years (Frodl et al., 2008). They obtained a brain scan at the beginning of treatment, treated individuals for depression, and then conducted another brain scan, to compare the change in brain volume in those who achieved remission of depression and those who did not. Achieving remission of depression was protective of the volume and functioning of brain structures, including the hippocampus. However, continuing to feel depressed was harmful to the hippocampus—experiencing symptoms of depression is toxic to the brain.

To examine what occurs at the level of neurons, Duman and Duman (2015) examined changes in dendrites of neurons when exposing an animal model to stress by holding animals in passive restraint for a certain length of time. Thereby creating significant helplessness for the animal to replicate the experience of depression in humans. And here are the results—the brains of these animals had significantly greater shrinkage in both the length and number of dendrites, demonstrating that stress, depression, and anxiety have a negative neurobiological impact.

Intertwined, Yet Separate: Anhedonia and Pleasure

In animal models, hedonic (pleasure) "hotspots" have been detected in brain regions that are not necessarily part of the depression circuit (Loonen & Ivanova, 2016; Berridge & Kringelbach, 2015). The limbic system is much more tuned into the experience of sadness, stress, and depression, while the cortico–striato–thalamo–cortical circuit is more involved with pleasure and reward-seeking behavior. The nucleus accumbens, in particular, is deeply involved in the experience of positive emotions, along with higher cortical structures such as the orbitofrontal prefrontal, cingulate cortex, medial-prefrontal cortex, and the insular cortex. Kringelbach and Berridge (2009) have closely examined these hedonic hotspots and found them to be surprisingly small in size: in humans, about a cubic centimeter or so.

The circuits in the brain that serve mental illness and mental wellness are to some degree intertwined but also maintain a degree of separateness. The human brain appears to follow the rule of "different strokes for different emotions," as evidenced by a groundbreaking study of how we perceive negative, neutral, and positive emotions (Greenberg, Carlson, Rubin, Cha, & Mujica-Parodi, 2015). In this functional imaging study of how different emotions are perceived, when uncertain or neutral emotions were provoked, the medial and lateral prefrontal cortex are preferentially activated. Aversive emotion induction led to increased activity in the anterior insula, and positive emotions excited the caudate and the anterior cingulate cortex.

And different levels of mental wellness can change the functioning of the human brain. Yang and colleagues (2013) measured levels of dispositional optimism, a wellness trait, in subjects and then examined their brain using volumetric MRI. They found that more optimistic individuals had greater gray matter volume in the left thalamic, left pulvinar, and parahippocampal gyrus. What is more, when more optimistic individuals were exposed to negative stimuli, they had lower activation of the amygdala, a center of threat assessment, compared to less optimistic individuals—higher mental wellness acts as an antidote to negative emotions. And when viewing positive stimuli, individuals with higher dispositional wellness had higher activation of the anterior cingulate cortex, involved with mood processing—people with greater mental wellness can extract more pleasure from the good things in life.

This chapter has described the many ways our body is positively affected by mental wellness and negatively impacted by mental health disorders. The PNI system, comprising the HPA axis, ANS, and immune system, affects and in turn is affected by both physical and mental well-being. The neurobiology of wellness manifests throughout the body, from DNA to organ function, including the brain. Brain circuits that serve mental illness and mental wellness are intertwined but separate, and through them different levels of mental wellness can change the functioning of the human brain. It is our hope that this understanding will motivate you and help you apply the concepts of mental wellness in your practice, as we describe in Part 2 of this book.

PART 2

Principles of the Wellness-centric Clinician

Building on the review in Part 1 of the science behind the relationships between mental wellness and the body, Part 2 explores principles of mental wellness interventions that can help improve clinical outcomes and quality of life. We begin in Chapter 5 by exploring how five elements of mental wellness—exercise, optimized nutrition, optimized sleep, mindfulness, and social connectedness—can be used as wellness-centric tools to improve our patients' well-being. Chapter 6 examines what we consider the four pillars of mental wellness, the HERO wellness traits—happiness, enthusiasm, resilience, and optimism—and how to help our patients build their capacity for these crucial life-enhancing factors. Chapter 7 provides an overview of mental wellness programs available for clinicians, including our WILD 5 Wellness program, which we describe in further detail in Chapter 8. Chapters 9 and 10 round out Part 2 by offering ways to introduce mental wellness concepts and practices to patients and then to measure the positive effects they have, for your own and your patients' motivation and success.

CHAPTER 5

Five Elements of Mental Wellness

Wellness as a concept is easily understood but difficult to define. The *Merriam-Webster Collegiate Dictionary* defines *wellness* as "the quality or state of being in good health especially as an actively sought goal." And, as mentioned at the beginning of this book, World Health Organization's definition of *health* is "a state of complete physical, mental and social well-being, and not merely the absence of disease or infirmity" (WHO, 1948). Thus, wellness can be thought of as a state of complete physical, mental, and social well-being. The drive for wellness is shared by all human beings, an innate need, independent of one's race, sex, age, culture, or any other known variable. Wellness matters to both our mental and physical health and is clearly a modulator of inflammation (see Chapter 3).

In the last few decades, we have witnessed a huge decline in social connectedness, decreases in physical exercise, poorer diet quality, and the most significant shift in sleeping habits ever documented. Sadly, one of the victims of all of these profound changes appears to be mental wellness. Another indirect and profoundly worrisome issue is rising suicide rates. The United States is one of only two countries in the Western developed world to have an increase in suicide rates, while all other Western nations are experiencing a decrease. The continual decline of American wellness is a clear call to action for clinicians and society at large.

Five mental wellness practices introduced in Chapter 3—exercise, nutrition, sleep, mindfulness, and social connectedness—are "natural": humans have engaged in them from the dawn of time. However, with the presence of a psychiatric illness, patients tend to underutilize these wellness-centric tools and thus suffer a variety of negative consequences. Practicing these mental wellness elements exerts a positive effect on individuals: evidence reveals that engaging in each of these five wellness-centric interventions offers quick and significant improvement in mental wellness. As a wellness-centric clinician you can proactively recommend these interventions to enhance your patients' mental wellness and overall well-being.

These five interventions—exercise, mindfulness, sleep, social connectedness, and nutrition—are well studied. All possess significant scientific data on their ability to improve mental wellness. This chapter lays out a scientific case for why each of these interventions matter, and how each both diminish symptoms of illness and improve wellness.

Exercise

As a wellness enhancer, physical exercise has been appreciated for eons. But modern-day humans not only have forgotten this sage advice but also have collectively adopted a lifestyle that minimizes movement and physical exercise. The human body needs physical exercise for optimum living. Consider astronauts who spend time in space: after only a few days the lack of gravity and tight living quarters cause bones to lose density and muscles to atrophy, due to the lack of physical use.

As a society, we have become truly inactive—the industrial revolution has been very good to us in many ways, but not in our need for exercise. Speaking at the American Psychological Association's 117th annual convention, Steven Blair, one of the world's premier experts on exercise and its health benefits, called Americans' physical inactivity "the biggest public health problem of the 21st century" (APA, 2009). He noted that 25 to

35 percent of American adults are inactive—an astounding 40–50 million Americans, and that's not including those that are at best suboptimally physically active.

This problem is much worse in individuals with psychiatric difficulties. Nearly all psychiatric disorders include low motivation, low drive, low energy, and significant fatigue. Fraser and colleagues (2015), examining this issue in those with mental disorders, found that even though physical activity was generally low in this population, patients actually wanted to exercise and cognitively were aware of its physical health benefits. They also found that less than half of the patients knew about the mental health benefits of physical exercise. As a wellness-centric clinician, consider psychoeducation for your patients about the mental health and mental wellness benefits of physical exercise; they may be unaware of the positive influence it can have on both mental and physical well-being.

Physical exercise appears to positively impact brain health, a very important component of mental wellness. Intlekofer and Cotman (2013) reviewed the literature on the impact of physical exercise on the brain and found strong evidence of increased production of neurotrophic factors (which enhance neuron size, health, and functioning), increased angiogenesis, and increased synaptic plasticity and neurogenesis, particularly in the hippocampus, the "central processor" of the human brain. Physical exercise produced significant benefits in both size and function of multiple brain regions important in mental health and mental wellness, a "powerful stimulus that can countervail the molecular changes that underlie the progressive loss of hippocampal function in advanced age and Alzheimer's Disease." (Intlekofer & Cotman, 2013, p. 47).

Physical exercise also has a powerful mental wellness–enhancing effect. In a large, cross-sectional, non-interventional study across fifteen countries, with over 11,000 participants, Richards and colleagues (2015) found that happiness, an important component of mental wellness, is positively correlated to the amount of physical exercise: "high volume" exercisers reported

52% greater happiness as compared to sedentary individuals. This is powerful evidence of exercise's impact on mental wellness. In a prospective, randomized, controlled, interventional study, Khazaee-Pool and research colleagues (2015) used the validated Oxford Happiness Inventory to measure mental wellness in 120 older individuals (average age just over 70 years old): 60 randomized to receive a prescribed program of physical exercise and the other 60 to serve as a control group. Only the group randomized to physical exercise showed improvement in their levels of mental wellness ($p=0.001$). Even in individuals with the extremely challenging condition of cerebral palsy, Maher and colleagues (2016) found a higher level of physical activity was associated with a better quality of life and greater happiness. And Johnson and Acabchuk (2018) found that physical exercise figures prominently in factors that lead to a longer, happier life.

Some studies specifically examined the underlying biological mechanisms of how physical exercise improves well-being. It turns out that the description "runner's high" individuals report after exercise may be far closer to the truth than we previously realized. In a study of 11 healthy trained male cyclists who engaged in 90 minutes of intense exercise, 60 minutes of exercise at 55% of max heart rate, followed by 30 minutes of exercise at 75% of max heart rate, plasma levels of various endocannabinoids increased significantly after exercise (Heyman et al., 2012). Endocannabinoids are known to increase calmness, reduce anxiety, and increase mental wellness and well-being. Another study found higher levels of proenkephalin peptide F, an endogenous peptide that binds to opiate receptors in the brain and body, after versus before exercise (Kraemer et al., 2015). Endogenous opiates not only help with pain modulation, but also bring about a sense of well-being and enhanced mental wellness. A receptor binding study revealed even a single bout of exercise changed the occupancy of the cerebral opioid receptors, which could only happen if exercise produced endogenous opioids (Boecker et al., 2008). These individuals also reported significant improvement in their sense of mental well-being.

Although there are currently no specific dose-finding studies on exercise application for mental wellness improvements, we can leverage the large database on exercise and its mood lifting effects in major depression. Based on the known neurobiology of exercise, we expect the findings from the depression world to translate well to the realm of mental wellness improvement. The single best resource to guide us in this process is the Cochrane database review on exercise based on a meta-analysis of 25 different studies (Mcad et al., 2008). These are the salient findings about physical exercise and its impact on depressive symptoms:

· Exercise was remarkably effective in reducing depressive symptoms
· Even after the end of the formal intervention with exercise, exercise exerted a significant long-term residual positive impact
· Physical exercise was equal in efficacy to cognitive-behavioral therapy
· Physical exercise was equal to pharmacotherapy in its ability to improve mood
· Mixed exercise (aerobic plus resistance training) was the most effective, though every exercise modality was effective in its own right
· Exercise intensity matters—the greater the exercise intensity, the greater the benefits in improving depression
· Exercising twice a week has an impressive effect; exercising five times a week had an even larger effect
· Exercising regularly for several months produced the best results
· 20–30 minutes of exercise during each exercise episode produced significant benefits
· All age groups, young and old, benefited from exercise's beneficial effects on mood
· Both sexes showed similar improvements

There is every reason to believe that these findings would apply to mental wellness improvement as well.

We include specific physical exercise recommendations in our WILD

5 Wellness program (described in Chapter 7), and our own research shows that it is indeed a powerful mental wellness tool (reported in Chapter 8). We recommend 30 minutes of daily exercise of at least moderate intensity.

We recognize that for some beginning patients 30 minutes of exercise may seem like an insurmountable task. We have some suggestions to overcome this barrier:

- Recommend a "start slow but build up gradually" process. Accept even 10 minutes per day to begin with, and then suggest slowly increasing the duration and intensity of exercise.
- Offer coaching on the type of exercise that is safe and acceptable to the patient
- Obtain a physical examination and clearance from a healthcare provider prior to starting the exercise program

An enthusiastic and supportive clinician is perhaps the key ingredient needed in motivating a patient to start and maintain an exercise habit. We have found that clinicians who themselves are regular exercisers are more successful in motivating their patients to do the same. A coaching, supportive, and gently encouraging style adopted by a clinician is most likely to lead to success—after all, nearly all patients know exercise is good for them, and most likely have attempted to exercise on a regular basis in the past. Encouraging such patients to avoid seeing their past sub-optimum levels of exercise as an automatic signal that they will fail again in the future is a key task for the wellness-centric clinician. The road to success in developing a successful exercise habit is filled with twists and turns, and it is prudent for the clinician to accept this fact in order to avoid becoming frustrated with their patient's progress. Rather, the clinician should recommend a fresh start to their patients and offer the exercise recommendation non-judgmentally and with enthusiasm. Reasons for past failure should be gently and sensitively explored, so that lessons from the past can be learned in order to ensure a more successful future.

Since exercise clearly has wellness benefits, actively encouraging your patients to begin or increase exercise may be a simple way to improve their quality of life. Your patients may not be aware of the mental health and mental wellness benefits of physical exercise—you can use the principles in this section to offer psychoeducation for your patients about the positive influence exercise can have on both mental and physical well-being.

Nutrition

Food choices play a powerful role in our mental and physical health. We are what we eat, and this applies in both illness and health. The emerging sub-specialty of nutritional psychiatry is poised to take advantage of the burgeoning evidence of how the foods we eat both help treat psychiatric disorders and enhance mental wellness. Nutritional psychiatry, an emerging speciality within general psychiatry, essentially focuses on two major components of food, macronutrients and micronutrients, and seeks to optimize their ingestion to maximize their mental health benefits. But you do not have to be a nutrition specialist to offer your patients psychoeducation and direct suggestions for improved diet and its wellness-enhancing effects.

Nutrition and Mental Well-being

Substantial evidence reveals the relationship between the food ingested and mental health. Many studies have found that aspects of the Mediterranean diet, which is high in fruits, vegetables, fish, nuts, and whole grains and low in processed, fried, and animal-based foods, have positive effects on mental well-being. Munoz and colleagues (2009) examined the eating habits of over 8,000 individuals and found there was a direct, positive relationship between higher consumption of a Mediterranean diet and higher quality of mental and physical health, for both men and women.

Lesani and colleagues (2016) assessed happiness in over five hundred medical students in Iran, along with their intake of fruits and vegetables. Happiness was positively associated with the amount of fruits and vegetables consumed—the highest level of happiness was found in those who averaged more than 8 servings of fruits and vegetables per day. Yoshikawa and colleagues (2015) examined over 500 Japanese employees at a large company, measuring depressive symptoms and resilience, as well as frequency of fish consumption. High frequency of fish consumption was associated with lower depression scores and higher degrees of resilience, which might relate to omega-3 polyunsaturated fatty acids in fish. Muros and colleagues (2017) looked at the diet patterns of over five hundred 10-year-old children in Chile and found that higher adherence to a Mediterranean diet even among these children led to a higher association with self-esteem and self-concept.

The typical Western diet, compared to the Mediterranean diet, is associated with lower mental well-being. When Yoshikawa and colleagues (2016) examined the consumption of fried foods in 715 Japanese company workers, they found that higher ingestion was related to higher rates of depression and lower resilience. In a cross-sectional study of over ten thousand individuals, Bonaccio and colleagues (2018) assessed resilience utilizing the Connor-Davidson Psychological Resilience Scale and simultaneously obtained participants' eating habit scores for both the Greek and Italian Mediterranean diets. Greater consumption of Mediterranean-type or vegetable-based diets was positively associated with enhanced psychological resilience, whereas adherence to a Western diet was not. Those who ate a greater variety of fruits and vegetables had higher mental wellness and greater psychological resilience, likely related to greater intake of polyphenols and antioxidants.

Wellness Interventions for Nutrition

Research studies provide evidence to help us guide patients in changing their nutrition to improve their mental health. Parletta and colleagues (2017) randomized 152 patients suffering from depression to either a control group where they received social interaction, or an interventional group where they received regular hampers of food and fish oil supplements, elements of the Mediterranean diet. The interventional group had lower depression scores at three months, which they maintained at six months. Dowlati and colleagues (2017), in a prospective interventional study randomized women who recently had a baby and were vulnerable to postpartum blues to a control group or to receive a nutritional cocktail with tryptophan, tyrosine, blueberry juice, and blueberry extract. When they exposed these women to a known stressful activity (the sad mood induction procedure), those in the control group showed a robust increase in their sadness scores, but women who received the food supplements did not, demonstrating that the benefits of nutrition on mental health can be derived quickly.

Dr. Martha Morris is a professor in the department of Internal Medicine and director of the section of nutrition and nutritional epidemiology from Rush University Medical Center in Chicago. She and her colleagues have created the Mediterranean-DASH Intervention for Neurodegenerative Delay (MIND) diet (Morris et al., 2015). The diet is essentially a combination of the Mediterranean diet and the DASH (Dietary Approaches to Stop Hypertension) diet, which was originally designed to reduce hypertension and promote cardiovascular health, and is high in fruits, vegetables, and whole grains. Studies show that high adherence to the MIND diet leads to greater preservation of cognitive function and prevention of cognitive decline. The brain health impact of the MIND diet modification program was greater than either the Mediterranean or the DASH diets alone, making it better than the sum of its parts.

The MIND diet is highly directive and prescriptive. A MIND diet score for an individual can be easily obtained using a 15-item score card (Morris, 2015) which allows you and your patients to get a baseline score of eating patterns. The approach of the MIND diet is very patient friendly—no food items are banned. Higher scores on the MIND diet can be obtained by simply increasing the intake of certain foods and decreasing the intake of other foods. Over time, through gentle education and motivational interviewing, you can nudge your patients to move their weekly or monthly MIND diet scores higher and higher.

The MIND diet style of eating encourages certain types of food consumption, such as fruits, vegetables, and whole grains, and discourages others, such as fried foods and sweets. Adjustments can be made to the diet to accommodate an individual patient's diet preferences. For example, some patients do not or should not drink wine, and you should not encourage them to start drinking just to get a higher score. Rather, you can tell such patients to ignore item 15 and aim for their own highest score of 14. Similarly, some patients do not eat chicken; they can simply ignore the item for chicken and aim for a maximum score of 14.

The MIND diet, thankfully, helps prevent a "power struggle" between you and your patients. For patients who say, for example, they "simply can't live without cheese," encourage them to focus on finding other ways to improve their MIND diet score without sacrificing the foods they desire. So, discussing ways to decrease consumption of other unhealthy foods, and to increase consumption of healthy foods will improve their MIND diet score without them feeling deprived. This minimizes the power struggle over food choices. Because deriving mental wellness from nutrition is a lifelong process, a gentle, patient-centric approach is ideal, and the MIND diet fits well with this approach.

We recommend the MIND diet in our WILD 5 Wellness program (described in Chapter 7), and our experience using the MIND diet in clinical and research practice has been very positive. Patients find it easy to implement and appreciate making gradual changes to their eating habits. The average patient tends to have shockingly low scores—often in the 4- to 6-point range. With guidance and using the power of psychoeducation and motivational interviewing, you can help your patients double this score easily within a month or two. And remind your patients that perfection is not the goal—focusing on slow and sustainable changes in eating patterns takes away the usual apprehension patients often experience when discussing dietary changes with their clinicians.

Sleep Hygiene

If sleep does not serve an absolutely vital function, then it is the biggest mistake the evolutionary process has ever made.
—ALLAN RECHTSCHAFFEN

Of course, nature did not make a mistake in mandating that all animals sleep. Sleep is important for two different, yet interconnected reasons: to avoid diseases of the body and brain and to enhance wellness.

Unfortunately, modern Americans in general do not have good sleep health—we sleep less and more poorly than any previous generation. It appears that we have collectively adopted a host of bad habits that result in less sleep volume and low-quality sleep:

- Going to bed later and later
- Watching television until we fall asleep
- Bringing electronic devices to bed, causing overstimulation and suppressing melatonin due to emission of blue light
- Ingesting too much caffeine late in the day
- Consuming alcohol to "help us sleep" even though it does the opposite

This deterioration of sleep has led to significant problems, such as rising rates of obesity, increased rates of car accidents, and increased daytime fatigue. And it is not a coincidence that rates of depression and anxiety have gone up, and mental wellness has gone down as sleep health has declined. Both the mind and the body pay a price when we do not sleep well. Our own sleep is impacted by the sleep behaviors of those around us: couples, parents, children, roommates, and neighbors all impact one another's sleep health.

Implications of Poor Sleep

There is a bi-directional relationship between mental health and sleep, with each leading to and reinforcing the other. Van Dyk and colleagues (2016), upon examining the daily sleep patterns of a group of adolescents and assessing their mental health, found that good sleep leads to good mental health, and vice versa: good mental health leads to good sleep. This bi-directional relationship was apparent even on a day-to-day basis: as sleep quality changed every night, so did mental health the next day. In other words, every single night's sleep matters to mental health.

Jansson-Frojmark and Lindblom (2008) conducted a prospective, cross-sectional survey in a randomly selected population of 3,000 individuals from Sweden to find if there was a relationship between having anxiety or depression and eventual development of insomnia, and if the reverse was also true—if having insomnia was a risk factor for eventual development of anxiety or depression. They conducted these surveys at baseline and at the end of a year. They found a startlingly strong bi-directional relationship: those with anxiety had over four times the risk of also having impaired sleep, and those with depression had over twice the risk as people without these conditions. Furthermore, people who got poor sleep had twice the risk of developing anxiety and three and one-half times the risk of depression. This finding has been examined by Grandner (2017) who looked at the multilevel impact of poor sleep, as well as the positive benefits derived from good sleep health and found poor sleep does negatively impact mental health and the reverse is equally true.

Sleep and the Brain

The neurobiology of sleep reveals brain health and wellness are major beneficiaries of optimum sleep. Irwin (2015) convincingly argues that sleep is intimately tied to all members of the PNI system—the autonomic nervous system, the HPA axis, and the immune system. Even a single night of disrupted sleep can adversely impact the entire PNI system. Examples of PNI dysregulation created by sleep disruption include increased levels of inflammatory cytokines and heightened tone of the sympathetic nervous system. The downstream effects of this disruption help explain why people with poor sleep have a myriad of health problems, such as increased risk of cardiovascular disorders, diabetes, and even cancer. Interestingly, poor sleep can even impact an individual's response to vaccines and their ability to fight off viral infections.

Optimum sleep is critical to cognitive health. There is considerable evidence that during slow-wave sleep the brain consolidates memory at a molecular level (Sejnowski & Destexhe, 2000). Even one night of restorative sleep can help improve both memory and cognitive abilities such as attention, concentration, processing speed and executive functioning, but even one night of suboptimum sleep worsens memory and cognitive abilities. Yarnell and Deuster (2016) conducted an exhaustive review of the literature and found convincing evidence from multiple studies that poor sleep health negatively impacts performance in a host of important factors, such as stress resilience and driving capabilities, and poor sleep additionally increased pain, fatigue, negative mood, as well as compromised vigilance, decision making, and critical thinking.

Sleep Interventions

It is good to increase a patient's knowledge base about the importance of sleep, but giving them actual tools to improve sleep health is a far more effective intervention. Peach and colleagues (2018) evaluated over two hundred college students for sleep knowledge and sleep behaviors and used subjective measures and scales to determine their sleep amount and quality, as well as a wearable sleep device that nightly tracked the participants' sleep. Both objective and subjective measures improved in individuals with positive sleep behaviors, but simply possessing greater sleep knowledge did not have the same positive effects. In other words, just knowing about sleep hygiene practices is not sufficient in making an impact—rather, it is putting these learnings into practice that brings about positive sleep changes.

There is significant debate on the merits of individual sleep recommendations. Based on our own review of the literature on this topic, we selected six specific, measurable, and actionable sleep behavioral changes you can recommend to your patients (we also include these as part of our WILD 5 Wellness program, described in Chapter 7):

1. Avoid all electronic devices (e.g., television, smartphones, online games, tablets, computers, e-readers) 90 minutes prior to bedtime, due to the blue light they emit. Reading before bed should be upbeat and positive, avoiding disturbing material that may cause overstimulation.
2. Avoid napping during the day, which results in poor nighttime sleep.
3. Eliminate ambient light in the bedroom (e.g., light from a clock radio, cell phone, windows), using blackout shades and/or a night mask to block all light.
4. Enjoy a warm, relaxing bath or shower prior to bedtime.
5. Establish and stick to a regular bedtime each night, including weekends.
6. Avoid caffeinated drinks 10 hours before bedtime.

We advise patients to ultimately implement all 6 of these recommendations, but at a minimum we suggest nightly adoption of 4 or more of the 6 sleep hygiene practices. Based on our experience, most individuals readily identify at least 4 of 6 sleep hygiene practices they can apply to their lives. Occasionally, this proves to be difficult for a patient, and in such instances working collaboratively with the patient to identify even a few sleep hygiene techniques is appropriate. Accepting a "start slow but build up gradually" approach is acceptable. Of course, we should develop agreement with the patient that over time gradually integrating more positive sleep hygeine habits into their daily routine is advisable and achievable. In our studies (described in Chapter 8), objectively measuring sleep health using the Pittsburg Sleep Quality Index (PSQI), showed that 4 or more of these steps can significantly improve sleep health and wellness in as little as 30 days.

Mindfulness

Mindfulness is currently all the rage—you can hardly read a magazine or peruse a website without seeing something amazing about mindfulness' impact on the mind and body. Mindfulness is an ancient, Eastern philosophy with roots in Buddhist and Hindu traditions from Southeast Asia. Just a few decades ago mindfulness as a concept arrived in the Western countries, and there is now solid scientific evidence that supports its popularity.

For our purposes of mental wellness enhancement, mindfulness is an exceptionally useful tool. Jon Kabat-Zinn offers this definition of mindfulness: "Mindfulness means paying attention in a particular way: on purpose, in the present moment, and nonjudgmentally." (Segal, Williams, & Teasdale, 2013. p 38). Paying attention is the perfect antidote to distractibility and a wandering mind, which are both issues in a variety of psychiatric difficulties. Doing things "on purpose" distracts the mind from rumination. The present moment circumvents excessive rumination about the past or the future, which is often the cause of distress and directly harmful to mental wellness. Thinking nonjudgmentally prevents passing judgment, which can precipitate a depressive episode.

It is thought that states of non-awareness (being non-mindful) can lead to old patterns of thought, which can be negative and distressing. This non-mindful state understandably leads to heightened levels of depression, anxiety, insomnia, and general distress. On the flip side, the presence of mindful awareness cultivated by mindfulness practice can prevent the mind from slipping into negative patterns of thinking. It creates an altered state of calm, enhanced feelings of connectivity, and creative problem solving. The practice of mindfulness is not avoidance of distractibility; rather, it is being consciously aware of how the mind wanders, responding nonjudgmentally, and gently and intentionally bringing the mind back to focused attention.

Mindfulness and Mental Illness

The evidence regarding mindfulness' effectiveness in addressing mental illness is impressive. Evans and colleagues (2008) examined the application of mindfulness-based cognitive therapy in patients with full-blown generalized anxiety disorder and found it reduced the Beck Anxiety Index scores from 19 to 8.91, a 53% reduction in anxiety. Other measures, such as the Penn State Worry Questionnaire and Profile of Mood States Tension and Anxiety, also improved. Kim and colleagues (2010) studied patients with panic disorder and found that with a mindfulness intervention, even in the space of eight weeks, the Hamilton Anxiety Rating Scale scores improved, and the frequency of panic attacks decreased.

Even in treatment-resistant depression, studies demonstrate mindfulness' effectiveness as an add-on treatment. Kenny and Williams (2007) exposed 79 patients to eight weeks of mindfulness-based cognitive therapy. Using the Beck Depression Inventory scale, they found this intervention had a large effect size. Segal and colleagues from the University of Toronto (Segal et al., 2010), in a study of mindfulness-based cognitive therapy's ability to prevent relapse and recurrence of major depressive episodes, used an eight-week mindfulness training component, and then followed patients for months to assess the impact on future episodes of depression. Mindfulness-based practice was as effective in preventing a relapse as continuing an antidepressant treatment. In patients who stopped antidepressant therapy, mindfulness training exerted the same protection as ongoing medications in preventing a recurrence.

Mindfulness can impact anxiety as well as depression. Zeidan and colleagues (2014) studied 15 individuals who had never practiced mindfulness and for four days trained them to perform mindfulness meditation. Their anxiety decreased (and this change was associated with activation of the anterior cingulate cortex, ventromedial prefrontal cortex, and the anterior insula) in only 4 days.

Mindfulness and the Brain

A large scientific database helps us understand how this intervention works. Holzel and colleagues (2007) compared MRI assessments of 20 long-term mindfulness practitioners to non-meditators matched for sex, age, education, and handedness, and found larger gray matter volume in mindfulness practitioners, helping establish that there is a real neurobiological effect when individuals meditate.

And this change does not require a lifetime of meditation but can happen in a matter of weeks. In another study Holzel and colleagues (2010) enrolled a group of individuals who were stressed but otherwise healthy in an eight-week mindfulness-based stress reduction intervention. They imaged the amygdala, the organ involved with stress response that often functions excessively in stressed individuals, before and after the intervention. Individuals who experienced the greatest change in stress also had measurable changes in their brains: gray matter concentration had actually reduced in the right amygdala, and this biological change was positively correlated to changes in perceived stress. In yet another study by her team, Holzel (2011) enrolled 16 healthy, meditation naïve participants in an eight-week mindfulness program and measured hippocampal gray matter concentration using voxel-based morphology. Compared to a waitlist control group, these newly trained meditators had greater gray matter volume in the left hippocampus (a structure profoundly involved with processing of emotions and cognition) after eight weeks.

Overall, the effectiveness of meditation in making positive changes in the brain seems clear. In a review of the growing research database of brain imaging studies with mindfulness interventions, Tang and colleagues (2015) found the totality of the evidence strongly suggests that mindfulness studies reveal changes in gray matter volume in as little as eight weeks, and functional studies similarly revealed positive changes in network connectivity between various brain structures.

Not only physiological but also functional changes occur in the brain of individuals who practice mindfulness. Yang and colleagues (2016) taught meditation naïve individuals mindfulness meditation techniques and performed functional MRI as mental illness assessments before and after this intervention, to examine functional connectivity. These individuals had significant drops in depression and anxiety scores and showed an increase in the internal consistency between the precuneus and the temporoparietal junction and a decrease between frontal brain regions. These individuals also had decreased resting state connectivity between the pregenual anterior cingulate and dorsal medial prefrontal cortex—excessive connectivity between these "thinking" and "feeling" parts of the brain leads to excessive rumination, resulting in heightened depression and anxiety and reduced mental wellness. Because mindfulness practice can create this change even when a person is not currently meditating, this greatly suggests its utility in clinical practice.

Mindfulness also has an impact on the autonomic nervous system (ANS) and the inflammatory system. Kiecolt-Glaser and colleagues (2010) enrolled 50 healthy women, 25 novices, and 25 expert meditators in a complex but well-done study. They purposefully exposed participants to stressful conditions and examined their heart rate, obtained blood levels for the inflammatory marker interleukin 6 (IL-6), and assessed their level of positive affect. Expert mindfulness practitioners had a healthier ANS tone and immune system, both at baseline and after exposure to stress. Even when exposed to stress, expert meditators had a significantly better affective state and significantly lower IL-6 elevation. These results suggest that meditation and mindfulness practices are positive modulators of the ANS and the immune system.

Mindfulness and Mental Wellness

Mindfulness has a positive impact on mental wellness. Among 42 physician participants randomized to an 8-week mindfulness-based stress reduction program or a control group, Amutio and colleagues (2015) measured heart rate, a marker of ANS tone, which decreased in the intervention group. Levels of self-realization and mindfulness also increased, as did many other aspects of positive emotional states, such as being at ease and feeling peaceful, renewed, energetic, optimistic, and happy. Formal mindfulness teaching lasted only 8 weeks, but these physicians were followed for one year, and mental wellness kept improving even after the 8 weeks of formal training.

In another mindfulness intervention study, Erogul and research colleagues (2014) randomized first year medical students, a particularly at-risk population, to an 8-week mindfulness-based stress reduction program or to a control group. Stress diminished in the mindfulness group, and self-compassion was elevated (a mental wellness skill), compared to controls. Benzo and colleagues (2017) examined markers of mental wellness in 400 healthcare providers, to see which of them were associated with greater well-being. Self-compassion was significantly and independently associated with happiness, and this explained 39% of the variance; 95% of self-compassion's effects on happiness were explained by two elements: how participants coped with isolation and mindfulness.

We can summarize the most important things we have learned about mindfulness as follows:

- Mindfulness is effective in both reducing symptoms of mental illness and enhancing mental wellness.
- Mindfulness is not a particularly time-consuming activity. In some of our studies, we recommended only 8 minutes of guided mindfulness per day utilizing a free app.
- Mindfulness effects appear to be enduring.

In introducing mindfulness to patients, be aware that it can be intimidating—patients are often afraid that they will not "do it right." Gently emphasizing consistent practice, rather than perfect performance, may help them get started and stay on track. You can motivate your patients and help them with adherence, via education, coaching, and tracking their practices. Your patients will benefit from you educating them about the long-term psychological and neurobiological benefits of manintaining a consistent mindfulness practice. Mindfulness appears to be a gift that keeps on giving.

Social Connectedness

Bonding with others and social connectedness are a central need for human beings. It is as essential to our life as water and food, yet its potency in helping us thrive is often vastly underestimated. When social connectedness is suboptimal, we struggle with our mental health and mental wellness.

Social connectedness is so important for optimized mental wellness that its decrease in modern society is thought to be one of the prime reasons for increasing rates of depression, anxiety, despair, substance abuse, and even suicidality. Over the last few decades, individuals living in Western societies have demonstrably become more socially isolated. Loneliness, another descriptor of low social connectedness, is rampant. Reasons for this include the following:

- Working from home which reduces opportunities to connect socially
- Falling attendance at religious activities, adding to feelings of disconnectedness
- More people living alone, and stubbornly high divorce rates
- The arrival of computers, smartphones, and the internet, replacing direct human connections with pseudo-connectedness

Loneliness is a modern, self-inflicted tragedy of such epidemic proportions that, as mentioned in Chapter 1, the United Kingdom has created the cabinet-level position of Minister of Loneliness. The UK government believes, quite rightfully, that improving social connectedness will improve quality of life, decrease mental illness, and enhance mental wellness. Even though in the United States we are some decades away from having such concerted government efforts to fight the loneliness epidemic, you can address this issue now in your clinical practice.

Social Connectedness and Health

Quite literally, our life depends on our level of social connectedness. Holt-Lunstad, Smith, and Layton (2010) looked at various factors that decrease mortality across several conditions, among 148 studies with more than 308,000 patients. The number one condition that impacted mortality was the level of socialization—it had a greater effect than obesity or smoking. And social connectedness can act as a protective factor. Leigh-Hunt and colleagues (2017) reviewed the data from forty different studies on social connectedness and concluded that there is consistent evidence linking social isolation to worse cardiovascular and mental health outcomes. Cohen (2004) showed that more stress caused more depressive symptoms, yet social connectedness levels modulated depressive scores, driving them lower when social connectedness was high. Among individuals with coronary artery disease, Wang and colleagues (2006) showed that socially integrated individuals had less coronary artery blockage, even when they had comorbid depression.

These outcomes may relate to the strong positive feelings we get from socialization. To understand exactly what people are doing that generates positive or negative feelings, Killingsworth and Gilbert (2010) gave participants a smartphone device that would at random times ask them what they were doing and how they were feeling at that moment, on a 0–100 scale. The third highest positive feelings were reported during conversations with someone participants felt a deep connection to (number one was having sex, and number two was physical exercise), beating out other "feel-good" activities like playing a sport, listening to music, praying, and reading.

Research helps explain why this positive effect is so strong. Lieberwirth and Wang (2016) found that oxytocin and dopamine interact to regulate the bonding experience—if this bonding is impaired, levels of both of these neurotransmitters drop. This explains why we feel bad and dysphoric when we are separated from individuals with whom we are tightly socially bonded and why we literally crave being around those we love and share a strong social connection.

This craving for connection is so strong that the quality of emotional/social connectedness between parents and children impacts us for the rest of our lives. Guo, Mrug, and Knigh (2017) assessed children's level of emotional connectivity to their parents and then examined them decades later as adults, to see how their HPA axis functioned after exposure to experimental stressful situations. Deep social connectedness between parents and children were related to healthier HPA reactions to stress in adulthood.

Interventions for Social Connectedness

Social connectivity is changeable and improvable. Sheridan and colleagues (2015) randomized individuals with enduring and significant mental illness to a control group or to be educated about socialization and then asked to add two hours of social connectivity per week. After nine months, depression scores decreased in the intervention group. Kampert and Goreczny (2007) showed that all individuals, despite their impairments, crave social connectedness: over a thousand individuals with mental retardation reported a strong desire for increased community involvement and increased socialization. All human beings, regardless of who we are, truly yearn for connections with other people.

The elderly are very prone to isolation and loneliness, often due to physical limitations, but this too can be addressed. Jimison, Klein, and Marcoe

(2013) offered elderly individuals education on how to use a phone, tips on how to text, and how to access a web browser to make internet video calls to remain connected to family and friends. Although, as we mentioned above, this electronic connectivity is less substantial than direct face-to-face communication, the participants nonetheless reported an increased number of social contacts and increased total communication time as measured by e-mail, phone, and Skype usage.

We have also been conducting studies that involve enhancing social connectedness (described in detail in Chapter 8). We used scales to measure improvement in social connectedness before and after the intervention and offered a simple plan of enhancing social connectedness. We asked participants to meet or call a minimum of two friends or family members on a daily basis. We found significant positive results on the Social Connectedness Scale in all the studies conducted to date.

In discussing socialization with patients, we have found the concepts of micro- and macro-socialization help patients get a better handle on what types of social activities they should embrace in order to derive optimum mental wellness benefits. *Macro-socialization* refers to relationships and social engagements over an extended period of time with people and organizations we know well, such as spouses, family members, friends, religious groups, work events, political and non-political organizations, and so on. *Micro-socialization* refers to brief interactions with people we may not even know, such as smiling at people as they walk by, saying pleasantries to people we encounter, saying good morning to the barista at the coffee shop, or talking about the weather or local sports with fellow commuters while waiting for a bus. When practiced, these brief interactions also help diminish loneliness and enhance mental wellness. We recommend you encourage patients to engage in as many micro- and macro-socialization opportunities as possible.

There are clear biological and psychological benefits to improving socialization, and patients will benefit from developing both macro- and micro-socialization skills. With your guidance and prescriptive advice, your patients can quickly improve their socialization and reap tangible benefits to their mental health and wellness.

These five mental wellness interventions—exercise, nutrition, sleep, mindfulness, and social connectedness—are all well-researched and well understood wellness-centric interventions. There is clear scientific and neurobiological evidence supporting and proving the prowess of each of these five wellness-centric interventions in improving human wellness.

In clinical practice, it may be wise to avoid "picking and choosing" which of these interventions to offer. Each one has a non-overlapping biology, so it is prudent to offer patients the entire suite of these wellness-enhancing interventions. In fact, a positive "cross-pollination" effect occurs in individuals who engage in any of the wellness-centric interventions: there is a higher chance they will engage in other wellness-enhancing activities as well. For example, in a study of over fourteen thousand college students from 94 different undergraduate colleges, Vankim and Nelson (2013) found that socially engaged individuals are more likely to exercise and are therefore more likely to experience benefits with stress management and improved mental health.

With the large number of interventional studies supporting the utility of each of these mental wellness interventions, we are confident that by recommending each to your patients and coaching them to maintain these healthy practices, you will lead them to enhance their mental well-being.

CHAPTER 6

HERO Traits: Key Attributes of Mental Wellness

Over the last several years, as we have researched mental wellness interventions and applied them in our practice, we sought to identify particular traits that markedly improve with rising levels of mental wellness. When we examined the scientific literature, we looked for wellness traits that both demonstrated deficits in psychiatric disorders and improved with wellness-centric interventions. In both our research and our clinical practice, we have been repeatedly impressed with the importance of four key measures of mental wellness: happiness, enthusiasm, resilience, and optimism—what we call the HERO wellness traits. Our clinical and research efforts now center on these HERO traits as the four pillars of mental wellness.

Happiness, enthusiasm, resilience, and optimism play a central role in human functioning. As we describe in this chapter, research from multiple centers from around the world shows each HERO element is crucial in optimum functioning of both the human brain and human behavior. We all desire a life that is fulfilling, meaningful, and filled with happiness, enthusiasm, resilience, and optimism.

HERO Traits and Mental Wellness

Over our several years of research and clinical experience and a through in-depth examination of the published research, we have studied, developed, and practiced interventions to improve mental wellness. We have found that these four traits—happiness, enthusiasm, resilience, and optimism—share the following attributes:

- *Universality:* Each of these four wellness traits is desired by all human beings, no matter their cultural, racial or socio-economic background—they are universal needs.
- *Measurability:* These four attributes are easily measurable in patients from diverse backgrounds and are easily understood by patients and non-patients (i.e., they have high construct validity).
- *Deficit in mental illness:* Patients with psychiatric disorders display a decrease or deficit in each of these traits.
- *Biological basis:* There is a neurobiological, measurable, and demonstrable brain basis to all four of these traits, and their importance is well understood.
- *Changeability:* With targeted wellness-centric interventions, these four traits are demonstrably improvable.

Individuals with a psychiatric disorder are particularly vulnerable to significant decreases in the HERO wellness traits—what we call Wellness Deficit Disorder. Our national mental wellness survey shows patients with psychiatric illnesses have remarkable decreases in their HERO wellness traits (Jain et al., 2016[b]). Individuals with psychiatric disorders must deal with not only the painful symptoms of their illness but also the near universal sting of low mental wellness. But we have also found that wellness interventions improve these traits, often quickly and markedly, as we describe in detail in Chapter 8.

In this chapter we explore each HERO trait in depth, along with ways to help our patients strengthen them. We also describe the HERO Wellness Scale, a validated measure of mental wellness (Jain, Cole, Girard, Raison, & Jain, 2017[c]) that we use in our WILD 5 Wellness program, described in

Chapter 7. A copy of the HERO Wellness Scale is in the resource section of the book, and you are welcome to use it in your practice. With the HERO Wellness Scale you can identify wellness deficits and track your patients' improvement as you coach and motivate them toward increased happiness, enthusiasm, resilience, and optimism.

Happiness

The very purpose of our existence is to seek happiness.
—DALAI LAMA

Happiness is universally desired—this is one truth with no exceptions. Happiness was judged to be so valuable by the founding fathers of this country that in the Declaration of Independence they called it an "unalienable right": life, liberty, and the pursuit of happiness were seen as true equals. And pursuing happiness is now a common activity—just look at all the smartphone apps that tell us how to increase our happiness.

Research conducted over the last few decades has revealed that happiness, a key attribute of mental wellness, is indeed an important part of our well-being. In a survey of over 9000 college students in 47 nations, over half of the respondents rated the importance of happiness as a "9" on a 9-point scale; the average happiness rating was 8.1, making it the highest ranked among 21 variables, which also included love, wealth, health, and getting into heaven (Kim-Prieto, Diener, Tamir, Scollon, & Diener, 2005).

Research also shows that happiness has a "home address" in the brain, and that we devote large tracks of our brain to the pursuit of happiness. A literature review by researchers from Kyoto University in Japan showed that "functional neuroimaging investigations of happiness have consistently found that the induction of happy, as compared to neutral, emotions activated certain brain areas, including the anterior cingulate gyrus, medial parietal cortex (posterior cingulate gyrus and precuneus) and amygdala"

(Sato et al., 2015, p.1). These are some of the major structures involved in the neuroanatomy of the mood-generating and -regulating circuit. Moreover, a structural MRI study by these same researchers (Sato et al., 2015) showed that happier people had a significantly larger right precuneus region. And as mentioned in Chapter 5, "hedonic hotspots"—regions in the brain that strongly light up when pleasure is experienced—have been identified (Kringelbach & Berridge, 2009).

We also know that happiness is directly related to mental health. For example, individuals who live with schizophrenia, arguably one of the most debilitating of mental illnesses, have challenges with mental wellness and happiness. Pamler and colleagues (2014) assessed individuals with schizophrenia for baseline levels of happiness and found they reported lower levels of happiness compared to healthy controls, clear evidence of Wellness Deficit Disorder in these individuals. Reported happiness was also significantly associated with mental health-related quality of life, perceived stress, resilience, and optimism.

What makes us happy? D'raven and Pasha-Zaidi (2014) examined this question in university students in the United Arab Emirates. Seven themes emerged from their research, factors at the individual, family, community, and country level that modulate happiness levels:

Pleasurable activities increase happiness. In the D'raven and Pasha-Zaidi (2014) study, happiness was alterable both for the moment and over multiple days by engaging in certain pleasurable activities, such as watching television, traveling, physical exercise via group activities, enjoying flowers, acting, making others laugh, planning for the future, connecting with others, being smiled at (even by a stranger), and laughing with friends. You can suggest these types of activities to your clients to enhance their happiness. *Caution*: The heedless pursuit of hedonia, without thought and in a harmful manner, will understandably lead to sadness and unhappiness. Asking patients to increase pleasurable activities should be done with thought, to avoid damaging and harmful means. We suggest recommending healthy activities that hold genuine meaning for your patients; for example, solitary pursuits of happiness may work better in Eastern societies, and group activities in Western societies (Ford et al., 2015).

Happiness is derived from accomplishments and reaching goals. We derive great pride from accomplishing our goals. Successfully accomplishing difficult tasks improves our level of happiness (D'raven & Pasha-Zaidi (2014). Because human beings are hardwired to be goal-setters and task-oriented, accomplishing tasks often brings tangible rewards. And pride in self leads to enhanced happiness. You can leverage this theme when using mental wellness interventions with your patients: offer them achievable tasks to successfully accomplish as a direct happiness enhancer.

Individuals experience greater happiness when with friends and family. The concept of togetherness appears to be important to most, irrespective of culture or any other demographic variable. A group's happiness is as important as an individual's happiness, and interconnectivity between members influences each member's happiness. D'raven and Pasha-Zaidi (2014) found that a person's happiness had a ripple effect, extending out and positively influencing the happiness of others. Individuals also unconsciously "sampled" the level of mental wellness and happiness in other group members before deciding how happy they themselves were. Participants seemed to be aware that their own happiness affected others important to them. As a clinician, you can leverage the fact that many people are highly motivated to improve the happiness of their family and friends. Helping your patients understand that improving their own happiness can positively impact others may motivate them to make postive changes in their life.

Happiness is achieved through service and social responsibility. D'raven and Pasha-Zaidi (2014) found that volunteering, being socially responsible, and being charitable brings tangible rewards to individuals, including happiness. Exercising social responsibility was also a happiness enhancer. Voluntarily "doing the right thing" was associated with elevated mental wellness and happiness scores.

Happiness increases with involvement in religion and spirituality. Overall, D'raven and Pasha-Zaidi (2014) found that people who reported being religious and regularly engaging in religious group activities were happier. Besides feeling there is a higher power guiding and watching over them, individuals involved in these group activities increased social connectedness, which further enhances levels of happiness. Many religious congregations are also involved in social and community service, which offers another venue for elevating happiness.

Happiness is increased by a strong and supportive society with political stability. Students surveyed by the D'raven and Pasha-Zaidi (2014) study identified the positive impact a stable society with a stable political system has on wellness. In particular, the study cited Syrian students who experienced lower mental wellness as a result of heightened societal and political disruption in their country.

With happiness as a key component to mental wellness, we can help our patients increase their wellness by practicing behaviors that increase their happiness, including appropriate and socially acceptable pleasurable activities, enhancing self-control, reaching goals, and increasing social connectedness—which mesh well with the elements of mental wellness described in Chapter 5. The next chapter describes several mental wellness programs you can incorporate into your practice to improve your patients' happiness, including our WILD 5 Wellness program.

Enthusiasm

Nothing great was ever achieved without enthusiasm.

—RALPH WALDO EMERSON

Enthusiasm is a vital need for living life to the fullest. Dictionary.com defines *enthusiasm* as "absorbing or controlling possession of the mind by any interest or pursuit; lively interest"; its synonyms include *eagerness, ardor, fervor, passion, zeal, energy,* and *spirit.* Without enthusiasm, one merely exists and nothing more. It is as if the engine of life sputters when enthusiasm is low, like a car that has plenty of gas but no oil in the engine. Like a catalyst in a chemical reaction, it is not the main ingredient, but it makes things pop and sizzle.

Multiple psychiatric disorders are associated with a low level of enthusiasm, including anxiety disorders, depressive disorders, and psychotic disorders. In our survey of American mental wellness (Jain et al., 2016[b]), we found that individuals with a psychiatric disorder had unusually low levels of enthusiasm. The *Diagnostic and Statistical Manual of Mental Disorders* has codified it, albeit somewhat indirectly, into the diagnostic criteria of various psychiatric disorders. For example, the criteria for major depression include such items as "lack of desire," "lack of pleasure," and "low motivation"—all proxies for enthusiasm depletion.

Clinicians can lack enthusiasm as well. Burnout affects providers in mental health as well as those in all other areas of healthcare, including surgeons, nurses, and primary care clinicians. Luk and colleagues (2018) examined the issue of burnout in clinicians and found depletion of enthusiasm is indeed a major cause. Bhatti and Viney (2017) looked at how to transform the lives and careers of senior physicians and recommended retaining and elevating enthusiasm, even during difficult times, as an essential human need.

High levels of enthusiasm produce a spillover effect on other individuals. A three-year study by Alsharif and Qi (2014) examined which teacher traits students ranked as having the greatest impact on their ability to learn a difficult subject, such as medicinal chemistry. The single most impactful trait in the instructor was enthusiasm. Students ranked enthusiasm even higher than an instructor's credentials, knowledge base, or any other trait. Enthusiasm is contagious and has a positive impact not just on the person possessing it, but on the lives of those they touch. Cultivating enthusiasm in yourself may in turn enhance your patients' enthusiasm.

And patient enthusiasm impacts psychotherapy. A study of cognitive-behavioral therapy in patients with sub-threshold depression (Hayasaka et al., 2015) revealed that the greater the patient's enthusiasm for completion of their therapeutic homework, the lower their depression and anxiety. This study strongly suggests assessing for enthusiasm in your patients, and alleviating enthusiasm deficits to maximize outcomes.

Directly and proactively offering enthusiasm-enhancing tips to your patient may indeed improve outcomes. With experience and patience, we have learned that we can increase our patients' level of enthusiasm by helping them develop a sense of purpose: finding opportunities for success, being mindful, being socially connected, and engaging in positive psychology exercises—elements of mental wellness described in Chapter 5—definitely helps increase levels of sustained enthusiasm.

Resilience

We regard resilience as the backbone of the HERO family—it is resilience, defined by the American Psychological Association as "the process of adapting well in the face of adversity, trauma, threats, or significant sources of stress," that gives the other elements an opportunity to flourish. Attention to resilience is growing in the scientific literature, as evidenced by the exceptionally large number of publications addressing its importance. Although there is no common definition of resilience across this vast literature, after reviewing a full one hundred articles Aburn and colleagues (2016) found three common themes: rising above, adaptation and adjustment, and dynamic process. Robertson and colleagues (2016) found that a common theme to resilience is the ability to positively adapt to adversity. They reviewed the resilience literature among physicians and found positive interactions between personal growth and accomplishment in resilient physicians. Resilience was highly correlated to three critical traits: high persistence, high self-directedness, and low avoidance of challenges.

Resilience relates directly to brain function. Gupta and colleagues (2017), in an MRI study of 48 individuals, first measured subjective levels of resilience and then attempted to correlate it to brain volume. In high-resilience individuals they found significant associations with greater gray matter volume in the subparietal sulcus, intraparietal sulcus, amygdala, anterior midcingulate cortex, and subgenual cingulate cortex. All of these structures are important in controlling our emotions, cognition, and executive function. Thus, higher resilience is associated with greater brain volume in critical structures that control vital higher-level human functioning.

Resilience also relates directly to the psychoneuroimmunological (PNI) system, described in Chapter 4. Walker and colleagues (2017) examined biomarkers of resilience and found several possible candidates of potential utility in measuring human resilience, including heart rate variability, immune markers (such as cytokine levels, T and B cell counts, and macrophage counts), and cortisol levels—all affected by the PNI system.

Building resilience can be important for our patients. Bozikas (2016) found lower resilience levels were associated with a greater risk of depressive episodes in bipolar patients, and similar findings emerged in patients with schizophrenia. Lower resilience levels were associated with greater psychosis, and a lower ability to bounce back and reintegrate into society. Bozikas and Parlapani (2016) also noted a relationship with other HERO traits: "Schizophrenia patients with higher resilience levels and optimism showed higher levels of happiness that associated in turn with lower perceived stress and higher personal mastery."

MacLeod and colleagues (2016) found evidence that higher levels of resilience were associated with positive outcomes in physical and mental health, successful aging, and longevity. Our own mental wellness survey (Jain et al., 2016ᶜ) revealed that individuals with no mental health or chronic pain conditions, on a scale from a low of 0 to a high of 10, report an average resilience score of 7.2, compared to 5.9 among those with a mental health condition, an 18% decrease. Our survey and others (Jain et al., 2016ᶜ; Jeste, Palmer, Rettew, & Boardman, 2015) have shown that this relationship is circular: low levels of mental wellness and high levels of mental illness lead to low resilience, and low levels of resilience lead to higher mental illness risk and lower levels of mental wellness. By addressing both issues—treating mental illness and enhancing resilience through targeted interventions—you can effectively build resilience in your patients, which involves the following abilities and desires:

- To not give up in the face of adversity
- To persist in efforts to solve a challenge
- To be self-motivated in addressing challenges
- To find an inner coach to guide actions
- To face and solve challenges and not look the other way

Life circumstances can lower resilience, but life skills can counter these effects. Hart and colleagues (2014) examined the issue of resilience in nurses, who—like groups working in high-stress environments—are at risk for low resilience. They found that a challenging workplace, feeling psychologically empty, perceiving diminished inner balance, and a sense of dissonance in personal and professional life lowered resilience.

Hart and colleagues (2014) suggest several interpersonal skills to reverse the effects, including cognitive reframing (thinking differently about challenges), being more socially connected, and having a better work-life balance. You can coach these skills in patients to enhance their well-being.

The scientific community has now begun to study resilience interventions. Moffett and Bartram (2017) exposed 105 first-year veterinary students to a teaching intervention focused on building resilience via a variety of skills, such as drawing on past experiences, reaching out to support networks, and consciously changing perspectives. Postintervention resilience scores, obtained with the Connor-Davidson Resilience Scale, significantly improved over preintervention scores. Participants felt learning resilience building skills helped them both professionally and personally.

The take-home message for clinicians is that resilience can be quickly, efficiently, and significantly improved, which enhances patients' overall well-being. Simple, directive, and prescriptive resilience-building exercises, discussed in Chapter 7, demonstrably improve this essential wellness trait.

Optimism

Merriam-Webster's Collegiate Dictionary defines *optimism* as a frame of mind: "An inclination to put the most favorable construction upon actions and events or to anticipate the best possible outcome." Optimism is not an empty feel-good approach but more an attitude we consciously adopt to examine all possible outcomes from the present situation and then choose the most positive.

Optimism is a measurable and changeable wellness trait, but it is a complex concept. Many authors have attempted to describe optimism and establish how it impacts well-being. Kleiman and colleagues (2017) offer the following conceptualizations of optimism: the sense of positive expectations for the future, the optimistic attributions we give to events, an illusion of control, and a set of self-enhancing biases. They found different benefits among these four types of optimism. Positive expectations of optimism protect against recurrent depressive episodes, whereas optimistic attributions moderate against anxiety symptoms. Thus, it is ideal to encourage patients to develop a wide array of optimism-enhancing skills to successfully navigate life and achieve high levels of mental wellness.

Optimism is really a cognitive construct, a style of thinking that results in definitive behavioral change. Optimistic individuals exert more effort in life to live up to their optimistic view of the future, whereas pessimistic individuals disengage from efforts (Carver & Scheier, 2014). Possessing high levels of optimism is of great benefit to individuals. Among the general population, a thirty-year long, prospective study from Scandinavia (Daukantaite & Zukauskiene, 2011) showed optimism in adolescence best predicts satisfaction in life when these individuals reached their middle years. In fact, optimism beat out intelligence, household income, and school success in predicting later life satisfaction.

The brain benefits greatly from higher levels of optimism. Yang and colleagues (2013) conducted a voxel-based, volumetric study of the human brain of 361 individuals comparing levels of dispositional optimism to brain gray matter volume. They found the brains of the optimists had greater gray matter volume in clusters of areas involved in the processing of emotions, that included the left thalamic region, left pulvinar, and the left parahippocampal gyrus. Dolcos and colleagues (2016) found that higher optimism levels correlated to greater gray matter volume in the orbitofrontal prefrontal cortex, a region associated with experiencing less anxiety.

In addition to structural differences in the brain, optimism levels affect brain functionality and connectivity. Ran and colleagues (2017) measured levels of dispositional optimism in their subjects and studied connectivity of the ventromedial prefrontal cortex to other regions of the brain. They found optimism increased connectivity in the middle temporal gyrus and decreased connectivity in the inferior frontal gyrus, both key brain regions of the limbic system.

Optimism may indeed be a matter of life and death. Kim and research colleagues (2017) prospectively assessed more than 70,000 nurses for mortality after a baseline evaluation of their level of dispositional optimism. Individuals in the highest quartile of optimism had a 29% lower risk of mortality compared to those in the lowest quartile. Even after adjusting for age and health status, the statistical relationship between optimism and life expectancy held steady. The association was found in diverse causes of mortality, including cancer, heart disease, stroke, respiratory disease, and infection. This demonstrates the incredibly diverse, positive impact of optimism on human beings.

Evidence also reveals that both dispositional optimism and explanatory-style optimism are connected to better mental health. In a review paper, Forgeard and Seligman (2012) explored how optimism directly and indirectly elevates mental wellness and found that higher levels of optimism is associated with greater mental well-being, better physical health, and even greater occupational success.

Higher levels of optimism may also prevent individuals from developing a psychiatric pathology. Birkeland and colleagues (2017) examined the protective effects of possessing higher levels of optimism. They prospectively evaluated a group of individuals before, and then 1, 2, and 3 years after the tragic bombing in Oslo, Norway, in 2011. Possessing higher levels of optimism before the trauma decreased the level of arousal, numbing, and dysphoric arousal, all three important elements of post-traumatic stress disorder.

Medical specialties besides psychiatry have taken note of optimism's associations with better outcomes, even in the most seriously ill patients. A study of individuals with congestive heart failure found a clear and statistically significant association between dispositional optimism and heart failure–related quality of life (Kraai, Vermeulen, Hillege, Jaarsma, & Hoekstra, 2018). They suggested optimism may be an improvable risk factor.

The mechanisms by which optimism improves quality of life may relate to behavioral choices. Carver and Scheier (2014) conducted a thorough literature search and found that optimists exhibited the following behaviors:

1. Handle stressors better
2. Make better spouses and enjoy relationships more
3. Are more nurturing as parents and have children who handle stress better
4. Handle healthcare challenges and pain better
5. Catastrophize less about the future
6. Are less likely to smoke and more likely to exercise and eat healthy meals
7. Live longer, happier, and healthier lives

They also found no convincing evidence of negative effects of optimism, so you can feel fairly safe in helping patients achieve higher levels of optimism to enhance their mental wellness.

Carver and Scheier (2014) found that optimism levels in a human being tend to stabilize over time and individuals tend to live at the same level of optimism gifted to them by their genetics and early childhood experiences. However, with conscious effort and with proper psychoeducation and guidance, optimism is alterable for the better.

Optimism can also moderate effects of chronic pain. Hanssen and colleagues (2013) offered half of a group of university students an optimism-enhancing intervention of writing about and visualizing their best possible self. Those in the control group were instead offered a sham exercise. Then all subjects experienced the cold pressor task, an experimental model of pain induced by cold. Individuals in the optimism-enhancing intervention group reported lower pain intensity, revealing that elevated optimism does have a direct, inhibitory effect on pain intensity. Boselie and colleagues (2017) used the same technique to induce higher levels of optimism in individuals and found even pain-induced executive dysfunction and task shifting (the ability to smoothy and efficiently shift cognitive tasks) were diminished in the intervention group.

It is clear that enhancing optimism in our patients can have extensive benefits for their mental and overall well-being. Although we all possess a certain level of optimism, granted to us by our genes and our environment, interventional studies reveal that optimism, like its other HERO brethren happiness, enthusiasm, and resilience, is modifiable with effort and practice. As a wellness-centric clinician, by offering techniques, coaching, and encouragement, you have the opportunity to make a lasting impact on your patients' mental well-being in each of these key areas.

The HERO Wellness Scale

The HERO Wellness Scale (Figure 6.1) is a five item self-rated scale that allows you and your patients to obtain scores for each of the HERO wellness traits described in this chapter, as well as an overall mental wellness assessment, at baseline and periodically throughout the wellness interventions you and your patient choose (several are offered in Chapter 7). It is a Likert scale from 0 to 10, with 0 being the lowest and 10 being the highest/best score, which we have validated in research (described in Chapter 10). Patients can easily use the HERO Wellness Scale, which can also be helpful when introducing patients to the concept of wellness, by offering them a tangible list of attributes to consider (more in introducing wellness to patients in Chapter 9). Having this information, especially the ability to compare current scores with baseline, pre-intervention scores, demonstrates to patients that their efforts are paying off (more in measurement-based care in Chapter

HERO WELLNESS SCALE

*PLEASE CIRCLE **ONE NUMBER** FOR EACH QUESTION BELOW.*

1. On average, during the last 7 DAYS, how happy have you felt?

0	1	2	3	4	5	6	7	8	9	10
Not at all happy		Mildly happy			Moderately happy			Highly happy		Extremely happy

2. On average, during the last 7 DAYS, how enthusiastic have you felt?

0	1	2	3	4	5	6	7	8	9	10
Not at all enthusiastic	Mildly enthusiastic			Moderately enthusiastic				Highly enthusiastic		Extremely enthusiastic

3. On average, during the last 7 DAYS, how resilient have you felt?

0	1	2	3	4	5	6	7	8	9	10
Not at all resilient		Mildly resilient			Moderately resilient			Highly resilient		Extremely resilient

4. On average, during the last 7 DAYS, how optimistic have you felt?

0	1	2	3	4	5	6	7	8	9	10
Not at all optimistic		Mildly optimistic			Moderately optimistic			Highly optimistic		Extremely optimistic

5. On average, during the last 7 DAYS, how would you rate your mental wellness?

0	1	2	3	4	5	6	7	8	9	10
Not at all good		Mildly good			Moderately good			Markedly good		Extremely enthusiastic

SCORING: To calculate total score, add all circled numbers.

TOTAL SCORE: 0– 50

HIGHER SCORES INDICATE HIGHER LEVELS OF WELLNESS

SCORE

WILD 5☆ Wellness®
Wellness **I**nterventions for **L**ife's **D**emands

FIGURE 2.1: Tools to Examine the Neurobiology of Mental Wellness

10). Receiving such immediate feedback is highly motivating and leads to higher adherence with wellness practices. A copy of the scale is available in the resource section of the book.

There is incontrovertible evidence that individuals with higher levels of mental wellness live longer, healthier, and more fulfilling lives. As wellness-centric clinicians, we can offer our patients great benefits by helping them build HERO wellness traits in a tangible framework to conceptualize mental wellness. The HERO Wellness Scale allows both you and your patients to make progress toward enhanced mental wellness and better well-being.

CHAPTER 7

Mental Wellness Programs for Your Practice

This chapter describes four developed, researched, and widely-utilized mental wellness programs: Martin Seligman's Positive Psychotherapy, Dilip V. Jeste's Positive Psychiatry, Giovanni Fava's Well-Being Therapy, and our own WILD 5 Wellness program. All four programs provide powerful mental wellness interventions that can augment your treatment strategies. We describe each program, as well as some enhancing engagement strategies you can use with all four programs.

Positive Psychology and Positive Psychotherapy

Based on his acute awareness that simply addressing psychological distress was not enough, Martin Seligman created a school of thought now called positive psychology. Seligman is a first-rate researcher and clinician who has contributed significantly toward helping the public recognize that there is more to mental health than just the absence of psychiatric symptoms and that seeking positive wellness traits and building upon them are worthy goals.

Seligman and Csikszentmihalyi (2000) proposed a theoretical framework for positive psychotherapy that is called PERMA—positive emotions, engagement, relationship, meaning, and accomplishment:

Positive emotions such as happiness, contentment, pride, serenity, optimism, confidence, and gratitude

Engagement in activities that are deeply meaningful to an individual to a degree that they engender a state of "flow" when engaged in them

Relationships that are deep in quality and quantity of positive meaning, such as relationships with family and friends

Meaning, as in achieving a sense of purpose and seeing the value in contributions to self, others, and society

Accomplishment, meaning achieving success in a chosen area, feeling masterful and competent, and seeking deep, personal meaning from work, family responsibilities, vocation, or profession

Seligman's model does not reject any element of traditional psychology or psychiatry. He explains that human beings in distress possess "authentic strengths" that are as real as their symptoms of disease. His model also holds that these signature strengths are identifiable, measurable, and improvable, as all humans have an inherent capacity for growth.

Seligman's conceptualization of mental wellness has initiated a huge positive ripple effect in mental health. Here are just a few of the results from his work: the establishment of a master's degree program in positive psychology at the University of Pennsylvania, adoption of the PERMA model by the U.S. Army to help build resilience in soldiers, and integration of positive psychology elements into the curriculum of many schools and universities across America (Seligman, 2018).

Based on his model of positive psychology, Seligman created a formal mental wellness program called Positive Psychotherapy (PPT). This wellness program has been studied multiple times in various settings and has shown effectiveness even in highly challenging populations such as those with psychosis (Schrank et al., 2016). He and Tayyab Rashid have published a clinical manual on positive psychotherapy for practicing clinicians (Rashid & Seligman, 2018). The opening two sentences from the preface of their book precisely describes their approach:

An unspoken and untested premise of psychotherapy-as-usual is that when a client is encouraged to talk at length about what is wrong, this client will somehow recover. Positive psychotherapy (PPT) takes the opposite approach. It encourages clients to recognize fully what is right and strong and good in their lives and to deploy what is best about them in order to buffer against mental disorders. (pg. ix)

They go on to add: "PPT assesses, appreciates, and amplifies what is good about clients—without minimizing their distress—and uses these strengths as the levers of healing."

The theoretical foundations of PPT are based on Seligman's groundbreaking exploration of the role of positive psychology in a variety of populations, including those with and without psychiatric disorders. He found that individuals prize their positive attributes. It is partly the atrophy or absence of these positive attributes that leads to and perpetuates the symptoms of major depression. PPT pushes hard against the traditional view that the focus of treatment is just symptom resolution, instead focusing on building positive psychology skills.

The PPT manual (Rashid & Seligman, 2018) provides an excellent explanation of PPT's concepts, extensive scientific evidence supporting PPT's effectiveness in a wide range of clients, and resources to immediately start utilizing these tools in your practice. PPT consists of 15 semi-structured sessions that are broadly divided into three phases:

PHASE 1

Session 1: The clinician introduces the PPT model and the gratitude journal, and explains the concept of journaling focused on wellness and the importance of gratitude. The client's questions are answered, and the concept and importance of homework is explained.

Session 2: The clinician and client discuss character strengths and signature strengths, and the client creates a list of strengths by self-reflecting and obtaining feedback from family and friends.

Session 3: Practical wisdom is the focus of this session. The clinician addresses problem-solving skills, and the client is encouraged to apply these new skills to three situations to change outcomes for the better.

Session 4: In this session, titled "A Better Version of Me," the client creates and then implements a written plan, which utilizes signature strengths to proactively impact a life challenge or problem.

PHASE 2

Session 5: This session focuses on "open" and "closed" memories. The client writes down and processes memories using PPT skills and uses character strengths and signature strengths to look for more adaptive means to deal with these memories in the moment and in the future.

Session 6: Forgiveness is the theme of this session. The client uses PPT skills to explore situations where forgiveness might enhance mental wellness. Forgiveness letter writing is one of the skills explored.

Session 7: The theme is "maximizing versus satisficing." The clinician and client explore strengths of each approach and how maximizing everything can lead to heightened levels of distress. The client uses PPT skills learned up to this point to create a plan of health, choosing between maximizing and satisficing.

Session 8: This session is devoted entirely to helping the client build skills in developing gratitude. The clinician introduces two practices, the gratitude letter and the gratitude visit, and helps the client develop a plan to incorporate one or both of these practices into homework assignments.

PHASE 3

Session 9: This session focuses on hope and optimism. The client is encouraged to see the best possible, most positive, but still realistic outcome for any given situation. The clinician explains the temporary basis of challenges and adversities and the importance of hope—if one door closes, another one opens.

Session 10: Posttraumatic growth is the focus of this session. The clinician explores the concept of strength being derived from experiencing a trauma, which is a new concept for most clients. The client engages in an exercise of writing down a past trauma and exploring what was learned from the trauma that was a growth experience.

Session 11: Slowness and savoring are the two themes of this clinical encounter. The clinician discusses and encourages purposeful slowing down of pleasurable events and experiences and then savoring them consciously, as well as using mindful skills to develop these skills of slowing down and savoring.

Session 12: Positive relationships are discussed in this session. The client learns to identify and appreciate the strengths of others and creates a "tree of positive relationships." The clinician encourages an active discussion between the client and the individuals the client has identified as a positive relationship, with the goal of further strengthening those relationships.

Session 13: This session focuses on positive communication. The clinician and client explore various styles of responding to good news and how those styles impact satisfaction in relationships. The client practices a specific skill called active constructive responding.

Session 14: Altruism is the main topic during this session. The clinician and client explore the concept of the "gift of time" exercise and discuss a plan for execution.

Session 15: The final session focuses on meaning and purpose. Together the clinician and client discuss the concept of searching for and pursuing activities that bring real meaning and purpose to the client's life. The client explores a "positive legacy" exercise, thinking about what the client's legacy of goodness in life will be in the future.

Positive Psychiatry

A few years after positive psychology hit the American landscape, positive psychiatry made its appearence. Dilip V. Jeste deserves most of the credit for bringing positive psychiatry to the world's attention. When Jeste was elected president of the American Psychiatric Association in 2013, his presidential address was on the topic of positive psychiatry. He thus brought attention to this important topic to psychiatrists in the United States and overseas for the first time. He and his colleagues then published "Positive Psychiatry: Its Time Has Come" (Jeste, Palmer, Rettew, & Boardman, 2015), offering a definition of positive psychiatry: "The science and practice of psychiatry that seeks to understand and promote well-being through assessment and interventions involving positive psychosocial charecteristics in people who suffer from or are at high risk of developing mental or physical illnesses" (p. 1).

Jeste suggests four components to this model of wellness-centric psychiatry:

1. Examining outcomes that include positive mental health measures
2. Appreciating and focusing on psychological traits (resilience, optimism, personal mastery and coping, self-efficacy, social engagement, spirituality and religiosity, and wisdom including compassion) and environmental factors (family dynamics, social support, and other environmental determinants of overall health)
3. Studying the neurobiology of positive psychiatry constructs using tools such as MRI and biomarkers
4. Developing positive psychiatry interventions to both treat and prevent psychiatric disorders

Jeste and colleagues have further helped the field understand positive psychiatry by comparing and contrasting it to traditional psychiatry (Jeste,

Palmer, Rettew, and Boardman, 2015). While the goals of these two schools of thought overlap, Table 7.1 identifies six areas of differences.

TABLE 7.1 SIX AREAS OF DIFFERENCE BETWEEN TRADITIONAL PSYCHIATRY AND POSITIVE PSYCHIATRY

Area	Traditional Psychiatry	Positive Psychiatry
Targeted patients	Focuses on symptom reduction and treating those with an identified mental illness	Includes goals of traditional psychiatry but extends to those at high risk of developing mental disorders or to prevent recurrence
Assessment focus	Focuses purely on symptoms of psychopathology	Focuses on examination, measurement, and building of positive attributes and strengths
Research focus	Focuses on studying those with identified psychiatric illness, i.e., those who meet the high threshold set by *DSM*	Focuses on individuals with known *DSM* psychiatric illnesses but examines positive protective factors and how to further build on them to help patients
Treatment goal	Interested in providing relief to the point of remission of psychiatric illness and aims for relapse prevention	Shares all of these elements but also focuses on increasing well-being and focusing on posttraumatic growth
Main treatments	Psychotherapy and psychopharmacology	Behavioral change, psychosocial change, enhancement of wellness traits, and the application of specific mental wellness interventions
Prevention	Not an articulated goal	Embraces all three types of preventive care: primary, secondary, and tertiary prevention

Source: Jeste, Palmer, Rettew, and Boardman, 2015

When *Positive Psychiatry: A Clinical Handbook* (Jeste & Palmer, 2015) appeared, its foreword was written by Martin Seligman himself, the father of positive psychology. *Positive Psychiatry: A Casebook* (Summers & Jeste, 2018) is an edited collection on the topic that begins with a bracing foreword from George Vaillant, and then offers an impressive range of case applications of positive psychiatry in a variety of clinical scenarios.

Well-Being Therapy

Giovanni A. Fava, a psychiatrist based both in Italy and in the United States, is the founder of Well-Being Therapy (WBT). He has worked for the last two decades to promote the cause of combining mental wellness interventions with pharmacotherapy to help patients fully recover and flourish. As Fava is trained in both psychopharmacology and cognitive-behavioral therapy, he used both of these models to create his WBT framework.

Fava and colleagues' conceptualization of mental wellness is based on a balance and integration of the following five psychic forces (Fava, Cosi, Guidi, & Tomba, 2017):

- Autonomy
- Environmental mastery
- Perception of environment and others
- Growth, development, and self-actualization
- Positive attitude toward one's self

Fava considers the basic mechanism of cognitive therapy as following this paradigm:

situation → negative automatic thought →
negative emotions and distress

On the other hand, the basic mechanism of WBT is as follows:

situation → elevated feelings of well-being →
suppression of negative thoughts

In other words, the presence of elevated levels of well-being act as an antidote to cognitive distortions that lead to depression and mental suffering.

The following summarizes the tasks to be accomplished at each of the eight face-to-face sessions:

Session 1: The first session is to assess the patient's current and past mental health challenges and to establish that mental wellness is the prime focus of treatment. The clinician introduces a structured diary concept, how the client will use Likert scales to assess mental wellness activities engaged in each day, and the importance of daily homework.

Session 2: The second session is typically two weeks after the initial session and includes reviewing the well-being diary and exploring which experiences helped the patient feel better. The clinician introduces the concepts of optimum experiences and monitoring of thoughts and behaviors that interrupt well-being.

Session 3: Typically, session 3 follows in another two weeks and focuses on enhancing the patient's own understanding of what feelings and experiences improve well-being.

Session 4: In session 4, the clinician helps the patient change from observing to modifying behaviors that enhance well-being, including restructuring cognitive and behavioral impediments to well-being and laying out plans to address identified roadblocks. The clinician introduces psychological dimensions of well-being.

Session 5: This session focuses on examining which thoughts and behaviors interrupted the client's flow of well-being over the last few weeks. The clinician reviews and discusses diary entries on well-being experiences and continues helping the patient with cognitive restructuring.

Session 6: This session takes another leap forward by asking the patient to examine not just retrospectively, but in live situations, what interrupts their experience of well-being. The patient is encouraged to accept challenges to get exposure to situations they previously avoided. Concepts of self-acceptance and the value of positive relationships with others is emphasized.

Session 7: In this session the clinician and patient evaluate progress to date and discuss appropriate goal setting, as well as areas of psychological well-being that enhance mental wellness, such as environmental mastery, personal growth, purpose in life, autonomy, self-acceptance, and positive relationships with others.

Session 8: In this final session of WBT therapy, the clinician and patient assess both global and symptom-specific improvement. Barriers are reviewed, along with specific cognitive or behavioral solutions. The clinician strongly encourages the patient to continue working on the well-being skills and discusses the need for future booster sessions.

WBT is a well-designed, thoroughly researched well-being enhancement program. In one study, Fava and his colleagues (Fava, Rafanelli, Tomba, Guidi, & Grandi, 2011) focused on a particularly challenging group of patients with a *DSM* diagnosis of cyclothymia. It enrolled a total of 62 patients and randomly assigned 31 individuals to received cognitive-behavioral therapy (CBT) first and then WBT (CBT/WBT), and the other 31 patients received typical clinical management (CM). The CBT/WBT group received sequential therapy, and CM consisted of ten, 45-minute sessions every other week. An independent blind evaluator assessed the patients before treatment, after therapy, and at 1- and 2-year follow-ups. They utilized two scales to measure cyclothymia symptoms: the Clinical Interview for Depression and the Mania Scale.

Results from both scales revealed that CBT followed by WBT was numerically superior to CM, demonstrating that mental wellness enhancement does reduce symptoms of even tough-to-treat disorders like cyclothymia. The CBT/WBT sequential intervention also had a positive impact on comorbidities such as generalized anxiety disorder, obsessive-compulsive disorder, and body dysmorphic disorder. Thus, the therapeutic benefits of WBT appear to be broad spectrum.

In another study, Fava and colleagues studied twenty patients with *DSM* generalized anxiety disorder (GAD) who were devoid of comorbid conditions, and randomly assigned some of the patients to 8 sessions of CBT only, and some to sequential administration of 4 sessions of CBT followed by another 4 sessions of WBT (Fava et al., 2005). They found the 4-session add-on of WBT significantly and positively impacted outcomes, with numerically superior outcomes in both anxiety and depression.

In a review article on the role of WBT in the treatment of major depression, Fava and colleagues (2017) found that even in the most vigorously conducted, randomized, double-blind studies, WBT was effective. In their various publications, Fava and colleagues affirm our concern that psychiatric illnesses are not merely a collection of psychiatric symptoms but also states of wellness deficit.

The WILD 5 Wellness Program

As we described in the introduction to this book, although our professional background is quite traditional, we began asking why so many patients who achieved remission were still not well. Our exploration of this question led us to the world of wellness-centric interventions, which we began to use systematically and routinely to augment our treatment strategies. We started mostly on an ad hoc basis, offering patients advice on the importance of mental wellness, but without offering any specific tools or resources. Within a year, with patients still not making much progress toward mental wellness, we decided to create a formalized wellness-centric program that was simple, self-directed, prescriptive, and trackable, with measurable improvements:

Simple is often the best approach in improving wellness—a complex approach can be fraught with difficulties. We wanted clinicians from all practice settings to be able to apply the program, and we wanted patients with a range of psychiatric disorders and backgrounds to realize that achieving mental wellness is not complicated

HERO EXERCISES

HAPPINESS • ENTHUSIASM • RESILIENCE • OPTIMISM

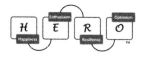

HAPPINESS & ENTHUSIASM ARE LINKED TO LONGEVITY

1. To increase your happiness, let's work on strengthening your happiness muscle. Take a moment and write down two positive things that you'd like to experience today. Also, two to three times today, find a few minutes to visualize and relish these positive experiences.

   a. _____

   _____

   b. _____

   _____

2. Having a goal or a project that inspires you will increase your enthusiasm. Write down two projects you find inspiring and set a start date. Put the date on your calendar with reminder alerts—make it happen and watch your enthusiasm improve!

   a. _____

   _____

   b. _____

> The HERO exercises are intentionally repeated every 8 days because repetition is crucial to learning and incorporating new ideas. After today, review your previous HERO exercises, as research shows that reflecting on past thoughts about wellness further strengthens and solidifies your HERO wellness traits.

Enthusiasm moves the world.
— Arthur Balfour

FIGURE 7.1: An example of a WILD 5 WELLNESS HERO exercise.   Source: the authors

DAILY JOURNALING FORM

Day #1 - Date: _____

EXERCISE	Exercise 30 minutes each day for 30 days, aim for at least moderate intensity	
Type of Exercise	Duration	_____minutes
Intensity	☐ Low ☐ Moderate ☐ High	

MINDFULNESS	Practice mindfulness at least 10 minutes each day for 30 days
Today's Guided Meditation(s)	

SLEEP	Implement 4 or more of the 6 sleep hygiene practices each day for 30 days		
Implemented These Sleep Hygiene Practices	☐ No electronics 90 min before bed	☐ Sleep mask or blackout shades	☐ Regular bedtime
	☐ No napping	☐ Warm bath/shower prior to bed	☐ Avoid caffeine 10 hrs before bed

SOCIAL CONNECTEDNESS	Meet or call at least two friends or family members each day for 30 days			
Today's Social Contacts	Friends		Family	
	☐ Call	☐ In-person	☐ Call	☐ In-person

NUTRITION	Log your daily meals/snacks/beverages/alcohol each day for 30 days		
Logged Meals/Snacks/Beverages/Alcohol	☐ Yes		☐ No
Strongly Recommended			
Implemented MIND Diet Principles	☐ Yes		☐ No
Practiced Mindful Meal Meditation	☐ Breakfast	☐ Lunch	☐ Dinner

TODAY'S PROGRESS	
My Barrier(s)	
My Solution(s)	

FIGURE 7.2: WILD 5 Wellness daily journaling form   Source: the authors

PARTICIPANT TRACKING FORM

Start Date: _____

	EXERCISE		MINDFULNESS		SLEEP	
	Did I exercise today following the FID principles?		Did I mindfully meditate at least 10 minutes today?		Did I implement 4 or more of the 6 sleep hygiene practices?	
	YES	NO	YES	NO	YES	NO
1	O	O	O	O	O	O
2	O	O	O	O	O	O
3	O	O	O	O	O	O
4	O	O	O	O	O	O
5	O	O	O	O	O	O
6	O	O	O	O	O	O
7	O	O	O	O	O	O
8	O	O	O	O	O	O
9	O	O	O	O	O	O
10	O	O	O	O	O	O
11	O	O	O	O	O	O
12	O	O	O	O	O	O
13	O	O	O	O	O	O
14	O	O	O	O	O	O
15	O	O	O	O	O	O
16	O	O	O	O	O	O
17	O	O	O	O	O	O
18	O	O	O	O	O	O
19	O	O	O	O	O	O
20	O	O	O	O	O	O
21	O	O	O	O	O	O
22	O	O	O	O	O	O
23	O	O	O	O	O	O
24	O	O	O	O	O	O
25	O	O	O	O	O	O
26	O	O	O	O	O	O
27	O	O	O	O	O	O
28	O	O	O	O	O	O
29	O	O	O	O	O	O
30	O	O	O	O	O	O
	YES	NO	YES	NO	YES	NO

FIGURE 7.3: WILD 5 Wellness patient tracking form   Source: the authors

WILD⁵☆ Wellness®
Wellness Interventions for Life's Demands

CONNECTEDNESS		NUTRITION		HERO	
Did I socially connect with at least 2 people today?		Did I log my meals, snacks, and beverages, including alcohol today?		Did I complete my HERO exercises today?	
YES	NO	YES	NO	YES	NO
O	O	O	O	O	O
O	O	O	O	O	O
O	O	O	O	O	O
O	O	O	O	O	O
O	O	O	O	O	O
O	O	O	O	O	O
O	O	O	O	O	O
O	O	O	O	O	O
O	O	O	O	O	O
O	O	O	O	O	O
O	O	O	O	O	O
O	O	O	O	O	O
O	O	O	O	O	O
O	O	O	O	O	O
O	O	O	O	O	O
O	O	O	O	O	O
O	O	O	O	O	O
O	O	O	O	O	O
O	O	O	O	O	O
O	O	O	O	O	O
O	O	O	O	O	O
O	O	O	O	O	O
O	O	O	O	O	O
O	O	O	O	O	O
O	O	O	O	O	O
O	O	O	O	O	O
O	O	O	O	O	O
O	O	O	O	O	O
O	O	O	O	O	O
O	O	O	O	O	O
YES	NO	YES	NO	YES	NO

or significantly time-consuming. The elements of the WILD 5 Wellness program—exercise, mindfulness, sleep, social connectedness, and nutrition, along with the HERO wellness traits—are all tried-and-true mental wellness–enhancing interventions. They are simple and, with your guidance, are easy for patients to incorporate into their lives.

Self-directed programs contribute to simplicity: they fit better into patients' schedules and reduce the number of clinician visits needed to achieve enhanced wellness—which also addresses clinicians' often overloaded schedules. This also makes the program easily available in multiple settings, including psychiatric and psychotherapeutic practices, as well as practices that do not directly focus on mental health, such as rheumatology and primary care.

Prescriptive advice, with specific steps and goals, is more effective than mere verbal recommendations. Giving patients detailed, prescriptive recommendations helps them better understand how to implement these wellness-centric practices. Providing an educational booklet or a handout focusing on an intervention gives patients enduring materials that they can review as needed. For example, giving specifics on how often and how long patients should practice meditation increases their likelihood of implementing the practice.

Trackable programs help encourage follow-through. Tracking daily practices and sharing the tracking form with others improves adherence, and patients learn a lot from reviewing their tracking forms.

Measurable improvements not only motivate patients and improve adherence, but it also helps clinicians assess for changes in wellness markers over time. As the famous management consultant Peter Drucker once said, "If you can't measure it, you can't improve it."

In developing this mental wellness program, our goal was to develop an effective program that could be incorporated into a range of mental health clinics and programs, with very limited time expenditure on the part of clinicians.

Our wellness-centric program is called WILD 5 Wellness, which stands for Wellness Interventions for Life's Demands, incorporating five wellness practices based on research outlined in Chapter 5: exercise, nutrition, sleep, mindfulness, and social connectedness.

Deeply influenced by the works of Fava and Seligman, in later versions of WILD 5 Wellness we complemented the program's five interventions with daily positive psychology exercises. Because of our interest in elevating the HERO wellness traits—happiness, enthusiasm, resilience, and optimism (discussed in Chapter 6)—the positive psychology daily exercises focus on these elements in rotation.

The WILD 5 Wellness program offers two practice options: a 30-day program called KickStart30 (Jain, Jain, & Burns, 2019[a]), and a 90-day program called LiveWell90 (Jain, Jain, & Burns, 2019[b]). The KickStart30 program involves a month of daily exercises, and the longer LiveWell90 program starts with the KickStart30 program in the first month and then tapers off the exercises to five days each week in the second month, and then three days each week in the third month, striving for a sustainable wellness practice. Clinicians report that many of their patients prefer KickStart30 over LiveWell90 because they initially feel more comfortable making a 30-day commitment.

The WILD 5 Wellness program is self-directed, offered in a workbook format, does not require ongoing clinician involvement. Both the KickStart30 and LiveWell90 workbooks are self-contained with everything a person needs to start and complete the program (details in the resource section of this book). Both the KickStart30 and LiveWell90 programs involve a prescribed list of wellness components to practice, a set of HERO (happiness, enthusiasm, resilience, and optimism) exercises, and daily journaling. We also provide a participant tracking form to encourage accountability and adherence, and the HERO Wellness Scale to measure wellness improvement (described in Chapter 6). A copy of the participant tracking form is available in the resource section in the back of this book.

Both the KickStart30 and LiveWell90 programs contain the following wellness practices, to be accomplished each day during the first 30 days and then, with the LiveWell90 program, tapering to 5 days and then 3 days each week for the second and third months:

> *Exercise:* At least 30 minutes of a moderate level of intensity—to help patients remember, we use the mnemonic "To be fit, you must FID," where FID stands for frequency (daily), intensity (moderate), and duration (30 min).
>
> *Nutrition:* Log all meals, snacks, and beverages, including alcohol. We also recommend the MIND diet and advise being as adherent as possible to this diet.
>
> *Sleep:* At least four of the six sleep hygiene practices:
>   1. Avoid all electronic devices 90 minutes prior to bedtime
>   2. Avoid daytime napping
>   3. Eliminate ambient light in the bedroom
>   4. Enjoy a warm relaxing bath or shower prior to bedtime
>   5. Establish and maintain a regular bedtime each night
>   6. Avoid caffeinated drinks 10 hours before bedtime
>
> *Mindfulness:* Practice at least 10 minutes
>
> *Social Connectedness:* Meet or call at least 2 friends or family members.

As you can see, the program is highly prescriptive: it specifies exactly what to do to meet the practice expectations for each element. The only exceptions are made for patients with chronic pain conditions or physical limitations; shorter exercise durations are permissible as necessary.

The HERO exercises are daily, two-item, positive psychology trait building exercises incorporating happiness, enthusiasm, resilience, and optimism as a foundational part of mental wellness. The HERO questions, which cycle through every 8 days, only take about 5 minutes to complete.

Reviewing answers to the previous HERO questions is also included as a reflective review to increase mindful awareness and thus strengthen internal HERO wellness traits. Figure 7.1 is an example of one of the HERO exercises, which involves two of the four HERO wellness traits.

One of the unique elements of the WILD 5 Wellness program is its tracking components. KickStart30 includes a daily journaling form (Figure 7.2) that takes about 5 minutes to complete. The form tracks specific information about mental wellness and captures useful information that will allow review of how the practices are progressing.

The WILD 5 Wellness program also includes a patient tracking form (Figure 7.3). This is a simple yes/no form that can be shared with clinicians, providing an opportunity to discuss what is working, receive positive feedback, and identify any barriers and challenges to develop a proactive plan to overcome these barriers. For example, if one of your patient's tracking form indicates that forgetfulness is a frequent cause of missing daily mindfulness practice, you can suggest that the patient set a daily reminder on their smartphone. If you note that a patient doesn't exercise on weekends, you can suggest that the patient ask a family member or a friend to join them on those days as a workout buddy.

Our research on the WILD 5 Wellness program indicates that it can lead to significant improvements in both illness and wellness markers in as little as 30 days. We describe this research in detail in Chapter 8.

Engagement-Enhancing Strategies

Over time, we have found that four motivational strategies—regular e-mails, wellness buddies, journaling, and handouts—enhance patients' engagement with their own wellness. Regardless of which approach you choose to enhance mental wellness in your patients, you may find these techniques helpful in your own practice.

Daily motivational e-mails are automatically sent to a patient's e-mail address (after obtaining consent, of course). Although this requires some upfront work, once done no further work is needed except to monitor the automated e-mail system you choose and perhaps fine-tune your messages. For our WILD 5 Wellness program we created 30 unique motivational e-mails that provide general information about one of the five mental wellness components and/or one of the HERO wellness traits, as well as encouragement for patients to track their daily participation using the participant tracking form. Our patients found e-mails both motivational and good reminders. Some clinics are now implementing WILD 5 Wellness supportive texting as another way to provide effective reminders and motivation.

We also encourage participants to have at least one wellness buddy. Studies show the presence of such a support system can dramatically improve adherence and produce significant benefits (Dailey et al., 2018; Winzer et al., 2019). Anyone the patient trusts and is close to can be a wellness buddy—a spouse, family member, a friend, or a co-worker. Patients check in with their wellness buddy regularly to let them know if they met their mental wellness goals. This helps patients stay on track with the wellness practices and increases social connection and positive reinforcement. Some of our patients have recruited their wellness buddies to do Kick-Start30 with them, as well as family members, friends, co-workers, and neighbors. Regardless of which wellness program you choose, you can encourage your patients to find wellness buddies to help them reach their mental wellness goals.

Journaling can also enhance the effectiveness of mental wellness programs. Very early in his research, Martin Seligman, the father of Positive Psychology, was struck by the power of journaling about topics like gratitude. He created a well-known gratitude exercise that involves creating a list of three things that make you feel gratitude. Compelling data reveal the beneficial effects of engaging in journaling as a wellness exercise. Redwine and colleagues (2016) randomized a group of individuals with heart failure to receive an 8-week program of gratitude journaling or to serve as a control group. After 8 weeks, those who had engaged in gratitude journaling had objective improvements in inflammation and heart rate variability, suggesting a positive impact on the inflammatory system and the autonomic nervous system.

Smyth and colleagues (2018) studied online positive affect journaling to examine if the practice helps both decrease mental distress and improve well-being. They conducted a controlled 12-week study in which the intervention group was asked to journal about various elements of positive affect for fifteen minutes for three days each week. Compared to the control group, the intervention group reported decreased mental distress, increased well-being, and less depression and anxiety after one month, and greater resilience after the first and second months.

Based on this research, in the latest version of the WILD 5 Wellness program, we added a wellness journaling component to build and strengthen these positive psychology traits. You can use our daily journaling form or help your patients develop their own journaling technique, with any of the wellness programs you choose.

And during our development, research, and practice with the WILD 5 Wellness program, we learned a very important lesson the hard way: patients remember less than twenty-five percent of what is discussed and recommended during clinical encounters, and over the course of 6 months, patients forget more than half of this already meager amount of information. This makes handouts critical for patient success.

We are increasingly convinced that wellness-centric interventions like the ones we describe here can be used by a wide range of clinicians to help improve the well-being of individuals. These mental wellness interventions appear to reduce inflammatory markers, reduce depression and anxiety, improve sleep, enhance HERO wellness traits, decrease chronic pain, and improve functionality. The four wellness programs described in this chapter—Positive Psychiatry, Positive Psychotherapy, Well-Being Therapy, and WILD 5 Wellness program—each have their own merits; at least one of them should fit your and your patients' needs. No matter which approach you choose, your patients' mental wellness will be well served. The four engagement-enhancing techniques—motivational e-mails, wellness buddies, journaling, and handouts—can work with any of these approaches to help patients follow through to reach their wellness goals.

CHAPTER 8

Research Supporting the WILD 5 Wellness Program

This chapter describes in detail the studies conducted to date demonstrating the effectiveness of the WILD 5 Wellness program in a variety of clinical and non-clinical populations. We used a combination of these well-studied measurement instruments in our various research projects on the WILD 5 Wellness program:

- Patient Health Questionnaire-9 (PHQ-9) to measure depression severity
- Generalized Anxiety Disorder-7 (GAD-7) to measure changes in anxiety levels
- Pittsburgh Sleep Quality Index (PSQI) to measure sleep
- Mindful Attention Awareness Scale (MAAS) to measure changes in mindfulness levels
- Sheehan Disability Scale (SDS) to measure disability
- Endicott Work Productivity Scale (EWPS) to measure work productivity
- Sleep Condition Indicator (SCI) to measure sleep
- Social Connectedness Scale (SCS) to measure the degree of social connectedness
- Eating and Appraisal Due to Emotions and Stress (EADES) to measure eating behaviors

- Dutch Eating Behavior Questionnaire (DEBQ) to measure emotional eating
- Brief Pain Inventory (BPI) to measure physical pain
- Cognitive and Physical Functioning Questionnaire (CPFQ) to measure cogntion
- World Health Organization Well-Being Index (WHO-5) to measure general wellness
- HERO Wellness Scale to specifically measure the mental wellness traits of happiness, enthusiasm, resilience, and optimism (described in Chapter 6)

We can divide our research program into three phases: Phase I, an early exploratory study in patients with a mental health condition, taking or not taking an antidepressant; Phase II, a large, diverse population study of patients with a mental health condition, chronic pain condition, or both; and Phase III, a more diverse population focused on improving mental wellness and cognitive and physical function.

WILD 5 Wellness Program: Phase I

In Phase I, the WILD 5 Wellness program's initial 30-day pilot study, 36 individuals enrolled and completed the study. Among these were 18 patients with a psychiatric disorder who were taking a psychotropic medication: 14 women and 4 men in the group of study completers, with a mean age of about 45 years. The other 18 community participants had no psychiatric difficulties but simply wanted to further improve their mental health and wellness: 14 women and 4 men, with a mean age of about 42 years.

Table 8.1 shows the results of this pilot study (Jain, Jain, & Kumar, 2015). Taken together, this Phase I study taught us the following lessons:

- The concept of mental wellness is well accepted by both patients and the public.

- Wellness interventions can quickly help reduce psychiatric symptoms in patients and further improve wellness in individuals with no mental health challenges. There was an across the board improvement in both psychiatric symptoms as well as wellness markers.
- A 30-day, self-directed wellness intervention is effective without a lot of time and guidance from clinicians.
- A program that is simple, prescriptive, and trackable is effective in improving mental wellness.

TABLE 8.1 WILD 5 WELLNESS PROGRAM, PHASE I: INITIAL 30-DAY PILOT STUDY (Jain, Jain, & Kumar, 2015): STUDY COMPLETERS (*N* = 36)

Measure	Instrument	Before	After	Improvement	P-Value
Patients with a psychiatric disorder, taking a psychotropic medication (*n* = 18)					
Depression severity	PHQ-9	11.1	7.0	36.9%	p=0.01
Anxiety	GAD-7	8.7	5.7	34.5%	p=0.01
Sleep	PSQI	11.7	7.6	35%	p=0.02
Emotional eating	DEBQ	38.4	31.8	17.2%	p=0.05
Well-being	WHO-5	8.8	13.6	54.5%	p=0.006
Community participants, with no psychiatric condition (*n* = 18)					
Depression severity	PHQ-9	5.8	2.8	51.7%	p=0.001
Anxiety	GAD-7	5.8	2.2	62.1%	p=0.001
Sleep	PSQI	5.8	2.8	51.7%	p=0.01
Emotional eating	DEBQ	32	26.5	17.2%	p=0.0004
Well-being	WHO-5	12.7	17.7	39.4%	p=0.0002

WILD 5 Wellness Program: Phase II

Our pilot results showed that we were on the right path, so we proceeded to Phase II testing. In this 30-day study (Jain et al., 2016[a]), 82 individuals who enrolled and completed the study had a self-reported psychiatric disorder. Additionally, in this Phase II program, 52 individuals who suffered from chronic pain (defined as pain present on more days than not for six months or longer) enrolled and completed this study. Nineteen of these patients were also taking opioid medications for their chronic pain. Based on lessons learned from Phase I, to expand the number of scales to measure change we also developed the HERO Wellness Scale (described in Chapter 6), which we validated in research (see Chapter 10 on measurement-based care).

Table 8.2 shows the positive results across all mental health disease and wellness markers at the end of 30 days. Statistical significance was reached on the MAAS mindfulness scale and the EWPS work productivity scale (Jain et al., 2016[a]). Table 8.3 shows results for the 51 individuals with chronic pain (Jain et al., 2016[b]). Across the board, the results revealed a clear and positive impact on both mental distress symptoms and mental wellness traits, as well as an impact on chronic pain and pain-related impairments.

TABLE 8.2 WILD 5 WELLNESS PROGRAM, PHASE II: A 30-DAY STUDY (*N* = 82; Jain et al., 2016a)

Measure	Instrument	Improvement	P-Value
Depression severity	PHQ-9	43%	p<0.0001
Anxiety	GAD-7	40%	p<0.0001
Sleep	PSQI	29%	p<0.0001
Emotional eating	DEBQ	14%	p<0.0001
Well-being	WHO-5	60%	p<0.0001
Happiness	HERO Wellness Scale	30%	p<0.001
Enthusiasm	HERO Wellness Scale	51%	p<0.001
Resilience	HERO Wellness Scale	63%	p<0.0001
Optimism	HERO Wellness Scale	45%	p<0.001

TABLE 8.3 WILD 5 WELLNESS PROGRAM, PHASE II: RESULTS FOR INDIVIDUALS WITH CHRONIC PAIN (*N* = 51; Jain, 2016b)

Measure	Instrument	Improvement	P-Value
Depression severity	PHQ-9	42%	p<0.0001
Anxiety	GAD-7	39%	p<0.0001
Sleep	PSQI	29%	p<0.0001

Emotional eating	DEBQ	15%	p<0.0001
Well-being	WHO-5	57%	p<0.0001
Happiness	HERO Wellness Scale	24%	p<0.001
Enthusiasm	HERO Wellness Scale	39%	p<0.001
Resilience	HERO Wellness Scale	52%	p<0.0001
Optimism	HERO Wellness Scale	39%	p<0.001
Worst pain	Brief Pain Inventory	18%	p<0.002
Average pain	Brief Pain Inventory	18%	p<0.001
Pain related sleep	Brief Pain Inventory	25%	p<0.001
Enjoyment of life	Brief Pain Inventory	24%	p<0.001

To determine what further changes would result from continuation of these wellness-centric practices, we invited our 30-day study completers to continue the WILD 5 Wellness program for another 90 days, and 35 individuals accepted. Their 90-day follow-up data showed clear and convincing evidence of maintenance of effect with both psychiatric symptom reduction, as well as elevation of mental wellness attributes such as happiness, enthusiasm, resilience, and optimism (Table 8.4). It confirmed that wellness-centric interventions are useful for both short- and longer-term utilization for the improvement of mental health and wellness.

TABLE 8.4 WILD 5 WELLNESS PROGRAM, PHASE II: RESULTS AFTER AN ADDITIONAL 90 DAYS (N = 35; Jain et al., 2016a)

Measure	Instrument	Score Before	After	Percent Change	P-Value
Depression severity	PHQ-9	5.2	5.2	benefits maintained	
Anxiety	GAD-7	4.7	4.7	benefits maintained	
Sleep	PSQI	7.3	6.9	benefits maintained	
Emotional eating	DEBQ	28.7	26.5	benefits maintained	
Happiness	HERO Wellness Scale	5.5	6.5	+18%	p=0.009
Enthusiasm	HERO Wellness Scale	5.1	5.9	+16%	p=0.02
Resilience	HERO Wellness Scale	5.5	6.1	+11%	p=0.08
Optimism	HERO Wellness Scale	5.8	6.4	+10%	p=0.1

Based on the Phase II data, we recognized that this mental wellness-enhancing program addressed the mental health needs of those with chronic pain, with mental illness, or with both conditions.

WILD 5 Wellness Program: Phase III

Phase III included two well-designed studies. The first study was conducted in collaboration with Tara Girard, director of the Health and Wellness Center at Beloit College, a small, private college in Beloit, Wisconsin (Girard et al., 2017). The participants were 41 college students who enrolled in the WILD 5 Wellness program (18 men and 23 women, with a mean age of 20.2 years, with a range of 18–25 years).

This phase of the WILD 5 Wellness program benefited from our results from Phases I and II. Students received daily motivational e-mails, and throughout the study were encouraged to contact the principal investigator if they had any questions. Students completed multiple scales before the study started and again at the end of the 30-day study. In Phase III we added the Cognitive and Physical Functioning Questionnaire (CPFQ) to include measures of cognition and physical functioning.

Table 8.5 shows the results of the study.

TABLE 8.5 WILD 5 WELLNESS PROGRAM, PHASE III:
BELOIT COLLEGE STUDY (N = 41 Girard et al., 2017).

Measure	Instrument	Before	After	Improvement	P-Value
Depression severity	PHQ-9	7.1	5.6	21%	p=0.1
Anxiety	GAD-7	8.2	6.6	20%	p=0.2
Cognitive and physical functioning	CPFQ	18.3	16.1	12%	p=0.01
Disability	SDS	6.2	4.9	21%	p=0.3
Well-being	WHO-5	12.4	15.0	21%	p=0.02
Happiness	HERO Wellness Scale	5.4	6.3	17%	p=0.06
Enthusiasm	HERO Wellness Scale	4.8	6.0	25%	p=0.01

| Resilience | HERO Wellness Scale | 5.5 | 6.3 | 15% | p=0.1 |
| Optimism | HERO Wellness Scale | 5.4 | 6.1 | 13% | p=0.1 |

This Beloit College study was highly instructive and produced across the board positive numeric, though not always statistically significant, changes. We were pleased to note that even in a vulnerable and stressed population such as college undergranduates, a prescriptive and simple wellness program can produce modest improvments in markers of psychiatric symptoms, as well as mental wellness. The degree of change in this population was less robust than some of our previous studies, and this perhaps reflects the level of stress endured by these individuals. We will in the future explore means to increase the output of wellness interventions in college students as they remain one of the most vulnerable segments of our population. The positive impact of this wellness program on physical and cognitive functioning was quite gratifying.

The second Phase III study was conducted by Donna Rolin and Saundra Jain as co-principal investigators (Rolin et al., 2018), and was supported in part from a grant from the Epsilon Theta chapter of Sigma Theta Tau International. The 37 participants all self-reported a mental health challenge, and included 4 men and 33 women, with a mean age of about 45.5 years (age range 23–79 years). The subjects were recruited from multiple sources—through private practice clinicians, flyers posted at a major university, and study posting on Clinicaltrials.gov. Once pre and post scores were obtained, they were analyzed for changes in mood (utilizing the PHQ-9 scale), anxiety (utilizing the GAD-7 scale), mental wellness (utilizing the WHO-5 scale), resilience (utilizing a 0–10 Likert scale), and cognitive and physical functioning (utilizing the CPFQ scale). The research team had decided to focus only on resilience changes as part of this data analysis, and other parameters of the HERO Wellness Scale were not analyzed. For this study we added two brief, daily positive psychology exercises to the mix—the HERO exercises (described in Chapter 7).

Table 8.6 presents our findings.

TABLE 8.6 WILD 5 WELLNESS PROGRAM, PHASE III: EPSILON THETA STUDY (*N* = 37; Rolin et al., 2018)

Measure	Instrument	Before	After	Improvement	P-Value
Depression severity	PHQ-9	10.7	6.6	38%	p<0.05
Anxiety	GAD-7	8.2	5.6	32%	p<0.05
Well-being	WHO-5	8.1	12.7	57%	p<0.05
Resilience	HERO Wellness scale	3.6	5.4	50%	p<0.05
Cognitive and physical functioning	CPFQ	26.6	17.9	33%	p<0.05

The Epsilon Theta chaper of Sigma Theta Tau International organization–supported study was broadly positive, with statistically significant improvements seen in all of the following—mood, anxiety, mental wellness, resilience, and finally, cognitive and physical functioning. The results of these two Phase III studies taken together clearly demonstrate that the WILD 5 Wellness program can positively impact multiple elements of mind and body functioning.

Post Hoc Analyses of Phase III Data

Before the full completion of the study, we had conducted an interim post hoc analysis of 25 individuals from the Epsilon Theta Phase III study (Jain et al., 2017[a]), 23 of whom were concurrently taking psychotropic medications. The subjects were recruited via word of mouth, by distributing flyers, and from direct referrals from mental health clinicians. We did so because we had a deep interest in seeing if this wellness program had an impact on the sub-components of the CPFQ scale. We were gratified to see that not only did the total score on the CPFQ scale show a significant improvement, so did each and every one of the seven items that are from the CPFQ scale. The seven individual items are: motivation/interest/enthusiasm, wakefulness/alertness, energy/focus/sustained attention, remember/recall information/finding words, and sharpness/mental acuity. Table 8.7 shows the results of this interim analysis.

TABLE 8.7 WILD 5 WELLNESS PROGRAM: POST HOC ANALYSES OF EPSILON THETA SUPPORTED STUDY- INTERIM ANALYSIS (*N* = 25; Jain et al., 2017a).

Measure	Instrument	Before	After	Improvement	P-Value
Cognitive and physical functioning	CPFQ	27.2	17.7	35%	p=0.00004
Depression severity	PHQ-9	10.8	5.1	53%	p<0.0001
Anxiety	GAD-7	7.3	4.8	34%	p=0.0001
Well-being	WHO-5	8.1	13.2	63%	p=0.0001

To determine if depressed individuals could benefit from wellness-centric interventions, we conducted another post hoc analysis of 52 participants from the phase II development program (Jain et al., 2017[b]). These participants self-identified as suffering from a mental health disorder and had a baseline PHQ-9 score of 10 or greater, signifying a moderate or greater severity of depression. Pre-post analysis for change and statistical significance was performed.

Table 8.8 summarizes the main results, demonstrating significant improvement in depression severity, anxiety, and well-being. The results also demonstrated improvement in the Sheehan Disability Scale, Brief Pain Inventory, Average Pain and Most Pain Perceived, Pittsburg Sleep Quality Index, Endicott Work Productivity Scale, and the HERO Wellness Scale measures of happiness, enthusiasm, resilience, and optimism (all p<0.05). Thus, even in patients with higher baseline symptom severity, wellness-centric interventions exerted significant, broad-spectrum benefits.

TABLE 8.8 WILD 5 WELLNESS PROGRAM: POST HOC ANALYSES OF PARTICIPANTS WITH MODERATE TO SEVERE DEPRESSION AND CURRENTLY ON A PSYCHOTROPIC MEDICATION, WITH A PHQ-9 SCORE OF 10 OR HIGHER (*N* = 52; Jain, et al., 2017b)

Measure	Instrument	Before	After	Improvement	P-Value
Depression severity	PHQ-9	14.7	8.0	46%	p<0.0001
Anxiety	GAD-7	12.3	7.3	41%	p<0.0001
Well-being	WHO-5	5.9	11.2	90%	P<0.0001

To examine the effects of our program on patients with chronic pain by offering them a wellness-centric intervention as an augmentation strategy, we analyzed data for 19 individuals in this cohort (Jain & Jain, 2017) who had chronic pain and were concurrently taking an opioid medication. These individuals had an average age of 52 years, and 16 were also taking psychotropic medications, with 6 individuals reporting major depression, 5 reporting an anxiety disorder, 2 reporting bipolar disorder, and 4 reporting a sleep problem (Jain & Jain, 2017).

The data are presented in Table 8.9. The results revealed a clear and positive impact on both mental distress symptoms, as well as mental wellness traits. The WILD 5 Wellness program also had an impact on chronic pain and pain-related impairments. The Brief Pain Inventory showed that worst pain improved by 20% (p<0.002); average pain improved by 11% (p<0.001), and interference with activities improved by 18% (p<0.05). We are very encouraged by these results. Knowing that wellness interventions can even partly address the needs of chronic pain patients who are currently taking opioid medications is very good news.

TABLE 8.9 WILD 5 WELLNESS PROGRAM: POST HOC ANALYSES OF PARTICIPANTS WITH CHRONIC PAIN AND RECEIVING OPIOID THERAPY (N = 19; Jain & Jain, 2017)

Measure	Instrument	Improvement	P-Value
Depression severity	PHQ-9	50%	p<0.0001
Anxiety	GAD-7	44%	p<0.002
Sleep	PSQI	30%	p<0.001
Well-being	WHO-5	78%	p<0.001
Happiness	HERO Wellness Scale	25%	p<0.05
Enthusiasm	HERO Wellness Scale	23%	p<0.05
Resilience	HERO Wellness Scale	60%	p<0.05
Optimism	HERO Wellness Scale	35%	p<0.05

Other Experiences with the WILD 5 Wellness Program

A number of clinicians from around the United States and overseas have incorporated the WILD 5 Wellness program into their clinical practices—we have freely shared this program at no cost with our colleagues. They expressed their appreciation for the "hard" data we collected, which demonstrates the efficacy of mental wellness as an intervention worthy to be added to their other therapeutic offerings. We also learned clinicians appreciated that a limited amount of their time was required to implement the WILD 5 Wellness program.

We discovered that the WILD 5 Wellness program works for a broad spectrum of patients. Clinicians began offering this intervention to a diverse patient population very quickly, such as those who had recently received electroconvulsive therapy, have complex chronic pain syndromes, have treatment-refractory depression or anxiety, are receiving transcranial magnetic stimulation, or have a rheumatologic disorder such as rheumatoid arthritis. Even for these tough-to-treat populations, the feedback has been generally positive. Wellness-centric interventions appear to be a useful and appreciated intervention in multiple specialties. Positive feedback from many clinicians showed us the generalizability of wellness-centric interventions in a diverse group of patients and clinical settings.

This journey with the WILD 5 Wellness program has been exciting and productive, and we are happy to make the program available to clinicians wanting to research it or use it in their clinics. We appreciate the hundreds of patients who helped us better understand and refine this wellness-centric intervention, and we are also delighted that clinicians from multiple settings, from psychiatry to pain management, from rheumatology to primary care, have all found ways to integrate it into their practices. We will continue studying and applying this wellness-centric program in an even more diverse patient population, and would of course welcome your feedback and suggestions.

CHAPTER 9

Incorporating Mental Wellness into Your Practice

It is important we proactively address some potential challenges and pitfalls in the process of offering wellness interventions to patients. These challenges exist at the patient level, clinician level, and system level.

At the patient level, patients may be thrown off by a clinician-initiated conversation about mental wellness in a medication-focused clinical encounter. They expect the conversation to center around symptom reduction and medications, since this is the typical standard of care. In addition, patients may not understand that heightened mental wellness has proven benefits, such as counteracting mental illness symptoms, so they may be reluctant to embrace the wellness interventions. There are also barriers of adherence, in both the short term and long term. This chapter addresses these challenges in depth.

At the clinician level, training is a concern. As we have pointed out in previous chapters, most clinicians have received limited education and training regarding the importance of mental wellness, and even less training on the application of wellness-centric interventions. This is a tremendously limiting factor for most clinicians, and it is wise to acknowledge this gap in our professional training. We also discuss these solutions in this chapter.

At the system level, many practitioners work for large healthcare systems such as a health maintenance organization, Veterans Affairs, or a county mental health system, and within these systems may encounter pressure to be efficient by putting a premium on the number of patients seen daily, rather than focusing on the quality of the interaction. Many psychopharmacologists are also quite pressed for time, often having to see a patient every 15 to 20 minutes for "med checks." This leaves hardly any time for a meaningful conversation about mental wellness or wellness-centric interventions. It is important to acknowledge these system level challenges and recognize that they are not expected to disappear any time soon. In this chapter we offer some potential solutions that may help address these challenges.

Being cognizant of these barriers, and strategies to address them, will allow you to anticipate them and work toward overcoming them to help ensure that every patient you take care of receives maximum benefit from wellness-centric interventions.

Overcoming Patient Level Barriers

We believe most patients, with very few exceptions, benefit from wellness interventions. The vast majority of patients innately crave high levels of mental wellness—we consider this a universal truth. Often there is immediate buy-in from patients when a clinician comments on the importance of mental wellness. In over sixty collective years of clinical experience, we can think of very few exceptions to this. But many barriers stand in the way of our patients' journey toward optimal implementation of wellness interventions, which may stop them from fulfilling their goal of maximized mental wellness. You may encounter barriers when introducing the concept of mental wellness to your patients, and you will almost certainly encounter other barriers along the way as you coach your patients to develop and maintain wellness-enhancing behaviors.

Introducing Mental Wellness Concepts to Patients

The practice of psychiatry and psychotherapy is a combination of art and science. If you have an interest in mental wellness, you will need to consider not just the science behind wellness concepts and the practice of applying it in clinical encounters but also the art of introducing wellness concepts to your patients—and improving their motivation to engage in such practices.

In some ways, the initial introduction of the concept of mental wellness to patients determines the ultimate success of this encounter. Here we summarize four critical steps to ensure that the wellness-centric interventions have a high chance of success:

Initiate a wellness discussion at an appropriate time when the patient's psychiatric symptomatology is under fair control.

Use an approach that is supportive, educational, and enthusiastic.

Offer a full understanding of why wellness-centric interventions, along with other treatment modalities, are important in both the short and long term.

Offer appropriate wellness-centric resources and adopt a coaching style of communication.

Patients with psychiatric illnesses genuinely desire higher levels of mental wellness, and as described in Chapter 1, surprisingly often they rank it above the goal of mere symptom reduction. So, the key question is not whether, but when to introduce this conversation. It may be wise with some patients to defer the conversation until they are better able to benefit from the information. For example, patients who are acutely psychotic, in the midst of a manic episode, severely depressed, or in an acute intoxication or withdrawal state are not likely to receive great benefits. But for the most part, our experience suggests initiating this wellness conversation sooner rather than later. We have found taking this wellness-centric approach early in treatment creates a stronger bond between the clinician and the patient. We recommend initiating the wellness conversation as soon as possible, ideally during the first or second clinical encounter.

None of this is to say that focusing on symptom reduction is not important. To the contrary, it is almost always the first priority and the main goal of a clinical encounter. We have found that telling patients there are two therapeutic goals of treatment, symptom reduction *and* wellness enhancement, is typically well received and appreciated. One of the significant criticisms levied on modern psychiatry is the heavy use of medications and a singular focus on symptom reduction. Initiating a conversation about mental wellness early in the treatment process clearly communicates to your patients that you are holistic in your approach, not just a "pill pusher," and you are ultimately interested in a positive outcome regarding your patient's mental health.

Patients often do not expect a clinician, particularly one who prescribes medications, to talk about mental wellness. This is a radically new concept for many patients. Based on our experience, these are our practical tips to help facilitate this initial conversation:

- Inform patients that, as a caring clinician, you have a deep interest in their mental health. Explain that mental health is a combination of two things: the degree of mental illness symptoms an individual possesses, and the degree of mental wellness an individual possesses.
- Inform patients about wellness-centric interventions in an understandable and clear manner. Communicate that mental wellness is important and explain how wellness-centric practices help diminish the symptoms of mental illness.
- Inform patients that they and their clinical team can focus on reducing mental illness symptoms *and* improving mental wellness

at the same time. One does not need to occur at the expense of the other.

- Share with patients that wellness is a basic human right. Inform patients of the World Health Organization's definition of optimal health: health is not just a mere absence of illness but also the presence of wellness. This definition of health and wellness seems to help patients understand why wellness matters so much.

- Suggest that patients invite a family member or a friend to join them on their wellness journey. Often, the presence of a "wellness buddy" is crucial in ensuring success.

- Maintain a positive, supportive, encouraging, and understanding attitude. Modeling mental wellness for patients is critical.

Patient Barriers to Developing and Maintaining Wellness Practices

Once you've introduced the concept of mental wellness to your patients, your task turns to motivating and coaching them to buy into the wellness interventions and to maintain their wellness practices. These are the top 7 patient level barriers we have encountered over the years:

1. Lack of understanding regarding the importance of mental wellness
2. Wanting only a medication fix for mental health challenges
3. Illness severity preventing regular engagement in wellness practices
4. Chronic pain as a barrier to activity and motivation
5. Lack of support from family and friends
6. Frustration with the "slow progress" from wellness interventions
7. Start strong and finish weak—adherence challenges

We examine each of these barriers and offer practical tips in overcoming these challenges.

1. Lack of understanding regarding the importance of mental wellness. When psychiatric disorders are present, patients may be desperately focused on symptom reduction, particularly if they have suffered chronically. These patients may initially respond with confusion when you discuss the importance of mental wellness and may reject your suggestions. To help overcome this barrier:

- Appreciate and accept the patient's primary goal of symptom reduction.
- Educate the patient and members of the patient's support system on the two aspects of optimum health—mental illness and mental wellness.
- Enhance the patient's knowledge about the science of mental wellness—knowledge is power.
- Be patient—it takes time for a patient to fully embrace wellness strategies.

2. Wanting only a medication fix for mental health challenges.   Patients desperate to feel better crave relief. They may believe medication treatment is the only solution to their woes, and see reduction and elimination of psychiatric symptoms as the only goal of treatment, and therefore overly rely on medications for both the short- and long-term "fix." Although we, too, are strong proponents of appropriate psychopharmacological treatments of multiple psychiatric disorders, we are also strong advocates for symptom reduction psychotherapies such as cognitive-behavior therapy. Patients often suffer from the same malady that afflicts the medical establishment: believing that medication *alone* is the ideal treatment of psychiatric disorders and is the only way to keep these disorders from relapsing. To help overcome this barrier:

- Use motivational interviewing techniques to educate patients on why mental wellness matters (described below). Patients are often more receptive to wellness-centric interventions when these techniques are utilized.

- Reassure patients that wellness-centric care is not "anti-medication" or "pro-medication."
- Assure patients that wellness-centric interventions have demonstrated positive effects on global mental health.

3. Illness severity prevents regular engagement in mental wellness practices. Patients present to our office in various states of illness. Those with a higher degree of symptom acuity tend to have greater challenges, such as fatigue, low motivation, and cognitive impairment, which makes it difficult to engage in wellness-centric practices. We must be sensitive to the fact that depression severity may negatively impact a patient's ability to engage in wellness interventions. Despite their understanding of the importance of these practices, a severely depressed patient may simply be unable to fully embrace our suggestions—they are not simply being uncooperative, obstinate, or unaccepting. Patients may feel both frustrated and defeated in the face of these severe symptoms. To help overcome this barrier:

- In more severely ill patients, consider deferring discussion of wellness-centric interventions until symptoms are under better control.
- Psychopharmacology treatment may need to take the lead, with wellness-centric interventions taking a backseat for the time being.

Offer understanding and empathy to patients who truly want to engage in wellness-centric interventions.

Alert patients that once symptom severity recedes, it will then be the right time to begin a conversation about the importance of wellness-centric practices.

4. Chronic pain is a barrier. Chronic pain conditions are common in modern society. Increasingly, patients present to metal health clinics with a comorbidity of chronic pain. This "double jeopardy" condition makes it much more difficult for patients to take optimum advantage of wellness enhancement activities. In addition, the presence of comorbid chronic pain comes with a greater risk of insomnia, obesity, physical disability, impaired memory and concentration, and apathy, to name just a few. These are genuine and disabling patient level barriers that clinicians must be mindful of and manage well. To help overcome these barriers:

- Encourage patients to seek the very best available treatment for their chronic pain condition. Sometimes a friendly but firm nudge is the necessary catalyst for a patient to access better care for their chronic pain condition.
- Individualization of wellness-centric interventions is particularly important when taking care of patients with chronic pain conditions. For example, instead of exercising 30 minutes a day, encourage them to break down their exercise into more manageable chunks of time, e.g., two 15-minute blocks, or three 10-minute blocks. Another modification might be daytime naps (although this is not typically a good sleep hygiene practice). Be flexible in wellness prescriptions to help these patients succeed.
- Beware of a pessimistic attitude! Patients with chronic pain conditions already live in a space overflowing with worry, negativity, and pessimism. Communicate a sense of hope and optimism to help them stay on track, and tell them that studies of wellness-centric interventions have proven effective even in this complex, comorbidly ill group of patients.

5. Lack of support from family and friends.   A lack of awareness regarding the power of wellness-centric practices is evident not just in patients but in society at large, so patients may not receive ideal support from their family members and friends. Family members who lack knowledge about the positive impact of mental wellness on mental and physical health might see wellness-centric interventions as too "new age" or "too radical." Poor mental health may affect their ability to provide support. Those with poor eating and exercise habits may actively or passively oppose others changing their behaviors. When recommending wellness-centric practices, clinicians should actively inquire about these challenging barriers. To help overcome these barriers:

- If possible and appropriate, meet with the family/friends/significant others together with the patient. This can make a significant difference in creating a supportive team.
- Encourage patients to share wellness handouts and resources with family members and friends. These educational resources can act as catalysts in producing positive change.
- Recommend specific wellness-centric books for patients and their support systems. This may encourage and cement positive wellness-centric behaviors.

6. Frustration with the "slow progress" from wellness interventions. Some patients become frustrated because they incorrectly believe wellness-centric strategies are slow to work, which can be fueled by a pessimistic, nihilistic mindset induced by a psychiatric disorder. The evidence is to the contrary—many wellness-centric interventions are quite rapid in onset. For example, a single bout of physical exercise can measurably improve mood and cognition; a single night of improved sleep can positively impact the HPA axis and mood; a single mindfulness practice session can positively impact mood and mental wellness markers. Wellness-centric interventions also have the power to sustain these improvements. To help overcome these barriers:

- Gently educate patients about their misperception that wellness-centric interventions are slow to occur.
- Offer evidence from the patient's past, for example, "When you go for a walk, how soon do you feel better?" or "When you sleep bet-

ter for even one night, can you tell a difference in how you feel both mentally and physically?"

7. "Start strong and finish weak"—adherence challenges.   Adherence challenges are a common barrier to sustaining mental wellness practices. Initially patients may start out strong but quickly fade in effort and enthusiasm, often because of forgetfulness, lack of motivation, or poor time management. To help overcome these barriers:

- Alert patients to this issue at the very outset. For example, you may want to share the following with your patients: "I know you want to make changes and improve your mental wellness. Before we get started, I want to tell you about a very common problem you may encounter. Often patients start out strong but then they begin to slow down over time, or they simply stop their wellness practices altogether. Do you think this might be a problem for you? If you're worried this could occur, then let's take a little time and talk about it now. What can we do now to make sure that doesn't happen?" This approach lays out the challenges a patient will likely face and initiates a conversation on how to potentially prevent or, at the very least, minimize the problem.
- Use a tracking form to allow you and your patients a way to monitor adherence to their wellness practices. Sharing the tracking form increases accountability and improves adherence. A copy of the WILD 5 Wellness participant tracking form is included in the resource section of this book.
- Emphasize the importance of *creating* a behavior or habit. Encourage patients to schedule their new wellness practices and set reminder alerts. Explain about planning in advance—when, where, and which wellness interventions they will use, as this will increase the likelihood of success.
- Inform patients that the goal is not perfection but steady improve-

ment. Remind them to be kind to themselves as they begin making these changes, as change may not be easy. Encourage patients to avoid "all or nothing" thinking and to stick with their wellness practices if they miss a day or two.

· Be patient and gently encourage patients to reengage in wellness pursuits if they stumble along their wellness journey.

Techniques to Improve Patient Uptake of Wellness Interventions

Several approaches in clinical practice can improve patients' acceptance, adherence, and success as they relate to wellness-enhancing interventions: motivational interviewing, coaching, and using positive, reinforcing approaches.

Motivational Interviewing with Wellness Interventions. Motivational interviewing (MI) is an essential asset for any wellness-centric clinician. MI has a long tradition in clinical medicine, particularly in public and preventive medicine interventions, such as smoking cessation efforts. In psychopharmacology-based practices, the typical clinical encounter is decidedly paternalistic in nature: a clinician unilaterally formulates the problem, decides on an intervention, and expects the patient to accept it. Such encounters often leave patients feeling talked down to, reducing their engagement in treatment and leaving them with lower levels of motivation for change. As a result, they have lower rates of adherence to treatment recommendations, leading to higher relapse and recurrence rates.

The MI model addresses many of these challenges. It is designed to be a directive, collaborative style of interaction where the main goal is to discover patients' desire for change, identify specific barriers they face, examine how their internal belief systems could sabotage their behavior, and use the patients' own strengths to discover ways to move in the right direction.

The three elements of MI in patient encounters are (a) collaboration between clinician and patients, (b) evocation of a patients' beliefs in exploring useful and defeating thought patterns, and (c) patient autonomy in recognizing they are ultimately responsible for and recognized for all the successes they achieve (Apodaca & Longabaugh, 2009). We should aim to partner with an engaged, involved, educated, enthusiastic, and, of course, a motivated patient.

For example, in recommending the practice of mindfulness with MI, you first explore the beliefs your patient may have about mindfulness, understand the correct and incorrect beliefs your patient holds about mindfulness, and allow your patient to explore any barriers that may hamper their attempts to fully engage in mindfulness practice. You respectfully question false beliefs and help the patient change these false beliefs. This is a practical example of how MI is a true friend of the wellness-centric clinician.

MI, when combined with psychoeducation, significantly enhances a patient's motivation for change. MI is a prudent approach for improving your patients' adherence to a wellness-centric lifestyle.

Coaching With Wellness-centric Interventions.   Coaching is an appropriate approach to take when introducing, promoting, and instilling wellness-centric principles. This approach emphasizes the following set of skills:

- Educating patients regarding interventions
- Measuring traits before the intervention
- Offering a prescriptive intervention
- Offering encouragement and motivation
- Remeasuring traits after the intervention
- Planning for maintaining the intervention

Our WILD 5 Wellness program uses all of these principles in a non-confrontational, non-disease focused approach, and it resonates well with individuals who want to improve their mental wellness.

There is considerable evidence the coaching model is effective in creating pro-health behaviors, and there is good evidence coaching style interventions offer benefits to our patients (Wayne, Perez, Kaplan, & Ritva,

2015). Additionally, the coaching model is effective in dealing with common health challenges like obesity, which often occurs in individuals with serious and persistent mental health disorders like schizophrenia, bipolar disorder, depression, or anxiety disorders.

Many national and international programs take advantage of this coaching approach to wellness enhancement (Burhouse et al., 2015). In our clinical experience, a health coaching style along with MI is an ideal approach to improving mental wellness.

Positive Reinforcement and Motivation Enhancement. Taking a "carrot and not the stick" approach—incentives rather than disincentives, positive rather than a negative reinforcement—is ideal for wellness-centric practitioners (Switzer et al., 2017). An important component to improving mental wellness is to focus on enhancing motivation (Segar & Richardson, 2014). At their core, nearly all mental health conditions demonstrate motivation deficits—the very conditions we are targeting produce low motivation.

There are several approaches to overcoming motivational challenges. Treating the underlying psychiatric condition is critical: motivation often improves as the mental disorder recedes. Medications for psychiatric disorders may induce fatigue, contributing to motivation challenges. In most instances this can be addressed by altering doses or changing the medication to better fit the patient's needs.

Another powerful strategy in overcoming motivational challenges is encouraging patients to find a "wellness buddy." Encourage patients to ask a friend or a family member to go with them for walks, to the gym, to the yoga studio, grocery shopping, etc. This can increase motivation and thereby improve adherence to wellness-centric practices.

Patients with mood and anxiety disorders are often self-punishing for self-perceived failures. Reassure them that sub-optimum adherence is not a sign of failure. Rather, encourage them to see these adherence challenges as an opportunity for improvement. In other words, the "carrot" approach (encouraging, supportive, enthusiastic) is more productive than the "stick" approach (punishing, blaming, shaming), which should be avoided by patients, their wellness buddies, and of course by the clinician.

Overcoming Clinician Level Barriers

Over the last decade of conducting research in the field of mental wellness and teaching it to fellow clinicians, we have observed many clinician level barriers in creating a wellness-centric practice. Lack of professional education and training in mental wellness appears to be the most obvious barrier. Another major challenge is the fact many clinicians are extremely busy and overworked. We understand all of these constraints, which we too have personally encountered in our practice.

When we gently confront clinicians about the centrality of mental wellness in a person's life and point out that traditional psychiatry often ignores mental wellness, we usually find they are willing to consider our ideas and suggestions. So, perhaps the first practical tip to overcoming clinician level barriers is for clinicians to appreciate that *wellness is a fundamental human right and need.* As clinicians, it is our responsibility to address the mental health needs of our patients, which by definition includes both reduction of mental illness symptoms and elevation of mental wellness traits. Once you accept this rationale, you are better prepared to take the necessary steps to becoming a more wellness-centric clinician.

Another practical issue is the need for didactic education and practical training in wellness-centric practices. We hope this book serves the needs of clinicians who are interested in wellness-centric interventions but need further direction. Many mental health conferences are now offering one or more sessions on mental wellness, and we encourage you to avail yourself of these learning opportunities. The American Psychiatric Association has published a handbook on positive psychiatry (Jeste & Palmer, 2015) that is a valuable addition to our limited library of mental wellness resources.

We encourage you to utilize these resources and perhaps conduct in-services in your clinics to train fellow clinicians and staff. We recommend not limiting the training to just the prescribing members of the clinical team but to include all team members—psychotherapists, psychologists, counselors, nurses, social workers, nurse practitioners, physician assistants, medical assistants, and front office personnel. Because it is of such importance, no member of the clinical and practice team can afford to be ill-informed about mental wellness.

Overcoming System Level Barriers

Mental health systems focus exclusively on mental illness. The elaborate system established around the country to evaluate and treat millions of patients who have a variety of psychiatric disorders is highly commendable—psychiatric illnesses are some of the most common and disabling conditions afflicting human beings. However, this by default creates a barrier in providing a systematized approach to addressing mental wellness. Additionally, the financial models for the delivery of mental healthcare are structured to treat illness, with hardly any incentives to address or treat mental wellness deficits. As a result, clinicians focus almost exclusively on mental illness, which is a true loss for patients.

These system level challenges are longstanding and entrenched, but we have reason to be hopeful. In 2013, the president of the American Psychiatric Association, Dr. Dilip Jeste, embraced mental wellness as a platform issue. As a result, greater attention has been paid to mental wellness in psychiatry, probably for the first time ever at a national level. More and more private clinics around the country are adopting mental wellness as an added mission and are discovering patients are attracted to this model of addressing both mental illness and mental wellness.

The solution to these system level challenges is to identify champions for the cause of wellness in the various settings. Even a few such "wellness champions" in an organization can bring about change in even the most resistant clinical system of patient care. It is our hope that after reading this book and accessing the wellness-centric resources, you will broach this subject with your organization's decision-makers to bring about change.

We have helped many clinicians around the country incorporate wellness-centric interventions into their practices, and there have been relatively few hiccups in their implementation in both private practice and public-sector psychiatry. We are very encouraged by these projects and the successes achieved. Experience has shown that by overcoming these system-wide barriers, even with relatively modest efforts, mental health systems can successfully adapt and integrate a wellness-centric focus in practices.

A patient's journey toward enhanced mental wellness is often rocky and prone to occasional false starts, but with ongoing motivation and support most patients improve their mental wellness. Your journey in incorporating wellness-centric interventions in your own practice will also involve occasional challenges and barriers. It is our hope that we have offered both you and your patients practical tips and suggestions to help smooth the way toward a successful wellness-centric practice.

CHAPTER 10

Practicing Measurement-Based Care

Measurement-based care (MBC) is becoming a standard of care in medical practice, with a strong move in all medical specialties to incorporate MBC into every step of a patient's journey through the medical system. Despite some obvious shortcomings, MBC has been a force for good. It can be used for multiple purposes, including screening, outcome measures, and to detect and measure change after treatment. In fact, even the federal government now recommends MBC to demonstrate the value of the interventions offered to patients (Center for Medicare and Medicaid Services, 2019).

In general, mental health clinicians around the country have been slow to adopt MBC. Adoption rates have been low in the assessment and treatment of disorders as diverse as anxiety disorders, mood disorders, schizophrenia, and attention deficit hyperactivity disorder (ADHD) (Waldrop & McGuinness, 2017). There are several reasons for this reluctance, including lack of tradition of using scales and screeners, underappreciation of measurement-driven clinical decision making, and a general lack of education regarding MBC.

Mental health professionals may also be resistant to the use of MBC because unlike other specialties, mental health professionals have no objective disease measures. Compared with, say, diabetes mellitus, we do not have a blood test to measure our disease levels. Yet studies demonstrate that despite the lack of objective markers in psychiatry, the use of clinician- or patient-administered scales and screeners has significant validity and consistently leads to better patient outcomes. For example, the Texas Medication Algorithm Project has demonstrated that clinical decisions based on measures of ADHD severity lead to better outcomes than treatment as usual (Pliszka et al., 2006). The American Psychiatric Association, across its various guidelines, also enthusiastically recommends the use of MBC (APA Clinical Practice Guidelines, 2019).

For all the reasons outlined, we need to look beyond our specialties' heritage and consider changing our clinical behaviors to incorporate MBC. At the end of the day, improving patient outcomes is our united goal. If you are interested in adding wellness interventions to your patients' care, you should strongly consider the use of scales and screeners.

Scales for Measurement-Based Care in Psychiatry

The history of MBC in psychiatry is relatively short. The psychopharmacology revolution, which began in earnest in the early 1960s, motivated psychiatry to create scales to measure changes in psychiatric symptomatology. Until then, narrative description of cases was the norm.

As the care of depression gradually shifted from inpatient to outpatient care, there was a clear need for a scale that was more useful in both settings. Psychiatrists Stuart A. Montgomery and Marie Asberg created the Montgomery Asberg Depression Rating Scale, still in use today (Hobden et al., 2017). It has 10 items, compared to the most common version of the Hamilton Depression Rating Scale, which has 17 items. Neither of these two depression rating scales are widely used by practitioners.

Decades ago, Aaron T. Beck created cognitive-behavior therapy. To address the absence of MBC, he created a variety of scales, and two in particular have become quite popular: the Beck Depression Inventory and the Beck Anxiety Inventory (Richter, Werner, Heerlein, Kraus, & Sauer, 1998). He also validated the scales' utility, sensitivity, specificity, and patient acceptability through a number of trials. The Hamilton Anxiety Scale, with its somatic anxiety and psychic anxiety subscale (Maier, Buller, Phillip, & Heuser, 1988), has also been used for decades in clinical trials.

The National Institute of Mental Health has created a number of scales now considered the standard of care in both clinical practice and research. The Clinical Global Impression (CGI) scale is frequently used in mental health studies conducted around the world (Dunlap, Gray, & Rapaport, 2017). Two versions of CGI scales are available to clinicians: CGI-Improvement and CGI-Severity. Another gift from National Institute of Mental Health is the Abnormal Involuntary Movement Scale, created in the 1970s, after the field became concerned about tardive dyskinesia in patients exposed to antipsychotics.

As ADHD has gained prominence, this field too has developed an array of MBC instruments. Vanderbilt University created the Vanderbilt ADHD Diagnostic Rating Scale to both screen for and measure improvement in ADHD in children and adolescents (Xiao, Wang, Lou, & Zhong, 2013). For adult patients, the Adult ADHD Self-Report scale has been studied by Leonard Adler and colleagues (Adler et al., 2006) from New York University School of Medicine, which has good acceptability by both clinicians and patients.

The two most globally popular and most utilized patient self-rated scales in psychiatry are the Patient Health Questionnaire-9 (PHQ-9), designed for screening and measuring depressive symptoms, and the Generalized Anxiety Disorder-7 (GAD-7), designed for measuring anxiety, with a focus on generalized anxiety disorder. These instruments have been studied extensively for clinical use in multiple settings (Kronke, Spitzer, & Williams, 2001; Lowe et al., 2008) and are popular for several reasons: they are patient-rated so they do not require significant clinic or clinician time; they have good sensitivity and specificity; and they both are recommended by multiple guidelines around the world.

Scales for the Measurement-Based Care of Mental Wellness

As the field of mental wellness is young, few MBC instruments are currently available specifically to measure levels of mental wellness. Yet despite the infancy of this field, some instruments have been quite well-studied. For example, the Warwick-Edinburgh Mental Wellbeing Scale, created in 2007 (Tennant et al., 2007), is a validated measure that can assess mental wellness levels at a national or regional level, and can even be used for individual patient-level wellness assessment. It is a 14-item self-administered instrument, asking questions about thoughts and feelings over the last two weeks, with each item focusing on a different aspect of mental wellness. Because 14 items may be excessive for clinical use, the Short Warwick-Edinburgh Mental Wellbeing Scale has only 7 items. Although the scale was originally created to study mental wellness in the general population, many of us have adapted it for clinical use. (Readers interested in obtaining more details can easily access the scale at Warwick Medical School website devoted to providing resources on this excellent scale [Warwick Medical School, 2019]).

World Health Organization Well-Being Index

The World Health Organization Well-Being Index (WHO-5), a 5-item scale measuring wellness (Krieger et al., 2014), has been around since the early 1990s and has an impressive track record in the literature, with use in both medical and psychiatric settings. In 1948, the WHO defined health as not just the absence of disease but also the presence of wellness. As a result of this mission statement, WHO researchers initially created a long version of the WHO-5 Well-Being wellness scale. After extensive testing of this instrument they determined that five of the items appeared to be of particular value, resulting in the current 5-item scale to assess subjective quality of life based on the following five attributes of well-being: positive mood (good spirits, cheerful), feeling calm and relaxed, feeling active and vigorous, waking up feeling fresh and refreshed, and daily life filled with things of interest.

The WHO-5 is a brief scale, and its psychometric properties have been well assessed. As both clinicians and researchers we have found it exceedingly helpful. This scale has been used in both psychiatric and chronic pain studies. The WHO-5 is slowly gaining global traction and is being used by an increasing number of centers around the world. WHO-5 is available in multiple languages (WHO-5 Scale).

The HERO Wellness Scale

We found these various scales to be helpful in our research and clinical practices, but they still did not adequately capture what we thought was the essence of mental wellness deficits in our patients. We were impressed by how much of a deficit in happiness, enthusiasm, resilience, and optimism—the HERO wellness traits—existed in our patients, but we had no way to measure it or to quantify changes based on wellness-centric interventions.

We therefore created the HERO Wellness Scale, a five-item, self-rated scale ranging from 0 (least) to 10 (most). The first four items assess happiness, enthusiasm, resilience, and optimism; the fifth item assesses overall mental wellness. We designed and developed the HERO Wellness scale to cover a representative sample of the domain of mental wellness; it diverges considerably from WHO-5 scale items by specifically assessing for well-established positive psychology traits such as happiness, enthusiasm, resilience, and optimism. We and other researchers have now tested the HERO Wellness Scale's utilization in multiple studies, as we describe below. A copy of this validated scale can be found in the resource section of this book.

To ensure the scale has good reliability and validity for clinical and research utilization, we compared it to the WHO-5 scale, the gold standard wellness instrument, in adult college students (Jain, Cole, Girard, Raison, & Jain, 2017[c]). Eighty-four college students from a private, liberal arts college in Wisconsin enrolled in the WILD 5 Wellness program. Before the study started, and at the end of 30 days, participants completed both the WHO-5 Well-Being Index and the HERO Wellness Scale. Data indicated that the HERO Wellness Scale provided reliable results that can be used for patient-level assessment of wellness. Further details on the statistical data supporting the introduction of this new wellness scale are provided in the Appendix section of this book.

Including Measurement-Based Care with Wellness Interventions

Patients seem to appreciate clinicians asking about the presence or absence of positive mental health traits. In fact, one study asked patients to rank their preferences about what clinicians should ask them and found that they ranked being asked about signs of mental wellness *higher* than being asked about mental illness symptoms (Crawford et al., 2011). This same study asked patients what should be included in an ideal scale for mental health. Recommendations included that the scale should be based on patient-rated rather than staff-rated judgments, should include both "positive" as well as "negative" items, and should be comprehensive—neither too long nor too short.

Incorporating Measurement-Based Care in Your Practice

Despite patient appreciation for rating both positive and negative traits, you may encounter barriers to MBC implementation in your clinical practice. Below are five of the most common responses from clinicians and support staff when the issue of measurement-based care is raised:

1. If they aren't required, I'm not wasting my time using scales
2. I don't know which scales to use
3. The scales and screeners are too expensive, and I don't have the time and money to get them
4. Patients hate these forms and will refuse to fill them out
5. The scales and screeners are unreliable, so I don't see any point in using them

We address each of these responses in turn. As you will see, including MBC in clinical practice can be effective and rewarding, which will help you overcome any of these barriers you may encounter.

   1. If they aren't required, I'm not wasting my time using scales. It is important for you and your staff to recognize that scales and screeners are typically filled out by patients—instead of being a time waster, they are often a great time saver. What is more, MBC is near-universally recommended by guidelines and is increasingly being required in more settings courtesy of insurance companies, managed care, and the federal government. Medicare is beginning to request use of the PHQ-9 in geriatric patients with depression living in nursing homes. Many insurance companies are demanding MBC before providing coverage for certain medications or services. For example, depression rating scales are required before transcranial magnetic stimulation treatment is approved, and the Abnormal Involuntary Movement Scale is required before a VMAT 2 inhibitor medication is approved for tardive dyskinesia. In time, more clinical situations will mandate the use of MBC.

2. I don't know which scales to use. This is an understandable concern—the hundreds of mental health scales and screeners available can leave you and your staff feeling confused, and many do not have the requisite training in MBC. One solution is to adopt one scale per disease state or disorder and use it routinely until its use becomes second nature. If after gaining expertise you detect inadequacies with a particular scale, then experimenting with another scale makes perfect sense. Here are some suggestions for scales and screeners specific to certain disease states:

- PHQ-9 for depression severity
- GAD-7 for anxiety
- The Mood Disorder Questionnaire for bipolar disorder
- Adult ADHD Self-Report scale for ADHD
- WHO-5 for wellness
- The HERO Wellness Scale for mental wellness

3. The scales and screeners are too expensive, and I don't have the time and money to get them. Most scales are available at no cost and easily downloadable from the Internet, including those listed above. Some are available in multiple languages. True, some scales are copyright protected and can be both costly and time-consuming to utilize. Simply avoid using expensive scales until you develop expertise in using the free scales.

4. Patients hate these forms and will refuse to fill them out. Our experience regarding the use of scales and screeners reveals widespread support from patients, with comments like, "I'm glad I'm being asked to fill out these forms so my healthcare provider doesn't miss anything important" and "This screener helps me better explain to my clinician how I'm really doing." Educate patients about why you use scales and screeners. You'll find that most patients will gladly complete the forms when they are told doing so helps you better understand them and offer them the best possible care.

5. The scales and screeners are unreliable, so I don't see any point in using them. Many clinicians are concerned that patients will not understand the scale content or will randomly answer the questions, or that the scales are not reliable. In fact, these scales are often written at a sixth-grade reading and comprehension level, so most patients fully comprehend them. Be sure to examine the sensitivity and specificity of all scales you integrate into your practice. All of the scales mentioned above possess good statistical reliability and validity. Because mental wellness is an issue in all psychiatric disorders, we recommend offering patients a mental wellness scale at every visit.

Incorporating Measurement-Based Care with Wellness-Based Interventions

MBC appears to truly enhance patient outcomes. Below we summarize our suggestions on how to ideally use MBC when offering wellness-based interventions:

> *Use free scales and screeners.* Free scales and screeners are quite useful and have excellent statistical data backing their utility, so cost barriers are no longer an issue with the availability of free scales and screeners.
>
> *Use scales and screeners routinely and frequently.* Just as primary care clinicians measure blood pressure on a regular basis to check for

changes, conducting regular checkups using MBC can help you avoid challenges down the road.

Tracking forms are our friends, so embrace them. Scales and screeners are time savers for busy clinicians, and they improve clinical outcomes.

Train all members of the clinical team on the use of MBC. Everyone on the treatment team, no matter their role, is vital in ensuring MBC utilization is optimized. Having every member of the treatment team enthusiastic and knowledgeable about the use of scales and screeners undeniably magnifies the value these instruments bring to patient care.

Inform patients of the results of their scales and screeners. Once the scales and screeners are filled out and scored, share the results with patients. Scores often help convince skeptical patients that there might be a problem and can be used to motivate patients to improve their scores. And seeing improvement in scores can help motivate patients to continue or increase their wellness practices. Clinicians often report that using scales and screeners helps their patients become more active members in their own treatment.

Measure both mental disease and mental wellness levels. As we have repeatedly posited, nearly all clinical scenarios involve both presence of illness and deficits in mental wellness. This means using at least two instruments, one to measure disease specific symptoms and the other to measure mental wellness.

Measurement-based care is here to stay, and we happily welcome this development in mental health. Granted, clinicians already have much to do, but the use of scales and screeners can save time and offer patients better care with improved outcomes. Regardless of which approaches to wellness-centric care you choose, we urge you to find ways to integrate MBC in your practice and make it a regular component of all clinical interventions.

PART 3
Developing Your Wellness-centric Practice

To complement the review of the science behind mental wellness and the mind-body connection in Part 1, and the principles of mental wellness interventions in Part 2, here we discuss what we and others have encountered in implementing wellness-centric practices to help you sharpen your skills in offering such interventions to your patients. In Chapter 11, we summarize lessons learned from our research and practice with wellness interventions. We discuss practical applications of wellness interventions, including add-on treatments, and offer some tips to avoid common mistakes when applying these practices. Chapter 12 rounds out our journey into mental wellness by sharing success stories with mental wellness interventions from the perspective of both patients and clinicians.

CHAPTER 11

Using Wellness Interventions in Clinical Practice

Well-being can be learned but it requires practice.
There is no substitute for practice.

—RICHARD DAVIDSON

It is gratifying to see wellness become a well-accepted concept in the treatment of patients afflicted with psychiatric disorders—we simply cannot medicate ourselves out of the mental health crisis facing modern America. It is reassuring to know that, with practice, wellness is learnable, and its levels can be raised in a fairly short period of time.

It is our hope that this book will help you implement wellness interventions in your clinical practice, and in your own life, to enhance well-being for all. We also hope you will embrace these four salient points and integrate them into your clinical practice:

1. Wellness is important to all human beings, irrespective of the presence or absence of a psychiatric disorder.
2. Wellness levels are often lower than desired, and lower than what is needed for optimum functioning.
3. Wellness deficits cause impairment to an individual's mental and physical functioning.
4. With direction, effort, and practice most individuals can rapidly improve their wellness.

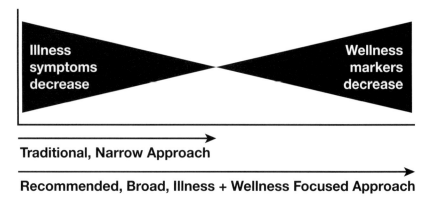

FIGURE 11.1: Traditional versus wellness-centric approach to mental health and illness.

The wellness-centric approach to treating our patients goes beyond sim-ply treating disease symptoms to embracing all aspects of well-being, as neatly summed up by Figure 11.1. When our patients come see us, they cer-tainly seek a decrease in their psychiatric symptoms and the associated suf-fering. Taking care of symptom reduction is only the first step. But merely achieving the absence of symptoms is not enough—we must also increase levels of wellness to inoculate our patients against relapse and enhance their well-being. And to do this, wellness must also be addressed with targeted, specific interventions. This broad therapeutic approach is associated with ideal short- and long-term outcomes in our patients.

This chapter outlines what we have gleaned from developing and using our WILD 5 Wellness program to enhance mental wellness in a broad range of populations. We first share findings from our multiple research studies in mental wellness and from our clinical practice. We then summarize practical applications for using wellness interventions in clinical practice and discuss how to utilize these interventions as an add-on to pharmacotherapy and psy-chotherapy. We end with a summary of key points to building a wellness-centric practice and offer some tips to avoid common mistakes when applying wellness interventions, to help you successfully incorporate wellness interventions into your practice. In the future, you may find this chapter a good refresher as you continue your journey as a wellness-centric clinician.

Lessons Learned from Our Research Efforts in Mental Wellness

Our national survey of 757 individuals taught us these key lessons:

- All human beings crave mental wellness
- Levels of mental wellness are generally lower than what most individuals desire
- The HERO wellness traits—happiness, enthusiasm, resilience, and optimism—are generally at sub-optimum levels
- Individuals suffering from a mental disorder have significantly low levels of wellness traits
- Chronic pain patients suffer from low levels of mental wellness
- Having both a mental disorder and a chronic pain condition exacerbates the wellness deficit

These results are a call to action for all clinicians, irrespective of background or specialty.

Our Phase I study with 18 patients and 18 controls (Jain, Jain, & Kumar, 2015), taught us the following:

- Individuals with a mental illness embrace mental wellness interventions, and their adherence is generally good
- If participants did adopt the wellness practices, their mental illness and mental wellness generally improve
- Participants without a mental health disorder also benefit from a wellness-centric program.

Adherence rates after the Phase I 30-day program revealed most of the practices had good average adherence to the five wellness interventions:

- Exercise: 20 / 30 days
- Mindfulness: 18.8 / 30 days
- Sleep: 24.5 / 30 days
- Social Connectedness: 28.5 / 30 days
- Nutrition: 23.5 / 30 days
- Average composite adherence 115.4 / 150 (SD=19.7)

The 18 individuals with a mental health challenge improved globally in their mental illness traits and showed significant improvement in mental wellness in just 30 days, with an intervention requiring little clinical time or effort. We also saw significant changes in mental wellness traits of the controls who had no mental health challenges.

We have now replicated these findings with larger numbers of individuals, from diverse backgrounds, in our Phase II and Phase III studies. Our data reinforce that simple, prescriptive, and trackable wellness interventions help reduce mental illness symptoms and improve mental wellness traits (Jain, Jain, & Kumar, 2015; Jain et al, 2016[a]; Jain, Rolin, & Jain, 2017[a]). These replicated results show us that these benefits are real.

Our findings were also replicated by a nurse practitioner in Arizona. As a candidate for a doctoral degree in nursing, he applied our mindfulness wellness intervention in his own research and had impressive results (Fong & Guthery, 2018). Among the 35 patients in his mindfulness intervention study, mean PHQ-9 score decreased from 16.7 to 12.9, a 23% improvement, (p=0.008) and mean GAD-7 score for anxiety decreased from 16.9 to 11.4, a 33% improvement (p<0.001).

Another important lesson was the impact of wellness interventions in a college population. Young adults attending college are vulnerable to stress and mental disorders and often suffer cognitively and physically from diminished levels of mental wellness. The application of the WILD 5 Wellness program at a private college in Wisconsin improved students' cognitive and physical functioning in 30 days.

Lessons Learned from Our Clinical Efforts in Mental Wellness

We have experienced both successes and failures over the last decade as we have offered wellness-centric interventions to our patients. Over time, we have learned from our experiences and have improved our wellness intervention skills, and our clinical outcomes have continued to improve.

Patients Embrace and Appreciate Incorporating Wellness Interventions

It has been gratifying to see the positive changes wellness interventions bring about in patients. Even patients who struggled for years with recurrent episodes of depression and/or anxiety have noticed a significant reduction in both the frequency and severity of such episodes. These wellness-centric interventions not only helped improve the degree of their symptomatology but also seemed to "vaccinate" them against future episodes.

Many patients used the word *empowered* when asked to describe their experiences with this wellness program. They said they felt empowered knowing there was more they could do to feel better than just taking medications. For many this sense of empowerment has been a transformative experience. Many patients incorporated these wellness practices into their daily lives, which has led to fewer relapses and recurrences of their psychiatric conditions. Wellness interventions indeed seem to offer long-term protection.

And a rather unexpected but welcome positive experience was how often patients who learned wellness interventions spread their new-found wellness behaviors to those around them. Often, as a result of patients' wellness practices, their family members, friends, and co-workers began adopting similar habits and behaviors.

Offering Wellness Interventions Enhanced Our Own Wellness and Work Satisfaction

In addition to benefiting our patients, offering wellness interventions to our patients has made us feel like more "complete" clinicians. We are no longer focusing solely on symptom control but have expanded our conversation to include the HERO wellness traits—happiness, enthusiasm, resilience, and optimism—and other aspects of mental wellness and well-being, along with symptom management and improvement. We now focus on something that matters deeply to our patients: their well-being. Changing the conversation to include mental wellness has vastly improved the therapeutic bond and alliance with our patients.

Our patients value and appreciate the resources we offer in our WILD 5 Wellness program: tracking forms, the HERO Wellness Scale, the WILD 5 Wellness mindfulness meditations, the HERO exercises, and others. These resources are "clinician extenders": they allow patients outside of sessions to review and solidify their learning, so we do not have to spend as much time educating patients. Tracking forms help improve their adherence and are a way to learn more about their wellness behaviors—what's working well and what's not.

Lessons Learned from Teaching Others About Wellness Interventions

One of the most striking things we have noticed from teaching other clinicians about wellness interventions is how positively it has been received. We have tapped into an unmet need: a near-complete dearth of any adherence tracking of wellness practices, or measurement of wellness levels. Our WILD 5 Wellness program offers direction regarding what to recommend to patients, as well as actual wellness resources. This helps clinicians not only talk to patients about exercise, sleep hygiene, and other wellness practices but also offers concrete suggestions and tools to follow through with these practices.

We have found that training seminars are more effective when we offer a combination of the science supporting the wellness interventions plus hands-on, step-by-step instructions on how to implement these wellness-centric interventions. We have both offered seminars and training sessions in various settings, such as professional society meetings, resident seminars, and faculty seminars in psychiatry and other specialties, in the United States and throughout the world: Canada, Mexico, Puerto Rico, Brazil, Argentina, Costa Rica, Columbia, Austria, Ireland, South Africa, Egypt, United Arab Emirates, and the United Kingdom. Universally, the reception to wellness as a concept has been extremely positive.

Practical Applications of Wellness Interventions in Clinical Practice

One of the most important lessons we have learned about wellness interventions in clinical practice is that the more we understand about the science of mental wellness, the more effectively we can help our patients. Understanding the scientific principles supporting these interventions is a huge asset. It will not only help you better target a patient's level of wellness, but it will also increases your passion to be an effective wellness-centric clinician.

The science of wellness can seem overwhelming, encompassing wellness epidemiology, effects on the HPA axis, autonomic nervous system, and immune system, as well as many other physical and mental health mechanisms and markers. But educating yourself step by step can enhance your understanding and motivation surprisingly quickly. The neurobiological sciences are a good place to start. Both microscopic and brain imaging studies have demonstrated the positive effects of higher wellness on brain structure and its functioning. Knowing these data expand our knowledge, enthusiasm, and drive to educate patients on the importance of wellness. As we have said before, knowledge is power.

Finding resources can be a daunting task, but resources are increasing in this growing field—and we hope this book contributes to your wellness armamentarium. We encourage you to visit the resource section of this book to explore the many wellnesses-centric options that are available to us clinicians. Psychiatry is disease-centric, and it is rare to find an article focusing solely on mental wellness published in a leading scientific journal. However, this situation is slowly changing, with occasional articles on mental wellness science and practice appearing in the mainstream journals, and more continuing medical-educational courses on wellness are being offered at professional meetings. We now even have a peer-reviewed journal that focuses on the science and practice of mental wellness: *The Journal of Happiness Studies*. As wellness becomes more incorporated into clinical practice, we anticipate that more and more educational resources will become available.

Here we summarize practical tips on using mental wellness interventions in your practice. These tips, combined with an understanding of the science behind these wellness-enhancing interventions, will augment your successful use of these interventions.

Patients Value Wellness More Than Symptom Reduction

Multiple research studies show that even patients with significant psychiatric pathology often rank their desire for wellness higher than their desire for symptom reduction. Understanding this fact is central to becoming a top-notch wellness-centric clinician. Psychiatric disorders are not just a mere collection of illness symptoms but are accompanied by a corresponding drop in wellness. Although offering mental wellness interventions at the outset of treatment may not be an appropriate intervention for some, keeping in mind that the basic human desire for wellness is universal, profoundly alters how we conceptualize patient needs.

Choose the Right Time and Approach to Introduce Wellness Concepts

Timing is everything when it comes to how and when we recommend wellness strategies. Ideally, we would evaluate all patients for their level of wellness and then offer specific wellness-centric interventions. But a patient's level of psychopathology should influence exactly when to recommend wellness interventions. There are multiple clinical scenarios where it might be appropriate to bring up the issue of wellness at the very first clinical encounter, but in other scenarios delaying such a conversation might make more sense if the patient is having acute or severe symptoms of their psychiatric disorder.

Once a patient is stabilized, however, wellness interventions have proven quite effective—even chronically ill but stable individuals benefit from wellness interventions. Multiple studies reveal the positive impact of wellness interventions in major depression, generalized anxiety disorder, and bipolar depression, to name just a few. Because remission rates remain low with psychopharmacological and therapeutic treatments, and relapse and recurrence remain high, wellness interventions are useful additions to our armamentarium, offering our patients holistic benefits ranging from symptom reduction to improved functionality.

Measure, Measure, Measure

A key to maintaining enthusiasm is to measure wellness—at baseline, and periodically thereafter. Knowing baseline scores and then monitoring progress with improving scores on a scale can be hugely motivating for both the patient and the clinician. Measuring wellness at the beginning of treatment (to establish a baseline) and frequently thereafter to monitor progress is key to maintaining enthusiasm for both you and your patients. Measuring progress not only helps you both understand changes in wellness levels but also lets you fine-tune your coaching and motivational interviewing to guide patients toward further progress. Any wellness instrument you are comfortable with and use on a regular basis is appropriate. We offer our HERO Wellness Scale and other tracking tools in the resource section in the back of this book as one way to establish baseline wellness levels and document progress.

Educate Patients About the Mental and Physical Health Benefits of Enhancing Wellness

Educated and empowered patients are in a better position to actively contribute to their own improved well-being. Unlike pharmacotherapy, where a patient can be a somewhat passive recipient of treatment, implementing wellness interventions requires patients to understand how the interventions will benefit them and to be actively engaged in their own treatment. Thus, providing this education is part of your charge as a wellness-centric clinician.

We recommend you take a mind-body perspective when educating patients about mental wellness. A mind-body approach is when a clinician explains to a patient that the mind is intimately connected to the body, and that a bi-directional relationship exists between the two. Another critical component of taking such a mind-body approach is to impress upon the patient that when they undertake a mind-based intervention (such as mindfulness practice), *both* their mind and body benefit, and if they were to initiate a body-based intervention (such as physical exercise), similarly, *both* their mind and body would benefit. You can expect patients on occasion to be initially confused—they too might be laboring under the misunderstanding that the only goal of treatment is symptom reduction. Reassure them that, while symptom reduction is an important goal of treatment, it is not the only goal. Psychoeducation about improving mental wellness traits should include helping patients understand that mental wellness further reduces mental illness symptoms, helps medication work better, and improves physical health. In our experience, taking a mind-body approach in educating patients on the positive impact of wellness on both mental health and the body improves patient acceptance and adherence.

Use Resources to Educate, Motivate, and Track Patient Progress

Resources make a wellness-centric clinician's job easier and more productive, and enhance patient understanding, motivation, and adherence. But when patients are not guided on which resources to use, they can be overwhelmed by the myriad choices that are of varying quality, particularly those available on the Internet. They often freeze, feel overwhelmed by the choices, and end up doing nothing. Here are some tips for you to avoid this outcome:

- Recommend printed or online wellness resources that you know well. We suggest only recommending resources you have deep familiarity with. Otherwise, your recommendations may sound hollow to the patient, and you may be unable to answer specific questions a patient may pose.
- Consider offering native language–specific resources for patients whose primary language is not English.
- Explore apps that focus on wellness interventions, such as exercise, sleep, nutrition, mindfulness, etc. Some of our favorite apps are mentioned in the resource section of this book.

Encourage Journaling for Patients to Enhance Their Mental Wellness

Keeping a diary and journaling is an essential component of wellness enhancement. Although it typically takes only a few minutes a day, journaling can have lasting effects on a patient's level of wellness, including decreased mental distress, depression, and anxiety, and enhanced resilience and mental and physical well-being. In the WILD 5 Wellness program we include a wellness journaling component to build and strengthen the HERO positive psychology traits. Regardless of the wellness intervention, any journaling or diary method (paper journaling or electronic media documenting) that you and your patients are comfortable with will allow that process to develop over time as patients progress in their wellness journey.

Using Wellness Interventions as an Add-on to Other Therapeutic Modalities

Wellness interventions are not intended to replace any other treatments. Rather, they are designed to work in concert with the other well-established therapeutic modalities, such as psychotherapy and psychopharmacology.

Excessive enthusiasm for any one therapeutic option is, generally speaking, harmful to our cause of optimized treatment. Wellness interventions have demonstrated effectiveness in multiple clinical paradigms, as monotherapy, as an add-on treatment to psychopharmacology, and in nonpatients who want to enhance their mental wellness. Wellness interventions can also be used as a sequential treatment option, after a course of cognitive-behavioral therapy or after stabilization of symptoms with medications. There is clear evidence that with higher levels of wellness come lower levels of mental illness symptoms and a lower risk of relapse or recurrence. So applying wellness interventions during treatment of virtually all patients, either early or later, is prudent.

Building a Relationship Between Medication and Wellness Practices

Most contemporary psychiatrists, psychiatric nurse practitioners, and physician assistants primarily offer medication therapies. Psychotherapy is being offered by very few of these professionals, as they are inundated by patients requesting psychopharmacotherapy services. Psychotherapy, usually supportive and typically cognitive-behavioral therapy, is generally provided by psychologists, social workers, licensed professional counselors, and other licensed mental health clinicians. This sad dichotomy in the delivery of mental healthcare appears inevitable because of heavy clinician workload and economic pressures.

But it doesn't have to be the case. Wellness-centric therapies improve medication outcomes and can be offered by all members of a treatment team, whether they are prescribing or non-prescribing clinicians, without requiring a great investment of clinical time. And there are several benefits for both patients and providers in taking this approach:

> Clinicians desire the best possible results from their medication treatments. Wellness-centric interventions have demonstrated their power as an augmentation strategy to help further improve

short-term outcomes. Disorder-related symptoms, such as depression, anxiety, and insomnia demonstrably improve, as well as the HERO wellness traits of wellness of happiness, enthusiasm, resilience, and optimism.

Clinicians want to obtain the best long-term outcomes from their medication treatments, and the lowest possible relapse rates. Wellness-centric interventions have demonstrated their power as an effective augmentation strategy to help further improve long-term outcomes.

Studies have demonstrated that there is no conflict, only synergy between medication treatment and wellness interventions.

Based on our experiences and those of other wellness-centric psychopharmacologists and psychotherapists, clinician satisfaction is increased when we offer this dual treatment approach of medication and wellness-centric interventions to patients. Adopting this more holistic approach signals to a patient that their clinician focuses on the "whole person." Our own satisfaction with clinical work was enhanced once we incorporated wellness-centric strategies into our practices.

For these reasons, we believe all mental health professionals, including the prescribing community, should incorporate wellness into their philosophy and clinical practices.

Offering wellness-centric interventions does not require a large investment of time. Because many medication visits are by necessity only 15–20 minutes, it is understandable why some clinicians are hesitant to add wellness interventions, given the already limited amount of time allocated to each patient. We offer these practical suggestions to help overcome issues with time constraints:

· Use a "start small, but build up gradually" approach, which can be easily adopted by the busiest of all clinicians, even during a short med check appointment. Emphasize that even minor but consistent behavioral changes can be hugely helpful.

- Offer wellness-centric interventions in short blocks of time. It takes only a minute or two to make a powerful wellness-centric recommendation during a clinical visit. Be specific and prescriptive, but brief. For example, recommending patients go for a 30-minute walk twice a week, or meditate for 10 minutes three times a week.

- Have printed materials available on a variety of wellness-centric interventions. Never underestimate the value of such resources offered by an enthusiastic, supportive wellness-centric clinician. The time required is minimum, but the benefits can be impressive.

- Post your own or others' non-copyright–protected wellness-centric educational materials on your website. It does take a little time initially to set this up, but doing it can be a huge time-saver in the long run.

- Be aware that not all patients in a psychopharmacology practice are appropriate for wellness-centric interventions. Patients with a high degree of symptom severity may be harmed by these interventions until they achieve a significant degree of symptom control. In such situations, defer offering wellness interventions until the patient is better able to take advantage of the wellness-enhancing interventions.

We firmly believe most psychiatrically ill patients receiving psychopharmacology treatments are candidates for wellness-centric interventions. Even chronically psychotic but stable patients with schizophrenia have benefited from wellness-centric interventions.

Building a Relationship Between Psychotherapy and Wellness Practices

The world of counseling professionals is large and diverse. For every medication prescribing clinician, there are perhaps as many as ten non-prescribing mental health professionals. And they come from multiple backgrounds: psychologists, licensed professional counselors, marriage and family therapists, clinical social workers, substance abuse counselors, etc. Nurses, in particular those who work in inpatient and partial hospital settings, often lead solo and group counseling sessions.

In this large world of non-prescribing professionals, there is generally an under-appreciation of the importance of wellness. This lack of awareness is likely due to their training, which is missing a focus on wellness. Just like psychiatrists, they are steeped in the culture of *DSM*, which means an exclusive focus on disease. This disease-only focus results in clinicians paying attention to symptoms of illness with little or no focus on wellness level assessments or on wellness trait enhancement.

Incorporating wellness-centric interventions can be an easy transition for most psychotherapists because it leverages many of the same perspectives and approaches as other forms of psychotherapy. In many cases, incorporating elements of wellness interventions into the range of psychotherapeutic approaches will be natural extensions of what you are already practicing. For example, many clinicians have been trained in the disease and symptom modifying techniques of cognitive-behavioral therapy, which heavily emphasizes elements such as psychoeducation, measurement-based care, and assigned homework, which are the very tools utilized with wellness-centric interventions.

Wellness-centric interventions can help psychiatric or psychotherapeutic approaches achieve even better outcomes. Wellness-centric interventions are not intended to replace anything in the psychiatric and psychotherapeutic armamentarium. Rather, the aim is to further reduce symptoms, and lower relapse and recurrence rates. Wellness interventions can help us offer our patients a comprehensive mental health treatment plan. Additionally, offering these interventions and explaining them to a patient are generally not excessively time-consuming activities. Plus, these interventions lead to improvements in social connectedness, work and home functioning, mindfulness, happiness, enthusiasm, resilience, optimism, and overall mental wellness—the spice of life that many of our patients are missing.

It is our sincere hope that you, as a mental health professional—whether prescriber or non-prescriber—will take to heart the science supporting wellness and integrate these wellness-enhancing interventions into your clinical practice. We are certain that you will find the addition of wellness-centric interventions will help improve not only your patients' well-being but also your own practice and quality of life.

Avoiding Common Mistakes when Applying Wellness Interventions

We have heard stories from clinicians who were initially very enthusiastic about utilizing wellness interventions but became frustrated when patients were not following through on their suggestions. We have found that some approaches are more effective than others in successfully encouraging patients to engage with wellness interventions. Here are a few suggestions:

> *Give wellness interventions appropriate time and respect in your patient interactions.* Advice on wellness is too often imparted as an aside, toward the end of an appointment, almost as an afterthought or a "throwaway" comment that is not particularly important but "might be nice to add if I have a minute or two left over." This inadvertently teaches the patient that wellness is not of prime import. Once you've decided it's appropriate to introduce wellness interventions to a patient, give this discussion appropriate time and respect during a clinical intervention, even when the focus of treatment is psychopharmacology. This will demonstrate to your patients that wellness is important and valued by you, which will

increase the likelihood that patients will see its importance and appreciate its value.

Avoid overemphasizing the value of wellness interventions in treating psychiatric pathology. It is a mistake to "oversell" a patient on wellness interventions, especially in patients with significant current psychopathology. This could potentially lead to you and your patients holding back from or delaying other appropriate treatments, such as psychopharmacology or cognitive-behavioral therapy. Wellness interventions, like all other interventions in clinical medicine, are best used judiciously in your practice.

Offer specific prescriptions for wellness interventions. In recommending wellness interventions to your patients, it is important to offer concrete, measurable, and attainable goals. Instead of simply saying things like, "You should exercise, it's good for you," or "You should practice meditation, it's good for your brain and your body and your wellness," please use a prescriptive approach. Explain the intervention fully and appropriately, and then offer targeted guidance and suggestions. Provide specific guidance on how patients are to apply these techniques and include room for them to work up to your recommendations, so they can build success rather than collect failures. For example, a recommendation for mindfulness might be something like, "This is a mindfulness app I recommend. To start, begin with 10–15 minutes a day. If that's too long, you can make it shorter. But its best to practice daily. And don't worry if you are doing it 'right.' Just practicing mindfulness is success."

Offer a full package of wellness interventions. Try to avoid picking and choosing a wellness intervention for a patient based on personal preference. Different wellness interventions will work better for some patients and not so well for other patients. This is why our WILD 5 Wellness program has multiple arms, and we encourage clinicians and patients alike to practice all of the wellness elements and to avoid picking and choosing any favorites.

Offer optimum coaching or monitoring. Coaching and monitoring are two essential skills for all wellness prescribers in mental health. The coaching model is particularly useful because you act as both a gentle teacher and an enthusiastic supporter of patients' efforts, while still offering suggestions on how to further improve their wellness skills. You can use the feedback from the patient tracking forms to tailor your coaching to every patients' needs.

Have patience with progress early in treatment. Human beings, generally speaking, do not tend to focus on wellness. Psychiatric illness may present extra challenges to a patients' ability to follow through. Understand that progress may be slow when patients initially learn wellness skills—try not getting frustrated, and coach your patients to avoid frustration, too. The typical wellness journey often starts out with a few false starts. When this happens, examine why a wellness intervention was not utilized appropriately, and then together with the patient, create a game plan to tackle this barrier head on. Gently encourage patients to reengage in their wellness practices.

Follow wellness principles in your own life. All human beings crave and place a high premium on mental wellness, and we clinicians are no different. Being a clinician is stressful work, and we too benefit from maintaining good mental health and wellness. We have found clinicians who model wellness for their patients also tend to be better prescribers of wellness-centric interventions.

All of these recommendations will help you better utilize wellness interventions in your practice. There is an art to becoming a wellness-centric clinician, and it requires practice. Just like with any other skill, experience is a great teacher. Using wellness intervention strategies in your practice will improve as you continually learn from your experiences.

Be patient, be a coach, be a cheerleader, and be a teacher as both you and your patients embark on the journey toward better wellness practices. Rome was not built in a day, and neither will your patients' journey toward wellness occur overnight. Take a positive and enthusiastic approach, set clear and achievable goals, and cheer every success with your patients along the way. This is an ideal approach to using wellness-centric interventions in mental health practice.

CHAPTER 12

Success Stories with Wellness Interventions

To round out the book, this last chapter aims to give you a patient-level, visceral sense of how wellness interventions actually affect individuals. There is value in hearing from the experiences of individuals, learning from their trials and tribulations, and applying these lessons to enhance the care of future patients.

Before sharing these patients' stories, we want to give you a taste of the success clinicians have achieved with wellness interventions. We offer descriptions of two clinicians' experiences with the WILD 5 Wellness program.

Clinicians' Observations of Success

Psychotherapist Kimberly Weaster, MEd, LPC-ACS, NCC, graciously shared her insights and observations after using the WILD 5 Wellness program in her practice:

> The wellness program has transformed my therapy practice, reducing the length of time clients spend talking about their lives and increasing the time clients spend living their lives. Drs. Jain have elegantly consolidated the 5 elements of a healthy life into a simple and powerful

model for living. The simplicity of this program belies the power of it. By focusing on nutrition, sleep, exercise, healthy social connections, and striving for life's purpose—however the individual defines these—people heal. I have consistently seen children, couples, adults, groups, and families lead healthier, happier lives by focusing their energies on the five wellness components.

Often clients are resistant to doing the work of therapy, and I have found them to be particularly resistant to wellness interventions. It is work to get better, and many people would rather talk about the work than do it. It is important to address this issue with clients during their first session. This way, clients are fully aware and are not struggling to deal with coming to terms with the work of healing on their own.

A pronounced strength of this model is the rapid healing of clients who are ready to change; conversely, in my experience those who are not ready to change quickly drop out of therapy and—although this is conjecture—likely do not make progress. In my opinion another strength of the wellness model is that it solves the potential ethical dilemma of keeping clients in therapy who are not making progress.

And yet, patients with seemingly intractable conditions can make significant progress with the program. Suzanne Grantham, PMHNP, a seasoned psychiatric nurse practitioner, referred many patients to early research on the WILD 5 Wellness program. Here are her thoughts on its impact on one of her patients:

When I was first introduced to the WILD 5 program, I was skeptical of its potential benefit. After all, wasn't I already teaching and encouraging my clients to exercise, eat healthy, be socially connected, stay present in the now and follow good sleep hygiene?

Weren't my clients already doing enough with psychotherapy and taking their medications to address their depression and anxiety? I approached the program with an attitude of, "It can't hurt. Maybe it could help."

However, my clients in the WILD 5 program quickly taught me that they were all capable of implementing wellness interventions and experiencing dramatic improvements in well-being as a result. What really struck me was that even my clients that were the most disabled by their depression and anxiety experienced significant improvements in well-being. I realized I had developed some learned helplessness as a clinician and had underestimated what my clients were capable of achieving.

One client who stands out in my mind was a man in his late forties who was on disability for depression. "Lucas" had spent at least 15 hours every day in bed for the past 5 years. He was socially isolated, physically inactive, pre-diabetic and lived on frozen food. Lucas had heroically endured many evidence-based medication trials and worked with numerous highly skilled psychotherapists without experiencing much benefit. Lucas was well educated and had over 10 years of sobriety under his belt.

Despite significant fatigue and depression, Lucas diligently practiced the wellness interventions in the program. He learned about nutrition and how to cook healthy simple meals. He pushed through his isolation and started reaching out to people daily and leaving his house daily. He forced himself to meditate even though initially he thought it sounded like a "woo-woo" form of torture.

At one point in the program, he became very ill from a virus and could not exercise or prepare healthy meals. He felt a lot of shame and frustration and almost gave up on participating in the program. Many of my clients hit a similar roadblock during the program and mistakenly believed they had "failed again," when actually they had just experienced a setback that they were capable of overcoming. With a little bit of support, Lucas was able to regain his footing and resumed his wellness behaviors.

Lucas experienced a lot of feelings of empowerment from his experience in the program. After 30 days in the program, he reported that his overall wellness had improved by 40%. A long-time participant in AA, Lucas experienced the program as providing him with a concrete set of strategies that could help him to "change the things he could change." Knowing that "it works if you work it," Lucas continues to practice the wellness behaviors over three years after he officially completed the program. Having learned that tracking his behaviors keeps him accountable, he documents his wellness activities on a Google doc he shares with me.

Forty pounds lighter with healthy cholesterol and fasting glucose levels, Lucas is no longer the socially isolated man he used to be. While he still suffers from depression and anxiety, he experiences far much greater feelings of well-being, belonging, and self-efficacy than he did in the past.

Suzanne's description outlines the positive impact patients can experience by integrating wellness-centric practices into their daily lives.

Patient Cases

The following stories demonstrate the range of diagnostic categories, degree of severity, and backgrounds of patients who have benefited from wellness interventions, in this case the WILD 5 Wellness program. Our aim is to illustrate the broad application of wellness interventions in improving quality of life. We hope these stories will both inspire and motivate you to integrate wellness interventions into your clinical practice. (Patient identifying information has been changed to maintain confidentiality.)

Melissa: Major Depression and Social Anxiety Disorder

Melissa was a 23-year-old single Caucasian female who suffered from social anxiety disorder and major depressive disorder since her early teens. Although actively engaged in therapy with a skilled psychologist and her psychotropic medication was being managed by a seasoned adult psychiatrist, she remained hugely symptomatic and impaired in nearly all domains of functioning. She remained actively engaged in psychotherapy treatment and tried a vast number of pharmacological treatments.

With the encouragement of her treatment team, Melissa enrolled in a 90-day WILD 5 Wellness study (LiveWell90). She had many of the expected initial trepidations—"it will be too hard to do; it won't work for me; I will fail at one more thing"—but agreed to give it a try. She was attracted to the structured nature of the program, its accountability components, and the ability to measure changes in wellness before and at the end of the wellness program—"I want to see if I get better or not." At the urging of her psychologist, she asked a close friend to become her wellness buddy.

The initial few days of wellness practices were a challenge for Melissa because she lacked drive and motivation at times. Having a wellness buddy was invaluable in getting her back on track. She struggled with the program's social connectedness element, given her social anxiety, as well as the practice of mindfulness meditation. But the daily logging and record keeping of her wellness practices slowly helped her overcome these barriers. She had made a commitment to her treatment team that she would give the program her best effort, and they were pleased that she was able to complete the 90-day program.

There were tangible benefits from her enhanced wellness. For example, Melissa enrolled in a few classes at college, began going out socially with friends, and timidly started dating. By the end of the 90-day program, her depression and anxiety measures both improved significantly. She did, however, report some difficulty with the mindfulness meditation practice, and her adherence with this practice was less consistent than with the other wellness-centric practices.

Table 12.1 shows Melissa's pre-post scores (at baseline and after the 90-days wellness program) for disease markers, impairment, and functional markers, which all improved. In addition, her HERO Wellness Scale individual item scores rose by 300–400%. Melissa's psychologist and psychiatrist were pleased that augmenting her current treatment with an integrated wellness program proved beneficial in terms of symptom reduction *and* wellness enhancement. Both clinicians appreciated that the wellness program is self-directed, thus not draining their practice resources, and because it is evidenced-based they felt confident recommending it. They both have encouraged Melissa to continue her wellness practices to cement the gains made so far.

TABLE 12.1 MELISSA'S PRE-POST PROGRESS

Measure	Instrument	Before	After	Improvement
Depression severity	PHQ-9	19	7	63%
Anxiety	GAD-7	16	6	63%
Sleep	SCI	5	14	180%
Emotional eating	EADES	27	66	144%
Cognitive and physical functioning	CPFQ	31	18	42%
Mindful awareness	MAAS	72	73	1%
Disability	SDS	10	5	50%
Social connectedness	SCS	14	38	171%
Well-being	WHO-5	4	5	25%

Melissa's case demonstrates that even fairly ill, treatment-refractory patients can benefit from augmentation with a wellness program and that providing patients with a simple, prescriptive, self-directed program can be effective. In addition, recruiting a wellness buddy is often an excellent suggestion. Large clinical gains are possible with wellness augmentation, and a thoughtful, encouraging, and motivating clinician can be invaluable to its ultimate success.

Joe: Bipolar Disorder, Social Anxiety Disorder, ADHD, and Panic Disorder

When Joe's psychotherapist called us to refer him to a wellness study, she openly expressed the concern he might "not do well" with wellness interventions, given his psychiatric history and his current level of disability. Before he became so ill, Joe was a bright, engaged, and well-adjusted individual, but his multiple psychiatric disorders had taken a large toll on his life. Now in his mid-50s, he had been diagnosed with bipolar disorder type I, social anxiety disorder, ADHD-inattentive type, and panic disorder, and had been in treatment for mental health challenges for almost thirty years. He experienced multiple hospitalizations for psychosis and suicidality and had tried several atypical anti-psychotics that were somewhat helpful but left him considerably unmotivated, sleepy, and fatigued—and he had gained nearly 60 pounds in the last ten years of treatment. His treating clinician noted that Joe mostly spent his time lying in bed and leaving the apartment only to come to his appointments.

Over his thirty years in treatment, Joe and his psychiatrist had tried nearly 50 different medication combinations. He was unable to work, received disability, and lived with a roommate. His body mass index (BMI) was 32, classifying him as obese, and his fasting lipid profile was elevated. He led a very sedentary life, and he reported eating predominantly fast food meals. According to his psychotherapist he was experiencing many vegetative symptoms of depression including slowed cognition, increased appetite, suicidal ideations, and increased time sleeping.

Joe began the KickStart30 program. As we oriented him to the wellness program, he was articulate and asked good questions. Much to our delight, he took to the program and found the workbook and its structure very useful in organizing his daily practices. Because of his inattentiveness and distractibility secondary to the ADHD, he greatly benefited from the step-by-step daily expectations set out in the workbook, and the need for regular documentation, which kept him on track. Instead of feeling constrained by the structure of the program, he felt liberated by it.

Table 12.2 shows Joe's pre-post scores. In addition to a reduction in symptoms, Joe also experienced an improvement in his mental wellness. His adherence was not perfect (Table 12.3), but perfection is not a goal of the 30- and the 90-day programs. Joe described the program as "very helpful" and considered physical exercise as his "most helpful" wellness strategy. He said his overall wellness improved 30% as a result of participating in KickStart30—his provider noted that in the ten years he had been seeing her, he had never shown a 30% improvement with medication alone.

TABLE 12.2 JOE'S PRE-POST PROGRESS

Measure	Instrument	Before	After	Improvement
Depression severity	PHQ-9	22	19	14%
Anxiety	GAD-7	13	11	15%
Sleep	PSQI	13	12	8%
Emotional eating	DEBQ	27	14	48%
Social connectedness	SCS	14	22	57%
Well-being	WHO-5	4	5	25%

TABLE 12.3 JOE'S ADHERENCE RATES

Element	Frequency		Percent Adherence
	Recommended Days	Actual Days	
Exercise	30	20	67%
Mindfulness	30	15	50%
Sleep	30	17	57%
Social connectedness	30	29	97%
Nutrition	30	25	83%

At this point, Joe is two years out from having finished his 30-day wellness program and continues to use most of his wellness interventions. He continues to track his daily practices, documenting and sharing the participant tracking form with his provider at each visit. He is walking 10,000 steps per day, is socializing more regularly, and is dating for the first time in 15 years. He follows a modified Mediterranean diet and over the last three years has lost significant weight: BMI is currently 23, and his fasting lipids are no longer elevated. Joe is described by his prescriber as stable, and his current medication regime consists now of only three medications—quite a change as compared to his previous medication lists.

Much can be learned from Joe's case. First, once again we see that even patients with severe impairment from their mental illness can benefit from wellness interventions—wellness enhancement may be a slow and rocky journey, but it is an achievable task. And, access to a structured wellness program strongly contributed to Joe's success: for 30 years clinicians told him to eat better, exercise more, socialize more, etc., but none of that was as effective as a simple guidebook that held him accountable for his daily practices. Wellness interventions can have long-lasting positive benefits for an individual. Good habits can be created in as little as 30 days, and if appropriately motivated, patients often continue these practices and receive ongoing benefits.

Shirley: Osteoarthritis, Rheumatoid Arthritis, Chronic Pain, Major Depression, and Generalized Anxiety

Shirley worked as a middle school science teacher for many decades, until chronic pain and depression forced her into early retirement. Now in her early seventies, suffering from chronic pain due to osteoarthritis (OA) and rheumatoid arthritis (RA), along with co-existing depression, generalized anxiety, and insomnia, she sought treatment. She currently receives her medical care from both her internist and her rheumatologist. She recently told her internist that she was feeling hopeless about her mental or physical conditions ever improving. Her internist, upon hearing her struggles with mental health, referred her to one of our wellness studies.

Shirley approached the WILD 5 Wellness study with a lot of trepidation. After all, as she reasoned with us on the phone, how is increasing her mental wellness going to help her deal with chronic pain, depression, anxiety, and insomnia? We explained to Shirley that wellness interventions were often "two for the price of one": they not only offer improvements in mental illness markers but also can positively impact both inflammation and its resultant impairments. Clearly skeptical, she nevertheless agreed to the wellness intervention, stating, "I guess I don't have much to lose, and my doctor really seems to think it will help me."

Because of her significant pain and skeletal impairments caused by her OA and RA, we modified the daily exercise requirement to suit her abilities. Much to her credit, Shirley wholeheartedly threw herself into the wellness program. She wrote to us just a week after starting the program to state she was amazed that her sleep showed significant improvement and she even had less pain. She wrote that she felt empowered and ready to engage in the wellness program. We were obviously pleased to hear her report and encouraged her to continue.

TABLE 12.4 SHIRLEY'S PRE/POST PROGRESS

Measure	Instrument	Before	After	Improvement
Depression severity	PHQ-9	14	8	43%
Anxiety	GAD-7	15	9	40%
Pain (worst)	BPI: Q3	7	4	43%
Emotional eating	DEBQ	60	114	90%
Social connectedness	SCS	21	48	129%
Well-being	WHO-5	10	17	70%
Happiness	HERO Wellness Scale	4	6	50%
Enthusiasm	HERO Wellness Scale	3	6	100%
Resilience	HERO Wellness Scale	3	7	133%
Optimism	HERO Wellness Scale	2	3	50%

By the time Shirley finished the study, she had achieved great improvements in both her psychiatric disease markers and the HERO wellness traits, as well as lessened pain (Table 12.4). She still contacts us every few months to share her progress: she reports she is continuing to do well and is experiencing global improvement in both her chronic pain symptoms and mental health.

Shirley's case illustrates that wellness interventions are effective in individuals who may have both mind and body disorders and symptomology. She demonstrates the rather quick benefits in both mind symptoms (e.g., depression, anxiety) and body symptoms (e.g., pain, fatigue) an individual can derive from such interventions.

A Patient's Personal Story of Success

Rheumatologist Hillary Norton referred one of her patients to a WILD 5 Wellness study. After completing the 90-day wellness program, this patient, a 66-year-old happily married woman who suffered from rheumatoid arthritis and depression for over two decades, provided a firsthand description of the ups and downs of changing lifestyle behaviors and moving closer to a wellness-centric life:

> I started the WILD 5 Wellness program without any expectations. I was only sure of two things: (1) I was sick and tired of being sick and tired, and (2) nothing I had done up to this point seemed to be getting me over the hump both mentally and physically. I am 66 years old, I have rheumatoid arthritis, I'm overweight, I've had insomnia since childhood, I have high blood pressure, anxiety/depression, and I was trying to deal with stress, basically like almost every other person out there. The program focuses on 5 vital areas of well-being, all of which were foreign to me. Nutrition—my basic food groups were sugar, caffeine, fat, and salt. Exercise—the only exercise I was doing most days was jumping to conclusions. Sleep—hmmm . . . what a concept. Socialization—like go out and socialize, oh dear, and now we come to Meditation—oh great!

Next, I'll be buying crystals and burning incense, I don't know how to sit, what do I do with my hands? Do I hum?

I decided that I would look at this new adventure as if I was going on a journey. I then prepared for my trip. I have my program guide which is like a tour book. I committed myself, that's like buying a non-refundable ticket, refrigerator and cupboards packed (like luggage), meditation tapes are downloaded (like a good book), new, broken-in athletic shoes (like a new outfit for traveling), mindfulness meditation time and location set (like an itinerary), friends/family notified (like informing them that I may need their help if I run into trouble), food log/journal ready (like places I'd like to eat), exercise plan (like places of interest).

Nothing makes you want to stick to something more than to share it with another person. Knowing that they will be asking how you're doing. I figured if I told a few friends about my new program then I was certain they would ask me how I was doing, and I didn't want to say I'd given up. My family was instrumental in this new lifestyle change. My kids always encouraged me and were interested to know about my progress. The verbal pats on the back are priceless. My dear husband joined me on my walks and occasionally his gentle urging got me to my feet. I don't know how it happened, but at some point I felt that if I didn't go for a walk somehow, I was impeding his progress (maybe some kind of reverse psychology was in play). Knowing I have their support and positive reinforcement, I can continue on my journey with confidence.

Food: oh no, I don't want to eat healthy stuff, it's boring. What a wonderful surprise! Eating tasty, healthy food is satisfying and filling. I love to cook, so why not just make the suggested foods interesting and tasty? I still miss my beans with salt pork, homemade tortillas, red chile, and fried potatoes. So, I decided to raise my favorite foods to a higher level. Now they have become special treats which have a higher status, like a Christmas cookie you only have during the holidays. Much more satisfying than a standard, go-to meal.

Exercise: I can't, I have RA, it hurts. I started out walking around my neighborhood. I walked like a penguin, and very slowly. There were many times I had to stop along the way, to catch my breath or to ask myself if I really wanted to continue or go back. I continued, I knew I would feel better about myself if I did. There have been times I have not been able to go for a 30-minute walk because of joint pain, but whatever amount of time I walk, it's better than not. I still walk like a penguin, but with purpose and on occasion I walk up to 40 minutes and at a quicker pace, feels good.

Sleep: Ahhh, that wonderful thing I hear so much about. Following the recommended six sleep hygiene practices helped tremendously. I still struggle with my insomnia, but I am sleeping more, and my quality of sleep is much improved.

Socializing: I text and email often but getting out to visit a friend or go to an event was becoming harder for me. I'm getting out more and enjoying myself.

Meditation: What is that? That was the biggest surprise and the best gift of the program. I love that it can be done anywhere, anytime, and it works! It's the best stress-reliever and pain-reducer I can do for myself.

I have to say that the HERO practices were challenging for me, especially the part when you're asked to write something positive about yourself. As I got further along in the program, I started to learn a lot about myself. I'm not too shabby. I'm not just the out of step, kooky, unfiltered person I see myself as—well, actually, I am that person, but I also have other qualities as well.

Being on the program has made me mindful, present, has increased my gratitude, my awareness, my listening skills. It has decreased my pain, my anxiety/depression, and has even regulated my high blood pressure. With each stick of butter I lose, I am able to walk more and feel better.

After the first 90 days I realized those were excursions. I'm not done, this is a lifetime journey. Some days are easier than others. I've gotten lost, frustrated, had to take a few detours, that lead to other detours, gone through tunnels hoping there was a light at the end only to find it was another train coming. I've had to learn to navigate uncharted paths, lost my footing, stumbled, and fallen. Surprisingly I've managed to get up again. All because I now have skills and tools to help me navigate through life.

Table 12.5 shows this patient's changes before and after participating in the 90-day wellness program. The HERO Wellness Scale shows this patient experienced the following pre-post improvements: happiness, 28%; enthusiasm, 80%; resilience, 100%; and optimism, 43%. And her rheumatologist reported that at the patient's last office visit her pre-post weight had decreased from 226 lbs. to 212 lbs. Her blood pressure had gone from a high of 138/88 down to 112/74. Her erythrocyte sedimentation rate, a marker of inflammation, had been at the highest 42 and was 25 at her last office visit. She reported that her RA pain had improved. In fact, her global assessment of pain at the follow up visit with her rheumatologist was 2/10, a sharp decrease from 9/10 noted at her previous office visit. We are happy to report that this patient continues enjoying her wellness journey.

TABLE 12.5 DR. NORTON'S PATIENT: PRE/POST SCORES

Measure	Instrument	Before	After	Improvement
Depression severity	PHQ-9	16	9	44%
Anxiety	GAD-7	14	7	50%
Pain (worst)	BPI: Q3	7	3	57%
Pain (least)	BPI: Q4	3	1	67%
Mindful awareness	MAAS	61	88	44%
Well-being	WHO-5	13	23	77%

These cases give you a glimpse of what is possible when augmenting your current treatment strategies with wellness-enhancing practices. These cases can all be considered "difficult" and perhaps even "resistant." Melissa and Joe had at best achieved sub-optimum results from their previous therapies, and Shirley and Dr. Norton's patient had significant physical as well as mental difficulties. For all four, adding a wellness program improved both their disease symptoms and their wellness levels, and we have every reason to believe that such programs can help many of your patients, too.

Final Thoughts from Authors

Adding wellness-centric interventions to routine care improves clinical outcomes in a wide array of clinical presentations. We and others have demonstrated such improvements in social connectedness, work and home functioning, mindfulness, happiness, enthusiasm, resilience, optimism, and overall mental wellness. All of these factors are indeed the spice of life. It is time that all of us healthcare professionals—prescribers and non-prescribers alike—examine the new science supporting the ancient and modern wisdom regarding wellness and integrate it into our clinical practices. After all, wellness interventions *do not replace* anything psychiatry and psychotherapy already offers its patients—rather, the *addition* of wellness-centric interventions helps psychiatrists and psychotherapists offer their patients even better outcomes.

As we end this book, we offer gratitude to you, dear reader, for spending time with us as we explored the world of wellness, happiness, enthusiasm, resilience, and optimism. We wish you, and your patients, all these HERO wellness traits in great abundance.

References

Aburn, G., Gott, M., & Hoare, K. (2016). What is resilience? An integrative review of the empirical literature. *Journal of Advanced Nursing, 72*(5), 980–1000. doi:10.1111/jan.12888

Adler, L. A., Spencer, T., Faraone, S. V., Kessler, R. C., Howes, M. J., Biederman, J., & Secnik, K. (2006). Validity of pilot adult ADHD Self- Report Scale (ASRS) to rate adult ADHD symptoms. *Annals of Clinical Psychiatry, 18*(3), 145–148. doi:10.1080/10401230600801077

Alsharif, N. Z., & Qi, Y. (2014). A three-year study of the impact of instructor attitude, enthusiasm, and teaching style on student learning in a medicinal chemistry course. *American Journal of Pharmaceutical Education, 78*(7), 132. doi:10.5688/ajpe787132

Amutio, A., Martínez-Taboada, C., Hermosilla, D., & Delgado, L. C. (2015). Enhancing relaxation states and positive emotions in physicians through a mindfulness training program: A one-year study. *Psychology, Health & Medicine, 20*(6), 720–731. doi:10.1080/13548506.2014.986143

APA website (2009). Physical inactivity poses great health risk to Americans, research shows. Retrieved June 21, 2019, from https://www.apa.org/news/press/releases/2009/08/physical-inactivity

APA Clinical Practice Guidelines. Retrieved June 21, 2019, from https://www.psychiatry.org/psychiatrists/practice/clinical-practice-guidelines

Apodaca, T. R., & Longabaugh, R. (2009). Mechanisms of change in motivational interviewing: A review and preliminary evaluation of the evidence. *Addiction, 104*(5), 705–715. doi:10.1111/j.1360-0443.2009.02527.x

Barker, E. (2018). Epigenetics, early adversity and child and adolescent mental health. *Psychopathology, 51*(2), 71–75. doi:10.1159/000486683

Bartekova, M., Radosinska, J., Jelemensky, M., & Dhalla, N. S. (2018). Role of cytokines and inflammation in heart function during health and disease. *Heart Failure Reviews, 23*(5), 733–758. doi:10.1007/s10741-018-9716-x

Benzo, R. P., Kirsch, J. L., & Nelson, C. (2017). Compassion, mindfulness, and the happiness of healthcare workers. *Explore, 13*(3), 201–206. doi:10.1016/j.explore.2017.02.001

Berridge, K., & Kringelbach, M. (2015). Pleasure systems in the brain. *Neuron, 86*(3), 646–664. doi:10.1016/j.neuron.2015.02.018

Bhatti, N., & Viney, R. (2017). Transforming the lives and careers of senior doctors: Retaining and harnessing skills and enthusiasm in difficult times. *British Journal of General Practice, 67*(663), 461–461. doi:10.3399/bjgp17x692813

Bhutan's Gross National Happiness Index. Retrieved June 21, 2019, from https://ophi.org.uk/policy/national-policy/gross-national-happiness-index/

Birkeland, M. S., Blix, I., Solberg, Ø, & Heir, T. (2017). Does optimism act as a buffer against posttraumatic stress over time? A longitudinal study of the protective role of optimism after the 2011 Oslo bombing. *Psychological Trauma: Theory, Research, Practice, and Policy, 9*(2), 207–213. doi:10.1037/tra0000188

Black, D. S., & Slavich, G. M. (2016). Mindfulness meditation and the immune system: A systematic review of randomized controlled trials. *Annals of the New York Academy of Sciences, 1373*(1), 13–24. doi:10.1111/nyas.12998

Boecker, H., Sprenger, T., Spilker, M. E., Henriksen, G., Koppenhoefer, M., Wagner, K. J., . . . Tolle, T. R. (2008). The runners high: Opioidergic mechanisms in the human brain. *Cerebral Cortex, 18*(11), 2523–2531. doi:10.1093/cercor/bhn013

Boen, C. E., Barrow, D. A., Bensen, J. T., Farnan, L., Gerstel, A., Hendrix, L. H., & Yang, Y. C. (2018). Social relationships, inflammation, and cancer survival. *Cancer Epidemiology Biomarkers & Prevention, 27*(5), 541–549. doi:10.1158/1055-9965.epi-17-0836

Bonaccio, M., Di Castelnuovo, A., Costanzo, S., Pounis, G., Persichillo, M., Cerletti, C., . . . Iacoviello, L. (2017). Mediterranean-type diet is associated with higher psychological resilience in a general adult population: Findings from the Moli-sani study. *European Journal of Clinical Nutrition, 72*(1), 154–160. doi:10.1038/ejcn.2017.150

Boselie, J. J., Vancleef, L. M., & Peters, M. L. (2017). Increasing optimism protects against pain-induced impairment in task-shifting performance. *The Journal of Pain, 18*(4), 446–455. doi:10.1016/j.jpain.2016.12.007

Bozikas, V., & Parlapani, E. (2016). Resilience in patients with psychotic disorder. *Psychiatriki, 27*(1), 13–16.

Burhouse, A., Rowland, M., Niman, H. M., Abraham, D., Collins, E., Matthews, H., . . . Ryland, H. (2015). Coaching for recovery: A quality improvement project in mental healthcare. *BMJ Quality Improvement Reports, 4*(1). doi:10.1136/bmjquality.u206576.w2641

Business Insider (2013). Venezuela Creates 'Vice Ministry Of Supreme Social Happiness' To Combat Sadness. Retrieved on June 24, 2019, from https://www.businessinsider.com/venezuela-creates-vice-ministry-of-supreme-social-happiness-to-combat-sadness-2013-10

Carek, P. J., Laibstain, S. E., & Carek, S. M. (2011). Exercise for the treatment of depression and anxiety. *The International Journal of Psychiatry in Medicine, 41*(1), 15–28. doi:10.2190/pm.41.1.c

Carlson, L. E., Speca, M., Faris, P., & Patel, K. D. (2007). One year pre–post intervention follow-up of psychological, immune, endocrine and blood pressure outcomes of mindfulness-based stress reduction (MBSR) in breast and prostate cancer outpatients. *Brain, Behavior, and Immunity, 21*(8), 1038-1049. doi:10.1016/j.bbi.2007.04.002

Carver, C. S., & Scheier, M. F. (2014). Dispositional optimism. *Trends in Cognitive Sciences, 18*(6), 293–299. doi:10.1016/j.tics.2014.02.003

Celano, C. M. (2011). Secondary prevention of cardiovascular disease: CBT, in combination with standard care, is effective. *Evidence-Based Mental Health, 14*(3), 81–81. doi:10.1136/ebmh1181

Center for Medicare and Medicaid Services (2019). Retrieved on June 21, 2019 from https://www.cms.gov/medicare-coverage-database/details/nca-decision-memo.aspx?NCAId=251)

Cohen, S. (2004). Social relationships and health. *American Psychologist, 59*(8), 676–684. doi:10.1037/0003-066x.59.8.676

Crawford, M. J., Robotham, D., Thana, L., Patterson, S., Weaver, T., Barber, R., . . . Rose, D. (2011). Selecting outcome measures in mental health: The views of service users. *Journal of Mental Health, 20*(4), 336–346. doi:10.3109/09638237.2011.577114

Creswell, J. D., Taren, A. A., Lindsay, E. K., Greco, C. M., Gianaros, P. J., Fairgrieve, A., . . . Ferris, J. L. (2016). Alterations in resting-state functional connectivity link mindfulness meditation with reduced interleukin-6: A randomized controlled trial. *Biological Psychiatry, 80*(1), 53–61. doi:10.1016/j.biopsych.2016.01.008

Dailey, R., Romo, L., Myer, S., Thomas, C., Aggarwal, S., Nordby, K., . . . Dunn, C. (2018). The Buddy Benefit: Increasing the Effectiveness of an Employee-Targeted Weight-Loss Program. *Journal of Health Communication, 23*(3), 272–280. doi:10.1080/10810730.2018.1436622

Das, A. (2016). Psychosocial distress and inflammation: Which way does causality flow? *Social Science & Medicine, 170*, 1–8. doi:10.1016/j.socscimed.2016.10.001

Daukantaitė, D., & Zukauskiene, R. (2012). Optimism and subjective well-being: Affectivity plays a secondary role in the relationship between optimism and global life satisfaction in the middle-aged women. Longitudinal and cross-cultural findings. *Journal of Happiness Studies, 13*(1), 1–16. doi:10.1007/s10902-010-9246-2

De Almondes, K. M., Costa, M. V., Malloy-Diniz, L. F., & Diniz, B. S. (2016). Insomnia and risk of dementia in older adults: Systematic review and meta-analysis. *Journal of Psychiatric Research, 77*, 109–115. doi:10.1016/j.jpsychires.2016.02.021

Demiris, G., Thompson, H. J., Reeder, B., Wilamowska, K., & Zaslavsky, O. (2013). Using informatics to capture older adults' wellness. *International Journal of Medical Informatics, 82*(11), e232–e241. doi:10.1016/j.ijmedinf.2011.03.004

Demyttenaere, K., Donneau, A., Albert, A., Ansseau, M., Constant, E., & Van Heeringen, K. (2015). What is important in being cured from depression? Discordance between physicians and patients (1). *Journal of Affective Disorders, 174*, 390–396. doi:10.1016/j.jad.2014.12.004

Desmond, T. (2016). *Self-compassion in psychotherapy: Mindfulness-based practices for healing and transformation.* New York, NY: W.W. Norton & Company.

Diagnostic and statistical manual of mental disorders (5th Ed). (2013). Washington DC: American Psychiatric Association.

Dolcos, S., Hu, Y., Iordan, A. D., Moore, M., & Dolcos, F. (2016). Optimism and the brain: Trait optimism mediates the protective role of the orbitofrontal cortex gray matter volume against anxiety. *Social Cognitive and Affective Neuroscience, 11*(2), 263–271. doi:10.1093/scan/nsv106

Dowlati, Y., Ravindran, A. V., Segal, Z. V., Stewart, D. E., Steiner, M., & Meyer, J. H. (2017). Selective dietary supplementation in early postpartum is associated with high resilience against depressed mood. *Proceedings of the National Academy of Sciences, 114*(13), 3509–3514. doi:10.1073/pnas.1611965114

D'raven, L. L., & Pasha-Zaidi, N. (2014). Happiness strategies among Arab university students in the United Arab Emirates. *Journal of Happiness and Well-Being. 2*(1), 1–15. Retrieved June 19, 2019, from https://www.journalofhappiness.net/

article/happiness-strategies-among-arab-university-students-in-the-united
-arab-emirates

Duman, C. H., & Duman, R. S. (2015). Spine synapse remodeling in the patho-physiology and treatment of depression. *Neuroscience Letters, 601*, 20–29. doi:10.1016/j.neulet.2015.01.022

Dunlop, B. W., Gray, J., & Rapaport, M. H. (2017). Transdiagnostic clinical global impression scoring for routine clinical settings. *Behavioral Sciences, 7*(3), 40. doi:10.3390/bs7030040

Emerson, S. D., & Carbert, N. S. (2018). An apple a day: Protective associations between nutrition and the mental health of immigrants in Canada. *Social Psychiatry and Psychiatric Epidemiology, 54*(5), 567–578. doi:10.1007/s00127-018-1616-9

Erickson, K. I., Voss, M. W., Prakash, R. S., Basak, C., Szabo, A., Chaddock, L., . . . Kramer, A. F. (2011). Exercise training increases size of hippocampus and improves memory. *Proceedings of the National Academy of Sciences, 108*(7), 3017–3022. doi:10.1073/pnas.1015950108

Erogul, M., Singer, G., Mcintyre, T., & Stefanov, D. G. (2014). Abridged mindfulness intervention to support wellness in first-year medical students. *Teaching and Learning in Medicine, 26*(4), 350–356. doi:10.1080/10401334.2014.945025

Evans, S., Ferrando, S., Findler, M., Stowell, C., Smart, C., & Haglin, D. (2008). Mindfulness-based cognitive therapy for generalized anxiety disorder. *Journal of Anxiety Disorders, 22*(4), 716–721. doi:10.1016/j.janxdis.2007.07.005.

Fava, G. A., Ruini, C., Rafanelli, C., Finos, L., Salmaso, L., Mangelli, L., & Sirigatti, S. (2005). Well-being therapy of generalized anxiety disorder. *Psychotherapy and Psychosomatics, 74*(1), 26–30. doi:10.1159/000082023

Fava, G. A., Rafanelli, C., Tomba, E., Guidi, J., & Grandi, S. (2011). The sequential combination of cognitive behavioral treatment and well-being therapy in cyclothymic disorder. *Psychotherapy and Psychosomatics, 80*(3), 136–143. doi:10.1159/000321575

Fava, G. A. (2016). Well-being therapy: Current indications and emerging perspectives. *Psychotherapy and Psychosomatics, 85*(3), 136–145. doi:10.1159/000444114

Fava, G. A. (2016). *Well-being therapy: Treatment manual and clinical applications.* Basel: Karger.

Fava, G. A., Cosci, F., Guidi, J., & Tomba, E. (2017). Well-being therapy in depression: New insights into the role of psychological well-being in the clinical process. *Depression and Anxiety, 34*(9), 801–808. doi:10.1002/da.22629

Fong L.F. & Guthery A. (2018, October). *The Effects of Mindfulness on Depression and Anxiety.* Research poster presented at the 31st Annual US Psychiatric CongressMeeting, Orlando, FL.

Ford, B. Q., Dmitrieva, J. O., Heller, D., Chentsova-Dutton, Y., Grossmann, I., Tamir, M., . . . Mauss, I. B. (2015). Culture shapes whether the pursuit of happiness predicts higher or lower well-being. *Journal of Experimental Psychology: General, 144*(6), 1053–1062. doi:10.1037/xge0000108

Forgeard, M., & Seligman, M. (2012). Seeing the glass half full: A review of the causes and consequences of optimism. *Pratiques Psychologiques, 18*(2), 107–120. doi:10.1016/j.prps.2012.02.002

Fraser, S. J., Chapman, J. J., Brown, W. J., Whiteford, H. A., & Burton, N. W. (2015). Physical activity attitudes and preferences among inpatient adults with mental illness. *International Journal of Mental Health Nursing, 24*(5), 413–420. doi:10.1111/inm.12158

Frodl, T. S., Koutsouleris, N., Bottlender, R., Born, C., Jäger, M., Scupin, I., . . . Meisenzahl, E. M. (2008). Depression-related variation in brain morphology over 3 years. *Archives of General Psychiatry, 65*(10), 1156-1165. doi:10.1001/archpsyc.65.10.1156

Gallup, Inc. (2018, January 10). Gallup's Top Well-Being Findings of 2017. Retrieved June 20, 2019, from https://news.gallup.com/poll/224675/gallup-top-findings-2017.aspx

Gallup-Sharecare. (2018, February). State of American Well-Being: 2017 State Well-Being Rankings. Retrieved June 20, 2019, from https://wellbeingindex.sharecare.com/wp-content/uploads/2018/02/Gallup-Sharecare-State-of-American-Well-Being_2017-State-Rankings_FINAL.pdf

Girard T. M., Klawitter C., Lopez, S., Santos Esperanza, J., Nikora, R., Raison, C., . . . Jain, S. (2017, September). *Application of WILD 5, a Wellness Intervention at Beloit College, Wisconsin Student Population.* Research poster presented at the 30th Annual US Psychiatric Congress Meeting, New Orleans, LA.

Goh, J., Goh, K. P., & Abbasi, A. (2016). Exercise and adipose tissue macrophages: New frontiers in obesity research? *Frontiers in Endocrinology, 7*(65), 1–8. doi:10.3389/fendo.2016.00065

Grandner, M. A. (2017). Sleep, health, and society. *Sleep Medicine Clinics, 12*(1), 1–22. doi:10.1016/j.jsmc.2016.10.012

Greenberg, T., Carlson, J. M., Rubin, D., Cha, J., & Mujica-Parodi, L. (2014). Anticipation of high arousal aversive and positive movie clips engages common and distinct neural substrates. *Social Cognitive and Affective Neuroscience, 10*(4), 605–611. doi:10.1093/scan/nsu091

Gruber, J., Mauss, I. B., & Tamir, M. (2011). A dark side of happiness? How, when, and why happiness is not always good. *Perspectives on Psychological Science, 6*(3), 222–233. doi:10.1177/1745691611406927

Guo, J., Mrug, S., & Knight, D. C. (2017). Emotion socialization as a predictor of physiological and psychological responses to stress. *Physiology & Behavior, 175*, 119–129. doi:10.1016/j.physbeh.2017.03.046

Gupta, A., Love, A., Kilpatrick, L. A., Labus, J. S., Bhatt, R., Chang, L., . . . Mayer, E. A. (2016). Morphological brain measures of cortico-limbic inhibition related to resilience. *Journal of Neuroscience Research, 95*(9), 1760–1775. doi:10.1002/jnr.24007

Hanssen MM, Peters ML, Vlaeyen JW, Meevissen YM, Vancleef LM. (2013). Optimism lowers pain: evidence of the causal status and underlying mechanisms. Pain, Jan;154(1):53–8. doi: 10.1016/j.pain.2012.08.006

Harris R, Hayes SC. (2007). The happiness trap: how to stop struggling and start living: a guide to ACT. Published by Trumepeter Books. ISBN978-1-59030-584-3

Hart, P. L., Brannan, J. D., & De Chesnay, M. (2012). Resilience in nurses: An integrative review. *Journal of Nursing Management, 22*(6), 720–734. doi:10.1111/j.1365-2834.2012.01485.x

Hayasaka, Y., Furukawa, T. A., Sozu, T., Imai, H., Kawakami, N., & Horikoshi, M. (2015). Enthusiasm for homework and improvement of psychological distress in subthreshold depression during behavior therapy: Secondary analysis of data from a randomized controlled trial. *BMC Psychiatry, 15*(302), 1–11 . doi:10.1186/s12888-015-0687-3

Heinzelmann, M., Lee, H., Rak, H., Livingston, W., Barr, T., Baxter, T., . . . Gill, J. (2014). Sleep restoration is associated with reduced plasma C-reactive protein and depression symptoms in military personnel with sleep disturbance after deployment. *Sleep Medicine, 15*(12), 1565–1570. doi:10.1016/j.sleep.2014.08.004

Helliwell, J., Layard, R., & Sachs, J. (Eds.). (2017, March 20). *World Happiness Report 2017* (Publication No. ISBN 978-0-9968513-5-0). Retrieved June 20, 2019, from Sustainable Development Solutions Network website: https://worldhappiness.report/ed/2017/

Heyman, E., Gamelin, F., Goekint, M., Piscitelli, F., Roelands, B., Leclair, E., . . . Meeusen, R. (2012). Intense exercise increases circulating endocannabinoid and BDNF levels in humans—Possible implications for reward and depression. *Psychoneuroendocrinology, 37*(6), 844–851. doi:10.1016/j.psyneuen.2011.09.017

Hobden, B., Schwandt, M. L., Carey, M., Lee, M. R., Farokhnia, M., Bouhlal, S., . . . Leggio, L. (2017). The validity of the Montgomery–Asberg Depression Rating Scale in an inpatient sample with alcohol dependence. *Alcoholism: Clinical & Experimental Research, 41*(6), 1220-1227. doi:10.1111/acer.13400

Holt-Lunstad, J., Smith, T. B., & Layton, J. B. (2010). Social relationships and mortality risk: A meta-analytic review. *PLoS Medicine, 7*(7), e1000316, 1–20. doi:10.1371/journal.pmed.1000316

Hölzel, B. K., Ott, U., Gard, T., Hempel, H., Weygandt, M., Morgen, K., & Vaitl, D. (2007). Investigation of mindfulness meditation practitioners with voxel-based morphometry. *Social Cognitive and Affective Neuroscience, 3*(1), 55–61. doi:10.1093/scan/nsm038

Hölzel, B.K., Carmody, J., Vangel, M., Congleton, C., Yerramsetti, S.M., Gard, T., Lazar, S.W. (2011). Mindfulness practice leads to increases in regional brain gray matter density. *Psychiatric Research.* Jan 30;191(1):36–43. doi: 10.1016/j.pscychresns.2010.08.006

Hölzel, B. K., Carmody, J., Evans, K. C., Hoge, E. A., Dusek, J. A., Morgan, L., . . . Lazar, S. W. (2010). Stress reduction correlates with structural changes in the amygdala. *Social Cognitive and Affective Neuroscience, 5*(1), 11–17. doi:10.1093/scan/nsp034

Hoyman, H. S. (1975). Rethinking an ecologic-system model of mans health, disease, aging, death. *Journal of School Health, 45*(9), 509-518. doi:10.1111/j.1746-1561.1975.tb04527.x

Intlekofer, K. A., & Cotman, C. W. (2013). Exercise counteracts declining hippocampal function in aging and Alzheimers disease. *Neurobiology of Disease, 57*, 47–55. doi:10.1016/j.nbd.2012.06.011

Irwin, M. R. (2015). Why sleep is important for health: A psychoneuroimmunology perspective. *Annual Review of Psychology, 66*(1), 143-172. doi:10.1146/annurev-psych-010213-115205

Irwin, M. R., Olmstead, R., & Carroll, J. E. (2016). Sleep disturbance, sleep duration, and inflammation: A systematic review and meta-analysis of cohort studies and experimental sleep deprivation. *Biological Psychiatry, 80*(1), 40–52. doi:10.1016/j.biopsych.2015.05.014

Jain, R., Jain, S., Raison, C.L,, Maletic, V. (2011). Painful diabetic neuropathy is more than pain alone: examining the role of anxiety and depression as mediators and complicators.Current Diabetes Report. Aug;11(4):275–84. doi: 10.1007/s11892-011-0202-2

Jain R. & Jain S. (2017, September). *Chronic Pain Patients on Opioids - Examining the Impact on Pain and Mental Illness Symptoms After a 30-day WILD 5 Wellness Based Intervention*. Research poster presented at the 30th Annual US Psychiatric Congress Meeting, New Orleans, LA.

Jain S., Jain, R., & Kumar, L. M. (2015, September). *WILD 5 Wellness: Impact of a Five-Pronged (Exercise, Mindfulness, Sleep, Social Connectedness & Nutrition) 30-Day Wellness Program on Mood, Mindfulness, Sleep Behvior, Social Connectedness, Emotional Eating and Mental Wellness*. Research poster presented at the 28th Annual US Psychiatric Congress Meeting, San Diego, CA.

Jain S., Daniels, N., Grantham, S., Simpson, J. A., Veenhuizen, J., & Jain, R. (2016, October[a]). *Description of WILD 5 Wellness Program and Its Utility in Individuals Suffering from a Psychiatric Illness: Results from a 30-day Intervention and an Optional 90-day Extension Phase*. Research poster presented at the 29th Annual US Psychiatric Congress Meeting, San Antonio, TX.

Jain S., Daniels, N., Gonzales, A., Grantham, S., Simpson, J. A., Veenhuizen, J., & Jain, R. (2016, October[b]). *Effectiveness of a 30-day Wellness Program in Individuals with Chronic Pain, with and without Mental Illness*. Research poster presented at the 29th Annual US Psychiatric Congress Meeting, San Antonio, TX.

Jain S., Rolin D., & Jain R. (2017, September[a]). *Cognitive and Physical Function Improvements and Mood and Anxiety Improvements After Undergoing WILD 5 Wellness, a 30-day Wellness Intervention in Individuals Self-identified as Suffering from a Psychiatric Disorder*. Research poster presented at the 30th Annual US Psychiatric Congress Meeting, New Orleans, LA.

Jain S. & Jain R. (2017, September[b]). *Application of WILD 5, a Wellness Intervention in Individuals Taking Psychotropic Medications Yet Have a Moderate or Higher Severity of Depression (PHQ-9 Score of 10 or Higher)*. Research poster presented at the 30th Annual US Psychiatric Congress Meeting, New Orleans, LA.

Jain S., Cole, S. P., Girard, T. M., Raison, C., & Jain R. (2017, September[c]). *HERO Wellness Scale: Examining the Validity and Reliability of a New Mental Wellness Scale*. Research poster presented at the 30th Annual US Psychiatric Congress Meeting, New Orleans, LA.

Jain, S., Jain, R., & Burns, B. (2019). *WILD 5 Wellness KickStart30: A Proven 30-Day Mental Wellness Program*. Austin, TX: Self-Published. Retrieved June 21, 2019, from https://www.amazon.com/WILD-Wellness-KickStart30-Proven-Program/dp/1791658806.

Jain, S., Jain, R., & Burns, B. (2019). *WILD 5 Wellness LiveWell90: A Proven 90-Day Mental Wellness Program*. Austin, TX: Self-Published. Retrieved June 21, 2019, from https://www.amazon.com/WILD-Wellness-LiveWell90-Proven -Program/dp/1798210835.

Jansson-Fröjmark, M., & Lindblom, K. (2008). A bidirectional relationship between anxiety and depression, and insomnia? A prospective study in the general population. *Journal of Psychosomatic Research, 64*(4), 443–449. doi:10.1016/j.jpsychores.2007.10.016

Jeste, D. V., & Palmer, B. W. (Eds.). (2015). *Positive Psychiatry: A Clinical Handbook*. Washington, DC: American Psychiatric Publishing.

Jeste, D. V., Palmer, B. W., Rettew, D. C., & Boardman, S. (2015). Positive psychiatry. *The Journal of Clinical Psychiatry, 76*(6), 675–683. doi:10.4088/jcp.14nr09599

Jha, M. K., Minhajuddin, A., Gadad, B. S., Greer, T., Grannemann, B., Soyombo, A., . . . Trivedi, M. H. (2017). Can C-reactive protein inform antidepressant medication selection in depressed outpatients? Findings from the CO-MED trial. *Psychoneuroendocrinology, 78*, 105–113. doi:10.1016/j.psyneuen.2017.01.023

Jimison, H. B., Klein, K. A., & Marcoe, J. L. (2013). A socialization intervention in remote health coaching for older adults in the home. *2013 35th Annual International Conference of the IEEE Engineering in Medicine and Biology Society (EMBC)*, 7025–7028. doi:10.1109/embc.2013.6611175

Johnson, B. T., & Acabchuk, R. L. (2018). What are the keys to a longer, happier life? Answers from five decades of health psychology research. *Social Science & Medicine, 196*, 218–226. doi:10.1016/j.socscimed.2017.11.001

Kampert, A. L., & Goreczny, A. J. (2007). Community involvement and socialization among individuals with mental retardation. *Research in Developmental Disabilities, 28*(3), 278–286. doi:10.1016/j.ridd.2005.09.004

Kenny, M. A., & Williams, J. M. (2007). Treatment-resistant depressed patients show a good response to Mindfulness-based Cognitive Therapy. *Behaviour Research and Therapy, 45*(3), 617–625. doi:10.1016/j.brat.2006.04.008

Khazaee-Pool, M., Sadeghi, R., Majlessi, F., & Foroushani, A. R. (2015). Effects of physical exercise programme on happiness among older people. *Journal of Psychiatric and Mental Health Nursing, 22*(1), 47–57. doi:10.1111/jpm.12168

Kiecolt-Glaser, J., Christian, L., Preston, H., Houts, C., Malarkey, W., Emery, C., & Glaser, R. (2010). Stress, inflammation, and yoga practice. *Psychosomatic Medicine, 72*(2), 113–121. doi:10.1097/PSY.0b013e3181cb9377

Killingsworth, M. A., & Gilbert, D. T. (2010). A wandering mind Is an unhappy mind. *Science, 330*(6006), 932. doi:10.1126/science.1192439

Kim, B., Lee, S., Kim, Y. W., Choi, T. K., Yook, K., Suh, S. Y., . . . Yook, K. (2010). Effectiveness of a mindfulness-based cognitive therapy program as an adjunct to pharmacotherapy in patients with panic disorder. *Journal of Anxiety Disorders, 24*(6), 590–595. doi:10.1016/j.janxdis.2010.03.019

Kim, D., Kubzansky, L. D., Baccarelli, A., Sparrow, D., Spiro, A., Tarantini, L., . . . Schwartz, J. (2016). Psychological factors and DNA methylation of genes related to immune/inflammatory system markers: The VA Normative Aging Study. *BMJ Open, 6*(1), e009790, 1–10. doi:10.1136/bmjopen-2015-009790

Kim, D. A., Benjamin, E. J., Fowler, J. H., & Christakis, N. A. (2016). Social connectedness is associated with fibrinogen level in a human social network. *Proceedings of the Royal Society B: Biological Sciences, 283*(1837), 20160958th ser., 1–7. doi:10.1098/rspb.2016.0958

Kim, E. S., Hagan, K. A., Grodstein, F., Demeo, D. L., De Vivo, I., & Kubzansky, L. D. (2017). Optimism and cause-specific mortality: A prospective cohort study. *American Journal of Epidemiology, 185*(1), 21–29. doi:10.1093/aje/kww182

Kim-Prieto, C., Diener, E., Tamir, M., Scollon, C., & Diener, M. (2005). Integrating The diverse definitions of happiness: A time-sequential framework of subjective well-being. *Journal of Happiness Studies, 6*(3), 261–300. doi:10.1007/s10902-005-7226-8

Kleiman, E. M., Chiara, A. M., Liu, R. T., Jager-Hyman, S. G., Choi, J. Y., & Alloy, L. B. (2015). Optimism and well-being: A prospective multi-method and multi-dimensional examination of optimism as a resilience factor following the occurrence of stressful life events. *Cognition and Emotion, 31*(2), 269–283. doi:10.1080/02699931.2015.1108284

Kloiber, S., Ising, M., Reppermund, S., Horstmann, S., Dose, T., Majer, M., . . . Lucae, S. (2007). Overweight and Obesity Affect Treatment Response in Major Depression. *Biological Psychiatry, 62*(4), 321–326. doi:10.1016/j.biopsych.2006.10.001

Kopschina Feltes, P., Doorduin, J., Klein, H. C., Juárez-Orozco, L. E., Dierckx, R. A., Moriguchi-Jeckel, C. M., & De Vries, E. F. (2017). Anti-inflammatory treatment for major depressive disorder: Implications for patients with an elevated immune profile and non-responders to standard antidepressant therapy. *Journal of Psychopharmacology, 31*(9), 1149–1165. doi:10.1177/0269881117711708

Kraai, I., Vermeulen, K., Hillege, H., Jaarsma, T., & Hoekstra, T. (2017). Optimism and quality of life in patients with heart failure. *Palliative and Supportive Care, 16*(6), 725–731. doi:10.1017/s1478951517001055

Kraemer, W. J., Gordon, S. E., Fragala, M. S., Bush, J. A., Szivak, T. K., Flanagan, S. D., . . . Patton, J. F. (2015). The effects of exercise training programs on plasma concentrations of proenkephalin Peptide F and catecholamines. *Peptides, 64*, 74–81. doi:10.1016/j.peptides.2015.01.001

Krieger, T., Zimmermann, J., Huffziger, S., Ubl, B., Diener, C., Kuehner, C., & Holtforth, M. G. (2014). Measuring depression with a well-being index: Further evidence for the validity of the WHO Well-Being Index (WHO-5) as a measure of the severity of depression. *Journal of Affective Disorders, 156*, 240–244. doi:10.1016/j.jad.2013.12.015

Kringelbach, M. L., & Berridge, K. C. (2009). Towards a functional neuroanatomy of pleasure and happiness. *Trends in Cognitive Sciences, 13*(11), 479–487. doi:10.1016/j.tics.2009.08.006

Kroenke, K., Spitzer, R. L., & Williams, J. B. (2001). The PHQ-9: Validity of a brief depression severity measure. *Journal of General Internal Medicine, 16*(9), 606–613. doi:10.1046/j.1525-1497.2001.016009606.x

Lama, D., & Cutler, H. C. (1998). *The art of happiness: A handbook for living*. New York, NY: Riverhead Books.

Leigh-Hunt, N., Bagguley, D., Bash, K., Turner, V., Turnbull, S., Valtorta, N., & Caan, W. (2017). An overview of systematic reviews on the public health consequences of social isolation and loneliness. *Public Health, 152*, 157–171. doi:10.1016/j.puhe.2017.07.035

Lesani, A., Mohammadpoorasl, A., Javadi, M., Esfeh, J. M., & Fakhari, A. (2016). Eating breakfast, fruit and vegetable intake and their relation with happiness in college students. *Eating and Weight Disorders - Studies on Anorexia, Bulimia and Obesity, 21*(4), 645–651. doi:10.1007/s40519-016-0261-0

Lieberwirth, C., & Wang, Z. (2016). The neurobiology of pair bond formation, bond disruption, and social buffering. *Current Opinion in Neurobiology, 40*, 8–13. doi:10.1016/j.conb.2016.05.006

Lindqvist, D., Dhabhar, F. S., James, S. J., Hough, C. M., Jain, F. A., Bersani, F. S., . . . Mellon, S. H. (2017). Oxidative stress, inflammation and treatment response in major depression. *Psychoneuroendocrinology, 76*, 197–205. doi:10.1016/j.psyneuen.2016.11.031

Loonen, A. J., & Ivanova, S. A. (2016). Circuits regulating pleasure and happiness in major depression. *Medical Hypotheses, 87*, 14–21. doi:10.1016/j.mehy.2015.12.013

Lopresti, A. L. (2017). Cognitive behaviour therapy and inflammation: A systematic review of its relationship and the potential implications for the treatment of depression. *Australian & New Zealand Journal of Psychiatry, 51*(6), 565–582. doi:10.1177/0004867417701996

Löwe, B., Decker, O., Müller, S., Brähler, E., Schellberg, D., Herzog, W., & Herzberg, P. Y. (2008). Validation and Standardization of the Generalized Anxiety Disorder Screener (GAD-7) in the General Population. *Medical Care, 46*(3), 266–274. doi:10.1097/mlr.0b013c318160d093

Lieberwirth, C., & Wang, Z. (2016). The neurobiology of pair bond formation, bond disruption, and social buffering. *Current Opinion in Neurobiology, 40,* 8–13. doi:10.1016/j.conb.2016.05.006

Lucke-Wold, B. P., Smith, K. E., Nguyen, L., Turner, R. C., Logsdon, A. F., Jackson, G. J., . . . Miller, D. B. (2015). Sleep disruption and the sequelae associated with traumatic brain injury. *Neuroscience & Biobehavioral Reviews, 55,* 68–77. doi:10.1016/j.neubiorev.2015.04.010

Macleod, S., Musich, S., Hawkins, K., Alsgaard, K., & Wicker, E. R. (2016). The impact of resilience among older adults. *Geriatric Nursing, 37*(4), 266–272. doi:10.1016/j.gerinurse.2016.02.014

Maher, C. A., Toohey, M., & Ferguson, M. (2016). Physical activity predicts quality of life and happiness in children and adolescents with cerebral palsy. *Disability and Rehabilitation, 38*(9), 865–869. doi:10.3109/09638288.2015.1066450.

Maier, W., Buller, R., Philipp, M., & Heuser, I. (1988). The Hamilton Anxiety Scale: Reliability, validity and sensitivity to change in anxiety and depressive disorders. *Journal of Affective Disorders, 14*(1), 61–68. doi:10.1016/0165-0327(88)90072-9

Marx, W., Moseley, G., Berk, M., & Jacka, F. (2017). Nutritional psychiatry: The present state of the evidence. *Proceedings of the Nutrition Society, 76*(4), 427–436. doi:10.1017/s0029665117002026

Massetti, G. M., Thomas, C. C., King, J., Ragan, K., & Lunsford, N. B. (2017). Mental Health Problems and Cancer Risk Factors Among Young Adults. *American Journal of Preventive Medicine, 53*(3, Suppl 1), S30–S39. doi:10.1016/j.amepre.2017.04.023

Matsunaga, M., Isowa, T., Yamakawa, K., Tsuboi, H., Kawanishi, Y., Kaneko, H., . . . Ohira, H. (2011). Association between perceived happiness levels and peripheral circulating pro-inflammatory cytokine levels in middle-aged adults in Japan. *Neuroendocrinology Letters, 32*(4), 458–463. Retrieved June 20, 2019, from http://www.nel.edu/userfiles/articlesnew/NEL320411A11.pdf

Mead, G. E., Morley, W., Campbell, P., Greig, C. A., Mcmurdo, M., & Lawlor, D. A. (2008). Exercise for depression. *Cochrane Database of Systematic Reviews,* (4), CD004366. doi:10.1002/14651858.cd004366.pub3

Menezes, A. M., Murray, J., László, M., Wehrmeister, F. C., Hallal, P. C., Gonçalves, H., . . . Barros, F. C. (2013). Happiness and depression in adolescence after maternal smoking during pregnancy: Birth cohort study. *PLoS ONE, 8*(11), e80370, 1–8. doi:10.1371/journal.pone. 0080370

Moffett, J. E., & Bartram, D. J. (2017). Veterinary students' perspectives on resilience and resilience-building strategies. *Journal of Veterinary Medical Education, 44*(1), 116–124. doi:10.3138/jvme.0216-046r1

Morris, M. C., Tangney, C. C., Wang, Y., Sacks, F. M., Barnes, L. L., Bennett, D. A., & Aggarwal, N. T. (2015). MIND diet slows cognitive decline with aging. *Alzheimers & Dementia, 11*(9), 1015–1022. doi:10.1016/j.jalz.2015.04.011

Muñoz, M. A., Fíto, M., Marrugat, J., Covas, M., & Schröder, H. (2008). Adherence to the Mediterranean diet is associated with better mental and physical health. *British Journal of Nutrition, 101*(12), 1821–1827. doi:10.1017/s0007114508143598

Muros, J. J., Cofre-Bolados, C., Arriscado, D., Zurita, F., & Knox, E. (2017). Mediterranean diet adherence is associated with lifestyle, physical fitness, and mental wellness among 10-y-olds in Chile. *Nutrition, 35*, 87–92. doi:10.1016/j. nut.2016.11.002

Palmer, B. W., Martin, A. S., Depp, C. A., Glorioso, D. K., & Jeste, D. V. (2014). Wellness within illness: Happiness in schizophrenia. *Schizophrenia Research, 159*(1), 151–156. doi:10.1016/j.schres.2014.07.027

Pan, A., Sun, Q., Czernichow, S., Kivimaki, M., Okereke, O. I., Lucas, M., . . . Hu, F. B. (2012). Bidirectional association between depression and obesity in middle-aged and older women. *International Journal of Obesity, 36*(4), 595-602. doi:10.1038/ijo.2011.111

Panagi, L., Poole, L., Hackett, R. A., & Steptoe, A. (2018). Happiness and inflammatory responses to acute stress in people with Type 2 diabetes. *Annals of Behavioral Medicine, 53*(4), 309–320. doi:10.1093/abm/kay039

Parletta, N., Zarnowiecki, D., Cho, J., Wilson, A., Bogomolova, S., Villani, A., . . . O'Dea, K. (2017). A Mediterranean-style dietary intervention supplemented with fish oil improves diet quality and mental health in people with depression: A randomized controlled trial (HELFIMED). *Nutritional Neuroscience, 22*(7), 474–487. doi:10.1080/1028415x.2017.1411320

Pascoe, M. C., Thompson, D. R., Jenkins, Z. M., & Ski, C. F. (2017). Mindfulness mediates the physiological markers of stress: Systematic review and meta-analysis. *Journal of Psychiatric Research, 95*, 156-178. doi:10.1016/j.jpsychires.2017.08.004

Peach, H. D., Gaultney, J. F., & Ruggiero, A. R. (2018). Direct and indirect associations of sleep knowledge and attitudes with objective and subjective sleep duration and quality via sleep hygiene. *The Journal of Primary Prevention, 39*(6), 555–570. doi:10.1007/s10935-018-0526-7

Physical Inactivity Poses Greatest Health Risk to Americans, Research Shows. (2009, August 09). Retrieved June 19, 2019, from https://www.apa.org/news/press/releases/2009/08/physical-inactivity.aspx

Pliszka, S. R., Crismon, M. L., Hughes, C. W., Corners, C. K., Emslie, G. J., Jensen, P. S., . . . Lopez, M. (2006). The Texas Childrens Medication Algorithm Project: revision of the algorithm for pharmacotherapy of attention-deficit/hyperactivity disorder. *Journal of the American Academy of Child & Adolescent Psychiatry, 45*(6), 642–657. doi:10.1097/01.chi.0000215326.51175.eb

Ran, Q., Yang, J., Yang, W., Wei, D., Qiu, J., & Zhang, D. (2017). The association between resting functional connectivity and dispositional optimism. *Plos One, 12*(7),: e0180334, 1–13. doi:10.1371/journal.pone.0180334

Rashid, T., & Seligman, M. (2018). *Positive Psychotherapy: Clinician Manual.* New York: Oxford University Press.

Redwine, L. S., Henry, B. L., Pung, M. A., Wilson, K., Chinh, K., Knight, B., . . . Mills, P. J. (2016). Pilot randomized study of a gratitude journaling intervention on heart rate variability and inflammatory biomarkers in patients with stage b heart failure. *Psychosomatic Medicine, 78*(6), 667-676. doi:10.1097/psy.0000000000000316

Richards, J., Jiang, X., Kelly, P., Chau, J., Bauman, A., & Ding, D. (2015). Dont worry, be happy: Cross-sectional associations between physical activity and happiness in 15 European countries. *BMC Public Health, 15*:53, 1–8. doi:10.1186/s12889-015-1391-4

Richter, P., Werner, J., Heerlein, A., Kraus, A., & Sauer, H. (1998). On the validity of the Beck Depression Inventory. *Psychopathology, 31*(3), 160–168. doi:10.1159/000066239

Robbins M, Szapocznik J, Tejeda M, Samuels D, Ironson G, Antoni M.(2003). the protective role of the family and social support network in a sample of HIV-Positive african american women: Results of a pilot study. *J Black Psychol.* Feb;29(1):17–37.

Robertson, H. D., Elliott, A. M., Burton, C., Iversen, L., Murchie, P., Porteous, T., & Matheson, C. (2016). Resilience of primary healthcare professionals: A systematic review. *British Journal of General Practice, 66*(647), e423-e433. doi:10.3399/bjgp16x685261

Rolin D., Blakeley L., Tran C., Dudley R., Jain S., & Jain R. (2018, October). *Wellness Interventions for Life's Demands (WILD-5 Wellness): Exercise, Mindfulness, Sleep, Social Connectedness, and Nutrition - Improving Mental and Physical Health Through Holistic Daily Behavior Change.* Research poster presented at the APNA 32nd Annual Conference, Columbus, OH.

Roy, B., Diez-Roux, A. V., Seeman, T., Ranjit, N., Shea, S., & Cushman, M. (2010). Association of optimism and pessimism with inflammation and hemostasis in the multi-ethnic study of atherosclerosis (MESA). *Psychosomatic Medicine, 72*(2), 134–140. doi:10.1097/psy.0b013e3181cb981b

SAMSHA (2016). Creating a healther life. Retrieved December 11, 2018, from https://store.samhsa.gov/system/files/sma16-4958.pdf

Sato, W., Kochiyama, T., Uono, S., Kubota, Y., Sawada, R., Yoshimura, S., & Toichi, M. (2015). The structural neural substrate of subjective happiness. *Scientific Reports, 5*:16891, 1–7. doi:10.1038/srep16891

Schmaal, L., Veltman, D. J., Van Erp, T. G., Sämann, P. G., Frodi, T., Jahanshad, N., . . . Hibar, D. P. (2016). Subcortical brain alterations in major depressive disorder: Findings from the ENIGMA Major Depressive Disorder working group. *Molecular Psychiatry, 21*, 806–812. doi:10.1038/mp.2015.69

Schon, H., & Weiskirchen, R. (2016). Exercise-induced release of pharmacologically active substances and their relevance for therapy of hepatic injury. *Frontiers in Pharmacology, 07*, Article 283, 1–17. doi:10.3389/fphar.2016.00283

Schrank, B., Brownell, T., Jakaite, Z., Larkin, C., Pesola, F., Riches, S., . . . Slade, M. (2015). Evaluation of a positive psychotherapy group intervention for people with psychosis: Pilot randomised controlled trial. *Epidemiology and Psychiatric Sciences, 25*(3), 235–246. doi:10.1017/s2045796015000141

Schutte, N. S., Palanisamy, S. K., & Mcfarlane, J. R. (2016). The relationship between positive psychological characteristics and longer telomeres. *Psychology & Health, 31*(12), 1466–1480. doi:10.1080/08870446.2016.1226308

Segal, Z. V., Bieling, P., Young, T., Macqueen, G., Cooke, R., Martin, L., . . . Levitan, R. D. (2010). Antidepressant monotherapy vs sequential pharmacotherapy and mindfulness-based cognitive therapy, or placebo, for relapse prophylaxis in recurrent depression. *Archives of General Psychiatry, 67*(12), 1256–1264. doi:10.1001/archgenpsychiatry.2010.168

Segal, Z.V., Williams, J.M.G., & Teasdale, J.D. (2013). *Mindfulness-Based Cognitive Therapy for Depression.* New York, New York. Guilford Press

Segar, M. L., & Richardson, C. R. (2014). Prescribing Pleasure and Meaning. *American Journal of Preventive Medicine, 47*(6), 838-841. doi:10.1016/j.amepre.2014.07.001

Sejnowski, T. J., & Destexhe, A. (2000). Why do we sleep? *Brain Research, 886*(1–2), 208–223. doi:10.1016/s0006-8993(00)03007-9

Seligman, M. E., & Csikszentmihalyi, M. (2000). Positive psychology: An introduction. *American Psychologist, 55*(1), 5-14. doi:10.1037//0003-066x.55.1.5

Seligman, M. E. (2019). Positive psychology: A personal history. *Annual Review of Clinical Psychology, 15*(1), 1–23. doi:10.1146/annurev-clinpsy-050718-095653

Sheline YI, Sanghavi M, Mintun MA, Gado MH. (1999). Depression duration but not age predicts hippocampal volume loss in medically healthy women with recurrent major depression. *J Neurosci.* Jun 15;19(12):5034–43.

Sheline, Y. I., Mittler, B. L., & Mintun, M. A. (2002). The hippocampus and depression1. *European Psychiatry, 17*(Suppl 3), 300-305. doi:10.1016/s0924-9338(02)00655-7

Shelton, R. C., & Miller, A. H. (2010). Eating ourselves to death (and despair): The contribution of adiposity and inflammation to depression. *Progress in Neurobiology, 91*(4), 275–299. doi:10.1016/j.pneurobio.2010.04.004

Sheridan, A. J., Drennan, J., Coughlan, B., O'Keeffe, D., Frazer, K., Kemple, M., . . . O'Callaghan, E. (2015). Improving social functioning and reducing social isolation and loneliness among people with enduring mental illness: Report of a randomised controlled trial of supported socialisation. *International Journal of Social Psychiatry, 61*(3), 241–250. doi:10.1177/0020764014540150

Slade, M. (2010). Mental illness and well-being: The central importance of positive psychology and recovery approaches. *BMC Health Services Research, 10*:26, 1–14. doi:10.1186/1472-6963-10-26

Slavich, G. M., & Irwin, M. R. (2014). From stress to inflammation and major depressive disorder: A social signal transduction theory of depression. *Psychological Bulletin, 140*(3), 774–815. doi:10.1037/a0035302

Simon, G. E., Korff, M. V., Saunders, K., Miglioretti, D. L., Crane, P. K., Belle, G. V., & Kessler, R. C. (2006). Association Between Obesity and Psychiatric Disorders in the US Adult Population. *Archives of General Psychiatry, 63*(7), 824–830. doi:10.1001/archpsyc.63.7.824

Simon, G. E., Ludman, E. J., Linde, J. A., Operskalski, B. H., Ichikawa, L., Rohde, P., . . . Jeffery, R. W. (2008). Association between obesity and depression in middle-aged women. *General Hospital Psychiatry, 30*(1), 32–39. doi:10.1016/j.genhosppsych.2007.09.001

Smyth, J. M., Johnson, J. A., Auer, B. J., Lehman, E., Talamo, G., & Sciamanna, C. N. (2018). Online positive affect journaling in the improvement of mental distress and well-being in general medical patients with elevated anxiety symptoms: A preliminary randomized controlled trial. *JMIR Mental Health, 5*(4), e11290, 1-14. doi:10.2196/11290

Spinhoven, P., Elzinga, B. M., Giltay, E., & Penninx, B. W. (2015). Anxious or depressed and still happy? *PloS One, 10*(10), e0139912, 1–17. doi:10.1371/journal.pone.0139912

Sprecher, K. E., Koscik, R. L., Carlsson, C. M., Zetterberg, H., Blennow, K., Okonkwo, O. C., . . . Bendlin, B. B. (2017). Poor sleep is associated with CSF biomarkers of amyloid pathology in cognitively normal adults. *Neurology, 89*(5), 445–453. doi:10.1212/wnl.0000000000004171

Steptoe, A., Dockray, S., & Wardle, J. (2009). Positive Affect and Psychobiological Processes Relevant to Health. *Journal of Personality, 77*(6), 1747–1776. doi:10.1111/j.1467-6494.2009.00599.x

Suchdev, P. S., Boivin, M. J., Forsyth, B. W., Georgieff, M. K., Guerrant, R. L., & Nelson, C. A. (2017). Assessment of neurodevelopment, nutrition, and inflammation from fetal life to adolescence in low-resource settings. *Pediatrics, 139*(Suppl 1), S23–S37. doi:10.1542/peds.2016-2828e

Summers, R. F., & Jeste, D. V. (Eds.). (2019). *Positive Psychiatry: A Casebook.* Washington, DC: American Psychiatric Association Publishing.

Switzer, F. S., Cheung, J. H., Burns, D. K., Sinclair, R. R., Roth, P. L., Tyler, P., & Mccubbin, J. (2017). Carrots, not sticks. *Journal of Occupational and Environmental Medicine, 59*(3), 250–255. doi:10.1097/jom.0000000000000940

Tang, Y., Hölzel, B. K., & Posner, M. I. (2015). The neuroscience of mindfulness meditation. *Nature Reviews Neuroscience, 16*(4), 213–225. doi:10.1038/nrn3916

Tennant, R., Hiller, L., Fishwick, R., Platt, S., Joseph, S., Weich, S., . . . Stewart-Brown, S. (2007). The Warwick-Edinburgh Mental Well-being Scale (WEMWBS): Development and UK validation. *Health and Quality of Life Outcomes, 5*:63, 1–13. doi:10.1186/1477-7525-5-63

Thurnham, D. I., & Northrop-Clewes, C. A. (2016). Inflammation and biomarkers of micronutrient status. *Current Opinion in Clinical Nutrition and Metabolic Care, 19*(6), 458–463. doi:10.1097/mco.0000000000000323

Tough, S. C., Siever, J. E., Benzies, K., Leew, S., & Johnston, D. W. (2010). Maternal well-being and its association to risk of developmental problems in children at school entry. *BMC Pediatrics, 10*:19, 1–12. doi:10.1186/1471-2431-10-19

UAE Happiness - The Official Portal of the UAE. (2019, May 19). Retrieved June 21, 2019, from https://government.ae/en/about-the-uae/the-uae-government/government-of-future/happiness

UK Government, Press release. (2018, October 15). *Prime Minister Theresa May launches Government's first loneliness strategy* [Press release]. Retrieved June 21, 2019, from https://www.gov.uk/government/news/pm-launches-governments-first-loneliness-strategy

Van de Weert-van Leeuwen, P. B., Arets, H. G., Ent, C. K., & Beekman, J. M. (2013). Infection, inflammation and exercise in cystic fibrosis. *Respiratory Research, 14*:32, 1–10. doi:10.1186/1465-9921-14-32

Van Dyk, T. R., Thompson, R. W., & Nelson, T. D. (2016). Daily bidirectional relationships between sleep and mental health symptoms in youth with emotional and behavioral problems. *Journal of Pediatric Psychology, 41*(9), 983-992. doi:10.1093/jpepsy/jsw040

Vankim, N. A., & Nelson, T. F. (2013). Vigorous physical activity, mental health, perceived stress, and socializing among college students. *American Journal of Health Promotion, 28*(1), 7–15. doi:10.4278/ajhp.111101-quan-395

Vogelzangs, N., Beekman, A. T., Van Reedt Dortland, A. K., Schoevers, R. A., Giltay, E. J., De Jonge, P., & Penninx, B. W. (2014). Inflammatory and metabolic dysregulation and the 2-year course of depressive disorders in antidepressant users. *Neuropsychopharmacology, 39*(7), 1624–1634. doi:10.1038/npp.2014.9

Waldrop, J., & McGuinness, T. M. (2017). Measurement-based care in psychiatry. *Journal of Psychosocial Nursing and Mental Health Services, 55*(11), 30–35. doi:10.3928/02793695-20170818-01

Walker, F. R., Pfingst, K., Carnevali, L., Sgoifo, A., & Nalivaiko, E. (2017). In the search for integrative biomarker of resilience to psychological stress. *Neuroscience & Biobehavioral Reviews, 74*, 310–320. doi:10.1016/j.neubiorev.2016.05.003

Wang, H., Mittleman, M. A., Leineweber, C., & Orth-Gomer, K. (2006). depressive symptoms, social isolation, and progression of coronary artery atherosclerosis: The Stockholm Female Coronary Angiography Study. *Psychotherapy and Psychosomatics, 75*(2), 96-102. doi:10.1159/000090893

Warwick-Edinburgh Mental Wellbeing Scales. Retrieved June 21, 2019, from https://warwick.ac.uk/fac/sci/med/research/platform/wemwbs

Wayne, N., Perez, D. F., Kaplan, D. M., & Ritvo, P. (2015). Health coaching reduces hba1c in type 2 diabetic patients from a lower-socioeconomic status community: A randomized controlled trial. *Journal of Medical Internet Research, 17*(10), e224, 1–19. doi:10.2196/jmir.4871

WHO (1948). Preamble to the constitution of the World Health Organization as adopted by the International Health Conference; New York. 19-22 June, 1946; 1946. signed on 22 July 1946 by the representatives of 61 States (Official Records of the World Health Organization, no. 2, p. 100) and entered into force on 7 April 1948.

WHO-5 Website. Retrieved June 21, 2019, from https://www.psykiatri-regionh .dk/who-5/about-the-who-5/Pages/default.aspx

Więdłocha, M., Marcinowicz, P., Krupa, R., Janoska-Jaździk, M., Janus, M., Dębowska, W., . . . Szulc, A. (2018). Effect of antidepressant treatment on peripheral inflammation markers – A meta-analysis. *Progress in Neuro-Psychopharmacology and Biological Psychiatry, 80*(Part C), 217–226. doi:10.1016/j.pnpbp.2017.04.026

Winzer, E., Dorner, T. E., Grabovac, I., Haider, S., Kapan, A., Lackinger, C., & Schindler, K. (2019). Behavior changes by a buddy-style intervention including physical training, and nutritional and social support. *Geriatrics & Gerontology International, 19*(4), 323–329. doi:10.1111/ggi.13616

Xiao, Z. H., Wang, Q. H., Lou, T. T., & Zhong, L. (2013). Diagnostic value of Vanderbilt ADHD Parent Rating Scale in attention deficit hyperactivity disorder. *Chinese Journal of Contemporary Pediatrics, 15*(5), 348–352. Retrieved June 21, 2019, from http://www.zgddek.com/EN/Y2013/V15/I5/348

Yang, C., Barrós-Loscertales, A., Pinazo, D., Ventura-Campos, N., Borchardt, V., Bustamante, J., . . . Walter, M. (2016). State and Training Effects of Mindfulness Meditation on Brain Networks Reflect Neuronal Mechanisms of Its Antidepressant Effect. *Neural Plasticity, 2016*, Article ID 9504642, 1–14. doi:10.1155/2016/9504642

Yang, J., Wei, D., Wang, K., & Qiu, J. (2013). Gray matter correlates of dispositional optimism: A voxel-based morphometry study. *Neuroscience Letters, 553*, 201–205. doi:10.1016/j.neulet.2013.08.032

Yarnell, A. M., & Deuster, P. (2016). Sleep as a strategy for optimizing performance. *Journal Of Special Operations Medicine: A Peer Reviewed Journal For SOF Medical Professionals, 16*(1), 81–85.

Yoshikawa, E., Nishi, D., & Matsuoka, Y. J. (2016). Association between frequency of fried food consumption and resilience to depression in Japanese company workers: A cross-sectional study. *Lipids in Health and Disease, 15*:156, 1-5. doi:10.1186/s12944-016-0331-3

Zeidan, F., Martucci, K. T., Kraft, R. A., Mchaffie, J. G., & Coghill, R. C. (2014). Neural correlates of mindfulness meditation-related anxiety relief. *Social Cognitive and Affective Neuroscience, 9*(6), 751–759. doi:10.1093/scan/nst041

Zimmerman, M., Mcglinchey, J. B., Posternak, M. A., Friedman, M., Attiullah, N., & Boerescu, D. (2006). How should remission from depression be defined? The depressed patient's perspective. *American Journal of Psychiatry, 163*, 148–150. doi:10.1176/appi.ajp.163.1.148

Data on the HERO Wellness Scale's Statistical Parameters

Using scores from baseline data (N = 84), internal consistency, calculated using Cronbach's α, was excellent ($\geq$ .9) for the 5-item HERO composite, α = .93. For the corrected item-total correlations, all 5 items were adequate ($\geq$ .5), ranging from .67 (Resilience), .83 (Happiness), .83 (Enthusiasm), .85 (Enthusiasm), to .86 (Mental Wellness). The inter-item correlation matrix revealed all 10 correlations were statistically significant (p < .001) and ranged from .57 (Happiness with Resiliency) to .82 (Happiness with Mental Wellness).

Relationships between scale scores and other measures intended to assess same or similar constructs also provide convergent evidence of validity for the HERO Wellness Scale. A Pearson correlation coefficient, computed to assess the relation between the HERO composite scale scores and WHO-5 Well-Being Index scores at baseline (N = 84), indicated a statistically significant positive correlation, r = .79, p < .001. According to Cohen (1988), correlations > .50 represent a large effect size; with a correlation of .79, 62% of the variance of either variable is associated linearly with variance in the other. Although the HERO Wellness Scale and the WHO-5 Well-Being Index are not identical measures, correlations between individual HERO items and WHO-5 total scores at baseline were all statistically significant (p < .001): Happiness, .75; Enthusiasm, .74; Resilience, .54; Optimism, .71; and Mental Wellness, .74.

Thus, analyses of the HERO Wellness Scale demonstrated strong evidence of its reliability and validity, and a strong correlation with the WHO 5 Well-Being Index. If you wish to directly assess positive psychology traits such as happiness, enthusiasm, resilience, optimism, and overall mental wellness, consider using the HERO Wellness Scale for individual-level assessment.

Resources

WILD 5 Wellness Materials

- *Mindfulness guided meditations*

  WILD 5 Meditations is a series of guided meditations that Drs. Saundra and Rakesh Jain recorded for use in their clinical and research practices. These complimentary recordings are available to practicing clinicians to use in their own settings.

  www.wild5meditations.com

  1. Five-Minute Breathing Space (6:45)
  2. Mindful Breathing (15:00)
  3. Body Scan (15:00)
  4. A Moment of Gratitude (9:58)
  5. Happiness Meditation (11:37)
  6. Pain Meditation (13:00)
  7. Introduction to Mindful Meal Meditation (5:18)
  8. Mindful Meal Meditation (23:30)
  9. Mindful Moment with a Raisin (9:56)

- *HERO Exercises*

  The HERO Exercises ask participants to answer 2 questions daily, focusing on the HERO wellness traits of happiness, enthusiasm, resilience, and optimism, which positively impact overall wellness.

  https://www.wild5wellness.com/forms.html

- *WILD 5 Wellness Participant Tracking Form*

  The tracking form is an easy way to document daily wellness practices.

  https://www.wild5wellness.com/forms.html

- *KickStart30 workbook link*

  https://www.amazon.com/WILD-Wellness-KickStart30-Proven
  -Program/dp/1791658806/ref=sr_1_1?keywords=kickstart30&qid=15
  54301365&s=gateway&sr=8-1

- *LiveWell90 workbook link*

  https://www.amazon.com/WILD-Wellness-LiveWell90-Proven
  -Program/dp/1798210835/ref=sr_1_1?keywords=LiveWell90&qid=15
  61403872&s=gateway&sr=8-1

Measurement Scales

- *HERO Wellness Scale*

  The HERO Wellness Scale is a 5-item, self-report questionnaire for measuring overall wellness.

  https://www.wild5wellness.com/forms.html

- *Warwick-Edinburgh Mental Wellbeing Scale*

  The WEMWBS is a 14-item well-studied wellness scale that is used to examine societal and individual levels of wellness.

https://warwick.ac.uk/fac/sci/med/research/platform/wemwbs

- *PHQ-9*

  The PHQ-9 is a 9-item depression self-report questionnaire for the screening and measuring of severity of major depression.

  https://www.phqscreeners.com/

- *GAD-7*

  The GAD-7 is a 7-item anxiety self-report questionnaire for the screening and measuring of severity of generalized anxiety.

  https://www.phqscreeners.com/

- *MDQ*

  MDQ is a 15-question self-report instrument designed to screen for bipolar disorder.

  https://www.integration.samhsa.gov/images/res/MDQ.pdf

- *Adult ADHD Self-Report Scale*

  The ASRS is a checklist of 18 questions about symptoms that are based on the diagnostic criteria of the Diagnostic and Statistical Manual-IV assessing for Adult ADHD.

  https://www.hcp.med.harvard.edu/ncs/asrs.php

- *WHO-5 Well-Being Index*

  The WHO-5 is a 5-item, self-report instrument, assessing one's subjective quality of life based on positive mood, vitality, and general interest.

  https://www.psykiatri-regionh.dk/who-5/Pages/default.aspx

- *Mental Wellness Center*
  http://www.mentalwellnesscenter.org/

  The Mental Wellness Center is a non-profit organization recognizing mental illness as a community matter. They provide education and support to meet the immediate and future needs of youth, adults, families, and the greater community.

- *Mental Wellness Awareness Association (MWAA)*
  http://mentalwellnessawareness.org/

  The Mental Wellness Awareness Association is a state-wide non-profit corporation that focuses on education for prevention, early intervention, scientific research and cures of mental health problems.

Other Useful Resources

- *The MIND diet*
  https://www.ncbi.nlm.nih.gov/pmc/articles/PMC4532650/

  The MIND diet was created to help prevent dementia and slow the loss of brain function that may happen with age.

- *Wellness Apps*

  There are many types of wellness apps that offer health-related services across different communication devices.

  https://www.myfitnesspal.com/

  MyFitnessPal is a fast and easy way to track calories and log activities.

  https://www.headspace.com/

  Using science and technology, Headspace makes meditation easy to learn and fun.

https://www.stopbreathethink.com/

This emotional wellness platform is to help kids, teens and young adults build the emotional strength to tackle life's ups and downs.

https://happify.com/

Based on the science of happiness, Happify uses activities and games to build a more fulfilling life.

https://mobile.va.gov/app/cbt-i-coach

CBT-i Coach is for people wanting to improve their sleep habits. It is intended to augment face-to-face care with a healthcare professional.

Index